# Hope and Dignity

VIOLA A. LENOIR
APRIL 1, 1894

# Hope and Dignity

OLDER BLACK WOMEN OF THE SOUTH

TEXT BY EMILY HERRING WILSON

PHOTOGRAPHS BY SUSAN MULLALLY

FOREWORD BY MAYA ANGELOU

Temple University Press    Philadelphia

Temple University Press
Philadelphia 19122
© 1983 by Temple University
All rights reserved
Published 1983
Printed in the United States of America

Library of Congress Cataloging in Publication Data

Wilson, Emily Herring.
Hope and Dignity.

1. Afro-American women—North Carolina.
2. Afro-American women—Southern States.
3. Afro-American aged—North Carolina.
4. Afro-American aged—Southern States.
5. North Carolina—Social conditions.
6. North Carolina—Biography.
7. Southern States—Social conditions.
8. Southern States—Biography.
9. Oral biography.
I. Mullally, Susan.
II. Title.
E185.93.N6W54    1983        305.4'8896073'075        82-19437
ISBN 0-87722-302-5

*For the older black women of North Carolina,*

*who live with hope and dignity*

# Contents

Foreword / xi

Acknowledgments / xv

Introduction / xvii

Chapter 1. Precious Lord, Take My Hand / 3

Chapter 2. One Dime Blues / 13

Chapter 3. Green Animals around the Moon / 23

Chapter 4. mid·wife / 31

Chapter 5. Cool Buttermilk, Brown Gravy, and No Chickens
under the House: A Dream / 45

Chapter 6. *Esse Quam Videri* / 57

Chapter 7. In This Dark World and Wide / 67

Chapter 8. Sisters / 75

Chapter 9. Taking Low to No One / 85

Chapter 10. Ivory Towers and No Sidewalks / 93

Chapter 11. Seeing a Thing Through / 101

Chapter 12. As Long as You Give Us the Equal / 109

Chapter 13. A Woman on Wall Street / 121

Chapter 14. Mademoiselle / 131

Chapter 15. ". . . For Peace and Justice, Freedom and Dignity for All People" / 141

Chapter 16. You Follow Me? / 151

Chapter 17. I Was Glad When They Said unto Me,
"We Will Go into the House of the Lord" / 161

Chapter 18. When the Sun Goes Down, You're in a Valley like This,
and You Can Look Up to the Top and See the Sunrise / 169

Chapter 19. The Little Country Church / 177

Chapter 20. The World Can't Take It Away / 185

Epilogue / 191

"I leave you hope

.        .        .

I leave you love

.        .        .

I leave you racial dignity

.        .        .        ."

*From the Last Will and Testament*
*of Mary McLeod Bethune*


"In the midst of immense difficulties,
surrounded by caste, and hemmed in
by restricted economic opportunity,
let the colored mother of today build
her own statue, and let it be the
four walls of her own unsullied home."

*William E. B. Du Bois, 1912*

# Foreword

Some historians describe our species as helpless creatures, trembling unarmed in the path of history. "He who does not learn from history is doomed (*sic*) to repeat it." We are warned to be intimidated and threatened by our past; to be ashamed, bitter or so guilty as to be in bondage to the actions of our ancestors. Hence, we are so weighted by the burdens of the past, we are unable to quite bear the present and totally incapable of moving into the future with even the semblance of hope or a shred of healthy prospect. "I helped the Lord make me what I am," asserts Mrs. Eva Roundtree.

To assume that we are mere gingerbread toys at the mercy of a ravenous mean old witch called History, is to surrender our natural birthright, which seems to me to be the ability to change not only our world, our time, but ourselves.

The American legend of slavery and repression, of wars for freedom and wars for gain is imprinted most heavily on the Black American memory. For despite the battle's personnel, the locations of arenas, and the shifting fortunes of winners and losers, the slaves were not destined to be on the side of the triumphant. Yet, much to the amazement of some and the consternation of others, we have survived our history, and, thereby, offer a unique and moving testimony to our fellow travellers on this planet headed either for the stars or oblivion.

When asked directly, the survivors are seldom able to explain the miracle of their survival. Hidden in their oblique responses are universes of complexities and denials and fiction.

*"A lot of people say they can see my mother in me. Seems like I don't really recall it being too hard. Only I could hear my mother say 'Well, we've made it so far. We can make it on.'"* . . . Etta Baker.

Inevitably the question must be asked, "How did these people survive?" And before it is answered, a second and more scathing question poses itself, "Why? Why did this beleaguered, scorned and scourged group decide to survive?" For we know only the most base submit to living at any cost, and the contribution of love, dignity, humor and art informs the viewer that Black Americans are neither base nor, even following centuries of vilifications, are they debased. The Black American preacher and his audience create and understand gloriously poetic imagery.

*"And my attention somehow was drawed up at the moon, the ring around the moon.*

*"I thought everybody seen it, but no. The animals was going around the ring of that moon. I thought it was elephants, great big tall animals, and some different sizes and some big white horses. And I stood there looking at it, and the little boys said to me, 'Minnie, what you looking at?' I said, 'I'm looking at them elephants up there.' 'Elephants?' Then the other children come there and they went to looking. 'We don't see no elephants, don't see*

*no rings around the moon.' But it was a pa-*
*rade, going around the moon. I stood there*
*and looked. My mother was sitting on the*
*porch. I don't know whether she was looking*
*at them or not. But the children was a 'laugh-*
*ing at me because I saw those things, going*
*round the ring. She scold me. Say, 'You come*
*in the house and sit down, talking bout you*
*seeing elephants going round!' So I come in*
*and sit down, and there was this old lady right*
*next door to us, said, 'Let that child alone.*
*Leave her off.' Said, 'Maybe you don't see*
*them but God has showed her something that*
*He hasn't showed you.' Now when I close my*
*eyes I can see them.*

"Art is a mystery." . . . Minnie Evans.

The simplicity of the questions can mis-
lead us into thinking it possible to invent
direct and satisfying answers. This is pa-
tently not true.

Any society founded on the glaring con-
tradictions of emotional love for personal
freedom while maintaining a dehumanizing
slave system must necessarily produce social conditions not easily penetrable nor
simply explained.

In *Hope and Dignity* Emily Wilson and
Susan Mullally have offered some answers
to the question of Black survival. Wilson, a
good and recognized poet, travelled her
adopted State of North Carolina (she is
originally from Georgia) talking to older
Black women and listening to their responses. Interestingly, the women collected
in this book appear to be speaking more to
their ancestors and even to their unborn
progeny than to Emily Wilson and therein
must lie the book's success. For, since Wilson is White, it is natural to suspect anything Black people might say to her. (There
is the old saying among Blacks: "If white
people ask you where you are going tell
them where you've been.") It is a compli-

ment to Wilson to say that she was wise
enough to pose her questions then stand
aside so that the women could reflect pri-
vately on the pasts they have lived and even
those they wished they had lived.

Mullally's photographs are inspired and
to the point. She has demonstrated as
much sensitivity as Wilson and an equal
amount of poetic curiosity.

The subjects appear, as out of a mist,
suddenly clear and clearly mistresses of
their real and imagined times. They have
overcome the cruel roles into which they
had been cast by racism and ignorance.
They have wept over their hopeless fate
and defied destiny by creating hope anew.
They have nursed, by force, a nation of
hostile strangers, and wrung from lifetimes
of mean servitude and third class citizen-
ship a dignity of indescribable elegance.

"If I had it to do over," Mrs. Bryant explains, "I would just as soon have the days
of back yonder as today. I had. But I'm
sure the children can have so much more
and so much more easier till this is better
days for living but not the kind of living we
was brought up with. We had time to visit
each other, and had time to go see the sick
and didn't have no thoughts of putting nobody in the rest home. Maybe if there was
four or five working on the farm, one could
stay at the house and wait on that sick person. And it didn't put no bigger strain on
them. Now it seems like they have keyed
up themselves for fine houses, fine furniture, fine cars, fine everything until it takes
them both to work [the wife and the hus-
band]. But used to if the man had to be
sick, the woman with the neighbor's aid
could carry on. Or if the woman had to be
sick, the neighbors would help do the
chopping or do whatever she had been doing till she could get well. Now there's no

way that no one hardly, the way they've got themselves stretched out for wanting so much, that they can carry on as well as we did. When mother stays at home with the children and works with them, like I did, you near about know them. No way hardly they can fool you or nothing. I'm not giving myself no pat, but nobody worked more hours than I did."

These women are teachers comprehensively. Their accounts inform us that while life in North Carolina and in all the United States, has been hard for the Black woman (and man and child) it can be borne with dignity, and it can be changed by hope. Salutes to Wilson and Mullally, and humble thanks to all the women collected in this book. I understand them. They are my grandmothers.

Maya Angelou
January 18, 1983

# Acknowledgments

A project extending over three years and many thousands of miles has required us often to take advantage of the generosity of friends and strangers. Several institutions have also provided invaluable help. First of all, we want to thank the National Endowment for the Humanities for a two-year research grant without which we would not have been able to initiate and complete this work. We are also especially indebted to The MacDowell Colony for providing the time and place in which the narratives and photographs could be prepared. Reynolda House Museum of American Art in Winston-Salem, North Carolina, was another ideal place to work, and the encouragement of the director, Nicholas B. Bragg, was generous. Finally, the staff and resources of Wake Forest University and its library were often essential in our research.

While we cannot mention the many friends who supported our efforts, we particularly thank the Wilson family—Ed, Eddie, Sally and Julie—for their patience and support and Maggie Lee Martin for her many contributions to us all.

There are numerous people who have provided professional help. We would especially like to thank Eunice Johnson, who saw the manuscript through to its completion. We appreciate the advice of a number of photographers: Earl Dotter, Kristina Egan, Roland Freeman, Joanna Hudson, Neal Rantoul, and Jackson Smith. The staffs of several oral history programs were helpful: the Southern Oral History Program at the University of North Carolina at Chapel Hill, especially Dr. Jacquelyn Hall, Director; the Duke University Oral History program; and Ruth Edmonds Hill of the Radcliffe Black Women Oral History Project. Rodney Barfield, curator of an exhibit, "Black Presence in North Carolina," at the North Carolina Museum of History was the first person to supply us with a list of names of older black women in the state, and several of those he recommended are included in this book. George Holt and Glenn Hinson of the North Carolina Office of Folk Life Programs put us in touch with other women to be interviewed.

Essential research assistance was provided by Patricia Giles, Reference Librarian at the Z. Smith Reynolds Library of Wake Forest University. Introductions to publishers came from Margaret Supplee Smith. We benefited from the typing skills and suggestions of Ruth Werner Smith and Shirley Anders. And we especially appreciate the advice of our readers: Germaine Brée, Dolly McPherson, and Elizabeth Phillips.

After we began the project, we depended upon the help of a large group of people who broadened our understanding of southern black culture or introduced us to women in communities throughout the state. We acknowledge the assistance of all of these: Frank Adams, Simona Allen, Pendleton Banks, Richard Bardolph, Mary

Barnwell, Estelle Bass, Caroline Biggers, Pauline Binkley, Charles Irvin Bland, Joan Bluethenthal, Mildred Bostic, John Broderick, Geneva Brown, Minnie Miller Brown, McLeod Bryan, Robert Coles, Gertrude Conley, Jeannette Council, Douglas Covington, Elsie Daniels, Richard Dillingham, Edith Elliott, John Eslinger, David Evans, Martha Evans, Mutter Evans, Vivian Evans, Bertha Ferrebe, W. W. Finlator, Helen Freas, Shirley Frye, Cleonia Graves, Elizabeth Hair, Bernice Harrell, Willie Harvey, Esmeralda Hawkins, Harold Hayes, Ethel Herring, Jeanne Hoffman, Velma Hopkins, Guion Johnson, Elizabeth Koontz, Roberts Lasater, Dorothy Leavitt, Bessie Lee, Hattie and John Lee, Howard Lee, Artie Manson, Rhoda Metraux, Frances N. Miller, Helen S. Miller, Jeanelle Moore, James Nance, LaRue Pearson, Maulsie Phillips, Nona Porter, Anne Queen, Robin Reavis, Hattie Reid, Sylvia Lyons Render, Barbara Bynum Ross, Prezell Robinson, Dorothy Sargent, Celester Sellars, Robert Seymour, Jesse Simmons, Howell Smith, David Spear, Marion Spear, Nina Howell Starr, Connie Steadman, A. T. Stephens, Elizabeth Thompson, Beatrix Totten, Evelyn Underwood, Elizabeth Watson, Constance Watts, Alfred Wellons, Carter Williams, Cratis Williams, William Windley, Louise G. Wilson, Mildred Wilson, and Peter Wood.

Finally, our association with Temple University Press has been happy and productive, and we are especially grateful for the enthusiasm, faith, and skills of our editor, Candy Hawley.

# Introduction

*She filled up the streets of the city with her song, and when she joined the crowds of people, they stood together, like a community. She was tall and black, and her voice came from a deep place.*

Here was Street Scene, an annual festival of fall in Winston-Salem, North Carolina, in the Southern Piedmont, where the strong smell of tobacco floats over the city, and warehouses share blocks with office buildings and shops. Stages were set up in the downtown for entertainers, and thousands of listeners walked about. As one woman's singing echoed over the streets, people began to gather in front of her—teenagers, young families with children in strollers, businessmen in their muted suits. All of them became a continuous line, until the line broke. On the other side of the empty space there was a young man whose face and hands had been savagely disfigured by fire. No one rubbed shoulders with him; the emptiness around him seemed great.

The gospel singer took the microphone, which in fact she did not need so resonant was her voice, and she began to come down the steps from the stage onto the street and among the people. She moved along, encouraging her audience to sing with her, "When Jesus walks with me." Effortlessly, she moved and came to stand beside the young man in his circle of empty space. As she came nearer, the microphone picked up his voice, and it was good. Was it the voice

which had drawn her to him? No one else seemed to have heard him. She stood for a time, singing with him, and at the end, her arm was around his shoulder, her large body touching his thin one. The crowd had also moved closer together, one to another.

That was where the idea to celebrate the lives of older black southern women was born. Or it was one place. The figure of the gospel singer at Street Scene awakened in me the memory of another place and another time when I was a child in Columbus, Georgia. There, down Zion's Alley, I had watched in my silence the passage of black women, heard their low singing at work and at rest, and drawn comfort from the security which seemed to encircle their bodies. Whether washing clothes in the pots steaming in their front yards or holding children on their laps on the porches of their small houses or balancing vegetable baskets on their heads with the grace of dancers, these women were dominant images in the landscape of my southern childhood. I had carried inside me for more than thirty years that feeling about these women, and the gospel singer brought it again to the surface.

I began to think of a way for the women themselves to tell their own stories, and I also thought of conveying those strongly visual images through photographs. I discussed the idea for a book with Susan Mullally, a photographer with a special interest in portraits, and we went back in her portfolio to look at her pictures of black families in Cape Girardeau, Missouri, where she had visited her grandmother. There we found the same compelling images I had responded to on Zion's Alley. We had also had similar college experiences which had drawn us as observers of contemporary history, Susan's at the University of California at Berkeley during the Vietnam era when she had used her camera to document social and political change, my own in Greensboro, North Carolina, as a witness to the 1961 civil rights sit-ins. As we talked about our past experiences we agreed that we wanted to make a permanent record of life around us and that the American South was a good place to begin: the achievements and lives of women who had not been recognized in traditional histories would be our subjects. Thus we made the decision to undertake this study, a decision which would lead us more than 20,000 miles during the next three years. *Hope and Dignity* is the result of listening and seeing.

Because I have lived in North Carolina for the past twenty years, I knew the resources of the state and had made friends among the citizens. This seemed a good place to work, and we began in the fall of 1979. Besides the fact that North Carolina was home for me, there were other good reasons to focus our work here. There are large numbers of older black women in North Carolina who live close to the places of their births and whose families belong to the history of the South. The black community is represented not only in significant numbers but in significant institutions: many black academies and colleges were established around the turn of the century, some of which continue to be rep-

resented by alumni, faculty, and students. There are many archival records and special collections in libraries. And there are a great many churches, large and small, where membership goes back several generations. Black leadership in the state includes not only the officers of these institutions but extends to public service at the state and local levels. In addition to having an important black community, North Carolina has been "progressive" (as described by political scientist V. O. Key) in its social and political history. Our subjects were here, and access to them seemed promising.

North Carolina has an interesting mix of rural and urban centers, and the populations have not been disrupted by large-scale migrations. The old and the new often achieve a remarkable harmony. Producing a crop from the land—notably tobacco—is still a significant part of the state's economy; at the same time a half-dozen large urban centers have national and international business interests like banking and insurance. One can have a leisurely cup of coffee at the local cafe in Winton (population less than one thousand) where the waitress takes calls for the Sheriff while he finishes his breakfast; the radio plays to satisfied customers, "I've got Jesus on the radio and Daddy on the phone." Even in a city like Winston-Salem (population 150,000), where the tobacco and banking industries gleam in high glass buildings, there are signs of a "folk" life: the Farmers' Market on Saturday is a lively bustle of families selling sweet potatoes, beans and medicinal herbs; roadside stands offer fresh strawberries gathered that morning; and a pick-up truck weaves its way through city traffic, loaded with a freshly slaughtered pig. While some older people in recent years have come to call their highrise apartment building "home," many others still enjoy the pleasures of sitting on their front porches in neighborhoods where their parents were born. North Carolina, in other words, has a mixture of the past and present, accessible to an interested writer and a photographer willing to travel from Murphy to Manteo, as the natives describe the journey from the southwest corner of the state to the northeast corner.

Having chosen North Carolina, we agreed on a plan to meet women in their homes, churches, and communities, to spend significant time with each one, taping interviews, making photographs, and visiting. We began by asking for the names of women from church leaders, community organizations, groups like the Eastern Star, the NAACP, the YWCA, and senior citizens' clubs, newspaper reporters, schools, colleges, and universities, and civic leaders. We asked for the names of women who were over sixty-five years old and had lived most of their lives in the South. We were looking for contributions in a wide area— the home as mothers, wives, and grandmothers; the church as gospel singers, teachers, and ministers; the community as civil rights activists, group leaders, and members of senior citizens' clubs; the arts, and business and education. We compiled a list of about one hundred names, half of whom we selected for interviews. Those whose stories and photographs we included in this book were chosen because of their varied achievements and the richness of their narratives. Each one is an individual with particular talents and opinions, but she is also representative of a larger number of older black women of the South.

These women share a broad context of southern living, and their lives, which span most of this century, are exemplary of many others.

They live throughout North Carolina, in the Piedmont, the mountains, and on the coast, at country crossroads, in towns, and in the major cities. On the way to visit them, we passed farmland and unincorporated villages (where barbecue suppers are held to raise funds for the Volunteer Fire Department), and once we stopped on a cold morning to watch neighbors help a family slaughter hogs. Stretches of interstate are relieved by mountains, hills, and the rolling green of unspoiled acres, more of this good earth than city dwellers ever see. We were aided by directions from men leaning back in chairs against clapboard grocery stores and from friendly attendants at busy service stations, where customers still can buy a big Orange and a moon pie. In the cities we found the familiar national landscape of McDonald's and Kentucky Fried Chicken obliterating the distinctive identification of place with the American stamp of uniformity (the old Robert E. Lee Hotel in downtown Winston-Salem has been replaced by the currency of another Hyatt House).

Sometimes our visits lasted only for several hours. On many occasions, we were able to come back for several days of talking; we have known a dozen of the women in frequent visits, telephone conversations, and letters. Each time we returned, we learned more, often changing first impressions; sometimes the women asked to go back to an earlier question in order to tell us more than they had been willing to tell during the first visit. Often, of course, the women really began to talk to us after I had turned off the tape recorder and Susan had packed up her cameras. With each of the women our visits and conversations were as important as the recorded interviews and photographs. Many were purely "social"— taking Betty Lyons to visit the Dixie Classic Fair, playing the piano and singing hymns before the Reverend Sophia East's church service began, dining on wild game at the annual church supper with Viola Lenoir and Carrie Stewart, and joining the family for lunch at Maude Bryant's table. We tried to fit ourselves into their often amazingly busy lives. We were impressed that these women, after seven or more decades of living, remained full of energy, vitality, and curiosity. Whether they were still on the job—like Gatha Lassiter, who manages a meals program for senior citizens—or, like Viola Barnett, living quietly alone in retirement, they were women who retain an active interest in life.

How did we expect to be received by the women we visited? After all, we were not only strangers, but strangers with tape recorders and cameras. And we are white. Obviously, we could not work in a region where social separation of the races had long existed, indeed, continues to exist in many ways, and pretend that there were no barriers. We were asking to come into homes, to share family history, and to be trusted. Yet we knew that good manners and cordiality are still a part of the legendary southern hospitality, and we depended upon it.

Before we began our project we had talked with a young black college teacher about the relationships between races in the South (she had grown up in New Orleans). She had told us that as a child she was taught three postures to maintain with whites: first of all, be extremely courteous; second, never tell a white man or woman what you really think; and finally, laugh heartily when the white people leave in order to relieve the tensions. We thought a long time about the warnings. We discussed them with a number of the women we met and they recognized with some familiarity what the young woman had told us. But one of them said, "Black people have developed a second sense; they know when to trust and when not to trust. If they seem to trust you, accept it and trust them. Go on with your work." It was advice which we acted upon.

In visit after visit, we were warmly welcomed in the homes; the women were friendly and interested. If our visits started out with an awkward formality, they ended with laughter and good will. As I walked up onto the porch to interview Geneva Hunt after a telephone conversation in which she had agreed to see me, Mrs. Hunt remained in her chair, hesitated, looked at me a long time. I introduced myself, reminded her of my reason for coming, and waited. Finally, she said, "Well, I wasn't expecting you." I looked at her, I waited, I finally spoke. "Mrs. Hunt, you were expecting a black woman." Yes, she nodded, it was so. We laughed, lightly. We went inside and began to talk.

In a few instances, I was not as successful. I stood in the road a long time trying to persuade a retired teacher, cutting brush from her hedge, that she should sit down and talk with me, or, I suggested, we could work together and talk. No, she didn't like newspaper reporters and as soon as she saw me drive up, she was sure I was one of them. Friendly, but firm. On another occasion, I was refused an interview by a woman who had been the dietitian in the state Governor's Mansion for almost fifty years; she and other employees there had had to agree to the families' requests that they never discuss their jobs in the mansion. And I spent a year of visits trying to persuade a union organizer to talk with me, but the memories of the bitter red-baiting that she experienced during the union's organizing efforts made her wary of any further publicity.

We failed on another occasion to break down the barriers. We had gone to the coast to meet a woman in Camden, recommended to us as one of the outstanding black leaders of her community. Willie Harvey, a black woman and a strong advocate for community action, had described her to us: "She can sit still in a roomful of people and make no sound, and they can put anything before them and nobody moves until she stands up. Then they stand up." Yet when we visited her, we were not successful at engaging her in conversation. She shielded her mouth and face with her hands, referring questions to her daughter. We clicked off the recorder, put away the camera, and stayed for Cokes and cookies in her sunny yellow kitchen. Still, she revealed little of her self. We went back a second time to meet her at a convention for senior citizens at Nag's Head, and we saw that she had plenty of vitality to participate in the Seniors' Disco and plenty of friends. But we did not feel, even then, that we knew this woman. We asked Mrs. Harvey where we had failed. "You scared her to death," she told us, flatly. "How?" we asked in genuine dismay. "Because you are white," she answered. "And once the knife has cut, we always expect that it will cut again."

These were exceptions to our general success in gathering interviews, but they were instructive. When we read *Drylongso* by the distinguished black anthropologist John Langston Gwaltney, we were made more aware of our racial differences. In interviews with forty-one of his relatives and friends and their relatives and friends (all protected by fictitious names in the book) readers are told that black people do not trust white people: "You simply cannot be honest with white people." "We know white folks but they do not know us, and that's just how the Lord planned the thing. . . . Now they are the great ones for begging you to tell them what you really think. But you know, only a fool would really do that." These were sobering warnings, indeed. Fortunately, at the time we read them we had already had many good experiences which gave us confidence to continue. We are not naive enough to assume that our subjects would tell the same stories to a black interviewer; we accept the fact that no one tells anyone everything. Yet, because we believe in the relationships we established with the women we met, we believe in the "truth" of that they told us. We know that life is a "fiction," the supreme fiction, as poet Wallace Stevens described his art, and that what people choose to reveal about themselves has its own truth. It is the truth not only of their lives but of their imaginations. *Drylongso* revealed some truths. We believe that *Hope and Dignity* reveals others. We learned that sometimes people really do talk to strangers. And women will talk to women. Beatrice Burnett abruptly stopped her narrative one day short of completion and took it up again the next day, explaining, "I have to bring these things out." Theresa Bland told us details of family life which even brothers and sisters did not know, believing, "If a person is working on a psychological book, it's important to know all of this." Betty Lyons ended her narrative of her child's illegitimate birth by asking, "Is truth the light of the world?"

As Studs Terkel concludes after his hundreds of interviews with people all over America, "The privacy of strangers is indeed trespassed upon. Yet my experiences tell me that people with buried grievances and dreams unexpressed do want to let go. Let things out."

These texts and photographs present their own truths. Whenever possible, I have relied on transcriptions of the spoken narratives of the women themselves. As a writer, I have tried to describe their environments and their achievements in a context of time and place. My particular interest has been the way in which individual lives can be presented through images and events which symbolize a broad and representative American passage. The photographs and the texts are, in James Agee's description of his text and Walker Evans' photographs in *Let Us Now Praise Famous Men*, "coequal, mutually independent, and fully collaborative." Susan and I hope that through the spoken words of these women, a writer's interpretive responses, and a photographer's visual record these lives will be revealed. Our principal object is one which Wordsworth described for his poems in the Preface to *Lyrical Ballads*: "to choose incidents and situations from common life, and to relate or describe them throughout, as far as was possible, in a selection of language really used by men [and women], and, at the same time, to throw over them a certain coloring of imagination."

This morning as I write about black women of North Carolina, many of them are at home with their own thoughts and dreams as they stand at the kitchen window or sweep off the porch or tend a grandchild. Hear them now in their silence, as their minds move across history. In the stories which follow we come to know something of their failures and successes, their sorrows and their joys. North Carolina poet A. R. Ammons has written, "Have you listened for the things I have left out? . . . how can I tell you what I have not said: you must look for it yourself." Each of these women might well have concluded her story with such a question.

                                        Emily Herring Wilson

# Hope and Dignity

# Precious Lord, Take My Hand

## Eva Hill Roundtree / Mattie Shannon Smith

### Winston-Salem

*Precious Lord, take my hand,*
*Lead me on, help me stand;*
*I am tired, I am weak, I am worn;*
*Through the storm, through the night,*
*Lead me on to the light,*
*Take my hand, precious Lord, lead me home.*

Sunday morning, and the voice of the gospel singer fills the air. The faithful have gathered—at a white clapboard church on a country road, and in the shining new sanctuary of a city church. She stands before them, a special person whose gift, she believes, comes from God alone. Hers is a presence central to the service of worship, and by the power and glory of her voice she moves the congregation, sometimes in waves of emotion which bring weeping and a movement of bodies in the pews and aisles, sometimes in the deepest recesses of the listeners' spirits. Her place is the church, and she has chosen it over the bright lights of the stage and the temptation of fame and fortune. She sings that she may help bring others closer to God.

Eva Roundtree at the Fellowship Baptist Church in Winston-Salem and Mattie Smith at the Hanes C. M. E. Church in the same city are gospel singers who are frequent performers in church services, at funerals, and in guest concerts across the community. Mrs. Roundtree and Mrs. Smith are representative of hundreds of older women like themselves who grew up singing. They are artists, without formal training, who sing "in the spirit." Their older listeners enjoy the echoes of familiar spirituals and hymns absorbed into the gospel sound; the younger ones provide handclapping and rhythm, which echo the influences of blues and jazz. Mrs. Roundtree and Mrs. Smith often sing alone, or they

may be accompanied by a pianist or an organist, but each shuns the secular influences of tambourines, guitars, horns, and drums. They are not self-righteous about their preference and take no harsh attitude that other musicians who sing the blues are "sinful." Each believes that her voice can speak most directly to God.

The Bible Belt South, where Eva Roundtree and Mattie Smith have spent their lives, is a place where local radio stations broadcast evangelical preaching and where Sunday is a day of worship. Roads and highways have signs announcing the coming of Jesus. Bibles are left in public places; a verse from scripture may be handwritten on the wall of a small country store. These are not signs of the new, self-conscious Moral Majority which has attempted to dominate religion in the 1980s; they are born and bred in the poverty of the backwoods and in rooted families who believe that the South is America's spiritual child and who turn for guidance to the Lord. Evidence of the secular world is present in the South the same as in California or New Jersey. But there are still many church-goers like Eva Roundtree and Mattie Smith who worship the way they were taught in their childhood in the first decade of this century. And the gospel sound is powerful evidence that the old and the new are joined together. The explosion of voices in the forties singing the new "gospel" has not yet ceased to be heard. Even on the college campuses there are groups devoted to that old-time religion.

Eva Roundtree grew up in a musical family; her uncle played the reed pump organ, her sisters sang, and their mother sang and preached. Songs like "I'm Dwelling in Beulah Land" and "The Blood Done

Changed My Name" were family favorites; some of them were heard on records played on the wind-up victrola. Singing was a natural expression of their love of Jesus, and they loved Him in their home as much as in their church.

"When I joined the church as nothing but a child of eleven," Mrs. Roundtree remembers, "I gave the pastor my hand, but I gave God my heart. Then, you couldn't stop singing even if you wanted to. Me and my mother and sisters started singing thirty-nine years ago. We were out in my front yard under a big tree, we were sitting out there, the family, and we were singing. And I said, 'As good as y'all sing, we ought to organize a group,' and they laughed at me. And they said, 'What would you call us?' And I said, 'The Smiling Four.' And they fell out laughing. And that Sunday night we went to a great big church, and I slipped and wrote a note to the minister and said, 'You've got a new group of singers here known as The Smiling Four.' And I got up and went to singing, and then they did the most beautiful singing that you ever heard. And while I was sitting under that tree, the Lord gave me this song to sing, 'Don't Forget Your Family Prayer.' I wrote it in my mind, and that's what we sang.

*Don't forget your family prayer*
*Jesus wants to meet you there.*
*When you have gathered in the evening*
*Don't forget your family prayer.*

*Prayer will make you love everybody.*
*Prayer will keep you living just all right.*
*And when you have gathered in the evening*
*Don't forget your family prayer.*

"Long as you get the words," Mrs. Roundtree explains, "you can make you up a tune. There are so many true words in the song. This is my favorite. Prayer will keep your home together."

Mrs. Roundtree, born in 1906 on a farm in Taylorsville, North Carolina, a small Piedmont community, was one of twelve children, "raised up in the church." Their mother, Retta Hill, was an active church member all her life, and she was ordained as a minister in the Holiness Church after they moved to Winston-Salem when she was past sixty years old. "When she was ordained," Mrs. Roundtree remembers, "the minister said, 'She's supposed to have did this a long time ago.' But she said she wasn't going until the Lord called her; she wasn't going because people told her." One of Mrs. Roundtree's strongest remembrances is of her mother's last sermon, "Work on, pay day's comin' after a while." She says, "That still brings joy to me. I remember everybody in that church was just shouting and carrying on."

Mrs. Roundtree, like her mother, believes that you sing or preach "what the Lord lays on your heart. My mother said, 'Sing as long as the spirit tells you to, but don't keep on because they applaud. And some day you may have to go on by yourself.'" The Smiling Four did stop singing as a group after the deaths of the mother and one sister and the approaching old age and illness of another sister. But Eva Roundtree continues to sing, going on by herself.

*Jesus will never say no.*
*Jesus will never say no.*
*You can call Him in the morning,*
*You can call Him late at night.*
*But He never, will never, say no.*

"I've had so many ups and downs," she pauses. "And I've had so many burdens to carry. But when you get old and nobody wants you around, Jesus is near you. Without God, honey, we don't get too far. I'm not begging the Lord for nothing. I'm thanking Him for what He has done. You talk to the Lord and wait for the answer. And when you get to thinking about what the *Lord* can do, then you'll sing these songs. And don't tell nobody nothing but the Lord. You might get disturbed, you know. I just got disturbed last week, and I walked the length of this house and I said, 'I don't let nothing separate me from the love of God.' Last night I was singing this piece that come to me and everybody was talking to know what it was, and I just got kind of happy there, and I was just sitting there and thinking, and I sang:

*From the love of God*
*From the love of God.*
*I'll let nothing separate me*
*From the love of God.*

*From the love of God*
*From the love of God.*
*I'll let nothing separate me*
*From the love of God.*

*I've been tempted*
*And I've been tried.*
*But I'll let nothing separate me*
*From the love of God.*

*From the love of God*
*From the love of God.*
*I'll let nothing separate me*
*From the love of God.*

"I helped the Lord to make me what I am. A lot of times when people get disturbed in their mind and they tell everybody and ain't nobody going to tell it like you told it. And you can tell them how bad you feel, and they say, 'Oh, you're having it hard,' and they tell it. So I just made up in my mind when things in my own house sometimes ain't sugar all the time, but I have a great big house here, and I can go from room to room. I can walk from room to room, and it won't be just a little while everything's just as quiet. You just feel so good when everything goes all right when you think everything's wrong. Let God fight your battles. You hold your peace. Let God fight the battle, and He will face it. When you think nothing's coming your way, He'll just move in so nice. And that's the reason I serve the Lord. I get a blessing. Every day. Not one day, but every day. I get my blessing. I'm seventy-five years old. And so young people call and ask me and say, 'Mrs. Roundtree, such and such-a thing.' I say, 'Hold your peace, honey. Let God fight the battle.'

"Honey, I'm telling you the truth, singing lifted me. Cause I've been burdened. And I'd get up there and it'd look like then my burden would fall. And I'd sing, 'Soon I will be done with the trouble of this world.' And I'd say, 'Remove this, Lord, so I can get to be myself cause you can't do anything burdened.' I don't find no new ways of serving the Lord. Singing is just my talent. I've brought inspiration to this church. I've been blessed and over-showered with gifts from little children. I'm growing old and going out, and they're still coming. It doesn't take a great big fine church to serve the Lord. You are in a little place, and God will expand your love. When I go to church I don't look back to see anybody. Nobody in this church has money enough to pay me. God will pay us, if we're doing it from the heart. You know a lot of time people offer to pay me, and I tell them they can't pay me. God give it to me. God gave me that blessing. Some time people will ask me to sing while they be up living like we are, and the Lord will let me live to see them pass. They called me yesterday morning. Brother Key's wife passed and he said, 'You know, she told me what she wanted.' She told him in the hospital, say, 'All you got to do is just be sure you see Mrs. Roundtree.' I will sing 'Remember Me, When I've Come to the Setting Sun.' That's one that come to me. It come in my mind, and everybody hears it, they love it.

*Remember me when I've come to the setting*
*sun.*
*Remember me and think of some good I've*
*done.*
*Remember me and count my blessings one by*
*one.*
*Not just for me*
*But for the work that I've done.*

"When I got my religion, that was a long time ago. I was baptized when I was eleven years old. And you had to get down on your knees, honey, back in them days, and praying, and folks would be around you singing, until you really felt the spirit of God, and my mother and my father said you get down there and pray and don't care who jump up and shout over your head; unless you feel something, you stay right there. And that's what I did. I don't even know when I got up shouting, that's just how high the spirit carried me. Now when something comes to you, say, 'Go ahead, go ahead, and do that,' that's the Devil sometimes in you, and here comes a slow move. Just pass you one time, say 'Don't do that.'

It's not coming back to tell you don't do it. When that conscience tell you you don't do anything, don't do it. I went to work in New York. I prayed, 'Lord, guide my mind, and show me the way back home.' And I closed my eyes, and something come and laid a hand on my face and said, 'Go home.' And the next morning, I got up and I packed my clothes, I'm going home. God guided me to go home."

Mattie Shannon Smith, a decade younger than Mrs. Roundtree, was born in 1916 in Lancaster, South Carolina. She also grew up singing. She sang with her grandmother at home, and she sang working in the field. The first song she remembers singing in church was "I'm Gonna Wait on Jesus Till He Come." She learned some of the words from her father and older brother, but her talent was a "gift."

"I was brought up on a farm for about three years of my life," she begins, "and I learned to chop cotton, hoe tobacco and corn. At that time my mother was working in service, and I wanted to go live with my grandparents. And that's where I really learned to become a good worker in the field. I just loved it because it was a nice atmosphere out there, nice sunshine and plenty of fresh air, and you could look at the beautiful trees around the field that you was working in. My grandfather was a tenant on around twenty-five acres. I don't remember my grandmother ever doing any work other than in the house cooking. She'd always have two and three vegetables, made real nice white potatoes with plenty of butter. See, my grandfather would hire people to work, too, and she would have plenty of food for everybody. She would fix good corn bread, and she would churn. She had me churning. I'd do the churning and I got tired of it, but I didn't say anything. I just gone on and do that work. They had five cows, two horses, and two mules and had four hogs and twenty-five sheep. They would take the wool and sell it after they cut it off. See, this white man that owned the farm they was living on, he would take it and sell it. My grandfather would always come out. He never would go in the hole. He'd always be on the top.

"It was a beautiful place where we was living, beautiful shrubbery and flowers. There was six rooms in this house, and it had a real large porch to it. I shared a room with my first cousin. And my parents would come down visiting. The school was close to where my grandmother lived. It looked like a log cabin sitting out there. And in that same room was from the first on up to the seventh grade. The teacher was a beautiful sort of woman. I can look at her right now. When she prayed—at that time, they'd pray before they'd have class—she'd pray a good prayer every morning. Her name was Mrs. Lizzie Carpenter. And she was a very good teacher. I learned how to count money. And learned how to spell my name. I learned *that*, and that was the most important thing of all a person need to do. There's a lot of older people right now don't even know how to write their name.

"We moved to Winston-Salem when I was seven. I went to school for a while, but I preferred to work. I just got as far as the seventh grade. I needed to work at that time, I thought, to buy my own clothes. That's what I wanted to do, and I've been working ever since doing service work. I started out in the factory, tobacco factory. It was real dusty at that time. Real dusty where they do the stemming. I was four-

teen. They didn't care at that time how old you were so you were a good worker. I worked seven years in the factory. The supervisor was a white man. I've been treated fine by white folks all my days. I've been lucky. I likes for them to treat me like I treat them, too. I treat them just like I do my own children. That's what I likes. That's the kind of quality. Treat me like I treat you. It doesn't matter about what color they are. It's the heart, you know, the way you feel about a person. I've worked thirty years, and in between there, I'd sing. But I still worked.

"I was born with this talent. My older brother would teach me this vocal music, singing those notes. You sing without a piano. As a child I sang in the New Hope Methodist Church in Lancaster, South Carolina. I been singing ever since I was large enough. I've always been a brazen child. In Winston-Salem, I would sing at my church. And that's where I still sing, the Hanes Christian Methodist Episcopal Church. I sang last Sunday, 'Let God Abide.' The audience responds. They answer me, 'Amen.' Most everything I sing, they enjoy it. All spirituals, soul-stirring. Mrs. Roundtree and I both sing spirituals, but she sings it more like hymns, and I like the way she do. See, I have a girl play the piano with me. It has more rhythm but Mrs. Roundtree's has more soul. More fire with her, you know. She feels it! She can feel it, and I can feel it when she sings. I get a lot of joy when she sings. The spirit moves me. Sometimes I get emotional. You don't know what you're doing when the spirit gets you. People tells me what I did later. Sunday it was real emotional. When I get into a song, I don't know what's happening. One lady blacked out and was carried home. Another, they tell me, was happy all over the church. Sometimes you sits up with water in your eyes.

"The men of the church don't get into it like they used to. When I was growing up, there used to be a bunch of men down towards the front of the church leading a devotion service, and they would have a good time before the eleven o'clock service. But they don't do that anymore. There's so much temptations out there. So much discord, and clubs and things they go to. They don't have time, they don't feel like getting to church. They just forget it.

"I heard Mahalia Jackson at Shiloh Baptist Church. There was a big crowd, and we couldn't all get in. When she came, somebody had told her about me. When I was introduced, she said, 'You're the one the Pilgrims were telling me about, but you're prettier than I am.' I sang for her, and she said, 'I'll steal you away from here,' wanted me to go with her. But I'm rich and famous now. How rich can I get when I get Jesus? I sang with the Camp Meeting Choir. I was always the soloist for this choir, and that's the group that I started out traveling with. We was on the radio spot for about five years in place of Wings Over Jordan. They was overseas at the time. So we was broadcasting from coast to coast. That was in the early forties and on into the fifties. We started traveling, but we didn't stay long. I enjoyed traveling. We'd run into it rough, sometime, you know, about getting a place to stay. We stayed in a hotel and then homes most times. We went to black and white audiences, mostly in churches when we were singing to the white. We sang in Birmingham and Macon and in the state of Georgia, and South Carolina, that part of the country. We contested the Wings Over Jordan at Madison Square Garden. It means we sang

against them. See who we could whip singing! We won. We sang at Radio City Music Hall, and was there for about a whole day once making recordings, you know, records. So this Jew said, 'I want her to sing by herself.' And he said, 'I want to buy her from the choir.' And so my director said, 'Nooo! I want to keep her.' And he wanted to buy me out from the Choir to sing blues, but I rather prefer spirituals. I gets more joy out of singing spirituals. It gives you a message when you sing spirituals more than the blues. It's no use of me turning around now cause I'm sixty-two years old. I'm happier now than I've ever been in my life. I'm growing older, growing older in the spirit, child. Closer to the Lord. You've got to get closer. I'm not going to let nothing turn me around.

"The nation is getting weaker and wiser. You know, the kids now that's being born into this world, the younger race, they started this, wanting to have a right to do what they wanted to do. To be with the whites if they wanted to be with them, you know, sitting down eating there. They think their money spends just like the white man. If we're going to have children, we're going to be together. The Lord don't make no difference. He loves us all. And that's why I love Him, because He loves all and everybody. He's not going to love the Russians or the Italians or the French people or the Germans better than he loves the Americans. He loves us all the time, and so it won't be no separating. We'll all be together when we get to heaven."

For Mattie Smith, and for Eva Roundtree, another Sunday has come, and the service is over. The gospel singer comes down from the choir and moves among the people.

# One Dime Blues

## Elizabeth Moore Reid / Cora Reid Phillips
## Etta Reid Baker

### Caldwell County

The steady rhythm of the guitar floats over the hills of Caldwell County. Joined by the staccato voice of the banjo, the excited pitch of the fiddle, the breathlessness of the harmonica, it echoes down the years. In memory, we see once more the flashing feet and moving bodies of neighbors who have gathered in a dirt yard or in the barn or are clearing the worn wooden floors of an old shack for all-night dances under a Carolina moon. The six-foot, two-hundred-pound black man "of pure African blood," John Henry, towers like a ghost, reborn in the speed and splendor of the ballad frailed on the guitar by a mountain woman. The sounds of blues, jazz, and hillbilly converge in the song of "Corinna." The genius of Blind Lemon Jefferson comes alive again in "The Black Snake Moon." The musicians stroke their shining instruments, lay them carefully across their chairs, and rest. The jug is passed around, bodies cool in the deepening night, and the mountains send back the sounds, overpowering the sense of isolation, the endlessness of work, and the hours of loneliness passed by the families: the legacy of their parents and grandparents, whose tunes they make this night.

This is the setting for our introduction to a family of remarkable musicians, born in Caldwell County of mixed black American, white American, American Indian, and Irish descent, all kin to one another in more ways than they can remember. Gone now are the old ones, Sallie and Boone Reid, who learned from their parents the music they passed along to their eight children. Gone, too, is Theopolis Lacy Phillips, but his renditions of "Sally Ann" and "Shakin' the Pines in the Holler" survive. Fred Reid, age seventy-eight, has put aside his banjo now to sit on the porch, to roll another cigarette from Prince Albert tobacco, and to talk.

Three of the women in the family still "make" music. They are Cora Phillips, born in 1907, widow of Theopolis; Etta Baker, her sister, born in 1913, both children of Sallie and Boone Reid; and Elizabeth "Babe" Reid, their cousin and Fred's wife, born in 1910. They all live within twenty-five miles of each other—close enough for visits—Cora in Dulatown, Etta in Morganton, and Fred and Babe on the mountain near Collettsville. Etta's home is on a paved street in a town of about fifteen thousand; Cora, Babe, and Fred live on dirt roads in the country where the liveliest sounds are those of animals in the night.

On this mid-October morning, we are on the road to Collettsville, where they all first came from. We pass through the sleeping village, turn off Highway 90 and cross Franklin Creek. Chickens are roosting on the church steps; we wind our way up the mountain. The smell of skunk is strong enough to taste. Already the fields along the bottom are filled with the bleached shocks of corn and goldenrod. The sourwood is plenty red. We park the car and get out, struggling with cameras and other equipment. A woodshed is filled with newly split logs. Peppers hang on diminished plants. Watching us from overhead on their porch, Babe and Fred sit out our approach. As we walk towards them, crossing a plank over a small stream, Babe, like rural women, goes inside. Fred squints from under his Diesel Cat hat, stands up, spits off the porch, and tucks his fingers in his back pockets. We stumble, raise our heads, Fred grins, and Babe returns to stand in the doorway. When she is in place, we meet, and slowly the story begins, like a tune which has been played across the years.

Babe waits until we take a chair, then pulls one up to the doorway and seats herself. Fred begins talking about the weather, about hunting dogs and skinning squirrels, and shares his recipe for apple brandy (from Limbertwig apples) and woodchuck ("That's the best eating I know of anywhere"). Slowly, the talk turns to music, and he recalls marrying Babe. "Yeh, we'd meeting together of a Saturday night, oh, for ever so long before we was married. I was just looking on; finally, I just decided to settle down. We was playing all night. Sit up and play, and them old folks maybe go to bed, and we'd just play right on. That wouldn't stop us. I was playing the banjo, and Babe was playing a guitar, and she played a banjo, too. 'Johnson's Boys,' 'Sourwood Mountain,' 'Goin' Down the Road A-feeling Bad,' and 'Bully of the Town.' Oh, just anything in the world I wanted to play I would play. I just picked it up. I didn't ever read nothing. And I guess I could play nearly all night and not play the same tune. Now, my Daddy, he'd what we call 'fist it.' And I never could do that. I just played with them two fingers. Me and her [Babe] got the guitar down so fine, and she can prove it. She could be a'sitting like she's sitting now and holding the guitar in her hand and she'd be a'playing back yonder, and I could play up here. She'd be playing with her right hand back here and me with my left hand up here." Fred reaches out to demonstrate how he and Babe both played her guitar together. Then he draws back and says he can't play anymore, doesn't want to play anymore. "Looks like it's just gone away from me some way or 'nother," he complains.

Babe leaves Fred in a brooding silence,

and plays a tune. She moves through "Worried Blues," "One Dime Blues," "Crow Jane," "Bully of the Town," and "John Henry." When her fingers are still, she seems to want to say, "What more is there?" Babe's story is told in the sustained narrative of the music she makes. Like Cora, Etta, and Fred, she does not sing with her instrument. The guitar is her voice, the tunes the speech of a muted woman. Coaxed, she talks a little about her life. One of two children born on nearby Johns River to Mattie and Ishmon Moore, she went through eight grades in the one-room school house which was right below where she lives now on Franklin Creek. Her mother taught her to quilt, and it's one way she still passes a winter's night. She learned to play guitar when she was about twelve years old from watching Etta and Cora play. Soon they were playing together at parties, where families gathered after a corn husking or for a dance of the old reels and sets. Babe and Fred married when she was twenty-four and he was thirty-one. They had eight children, seven girls and one boy. "All my boys was girls," Fred laughs. All eight children live in North Carolina. When Fred retired from working for the town of Lenoir, the county seat of Caldwell several miles down off the mountain, they went back home to Collettsville, where "it's quiet." Fred says about any place in town, "I wouldn't have it if it was just give to me," and Babe nods. Now their life is spent sitting on the porch and tending a small garden, and in winter, which comes soon, near the Warm Morning stove. In the evenings when Fred has gone to bed, Babe sits and plays for herself, a solitary figure in a solitary place. In contrast, her songs sing of a livelier time.

When the conversation gets too long for

Babe, she looks off, then starts her fingers again, "Don't Let Your Deal Go Down." Then another, and another, and just as "One Dime Blues" comes back again, the weather suddenly changes; a mountain storm has come up. No one speaks, but we all move, taking our chairs inside, and Fred closes the door.

We sit in shadow and silence, listening to the thunder, watching the lightning cut across the small windows. We read the calendar advertising Ramon's Pink Pills, "a fine laxative," and admire the pictures of Babe's own children and others she has nursed. Babe has put her instrument away and now sits, her hands folded on her lap. Fred rolls a cigarette and smokes. We wait. "I always set quiet, the way I was learned, when it's thundering," he says. Then a long while later, "It sounds like it's coming back." Babe speaks for the first time in the hour, "It ain't done yet." As nothing is ever done, nothing is over; for the voices of the past, like thunder, are born again in the music of the next generation. The story will continue as the sun comes out, and Fred and Babe agree to drive down to Dulatown with us to see Cora. We pack up Babe's guitar, put some cheese and crackers in a sack for Fred, and get in the car and come down and across Franklin Creek.

Dulatown, it is said, was settled by a white plantation owner, Alfred Dula, who took a black slave wife after his white wife died. His children and their children and so on down the generations inherited his name and property, and now there is a large community of Dulas, Doolies, and Dooleys in both white and black families. Cora Phillips is one of the blacks of Dulatown whose fair skin suggests the past interrelationships of the two races. She is out in the yard feeding her chickens. She squints from under a denim cap and throws up her hands when she sees Babe and Fred. Fred and Cora do all the talking, chickens scratch in the feed, dogs nudge one another, and we wait with Babe. In a while, we all go into the house, filled with the fragrance of Cora's apple pie (made from apples on trees Cora and her husband grafted). Babe sits down and tunes up her instrument, begins "John Henry," and the sound sends Cora scrambling under the bed to bring out her guitar. Cora fusses over the tuning, more exact than Babe, and instructs her, "Seems like that's a little bit flat, Babe. Pull it closer to the fret. Now just a little key on that." Babe's style is to play without first tuning up, as if she wants to get on with the real music, but Cora fusses—with the guitar strings, with the stove, with the chickens. Cora likes things a certain way. Now she settles down to playing, then jumps up and borrows Fred's pocket knife, ties it to the neck of her guitar, and tightens it down. She explains that sometimes she uses a broken bottle neck on the strings, like her daddy taught her. Then she's into "Gone With the Wind."

"I learned to play sitting on Poppa's knee when I was three or four years old," Cora begins. "In our family we played together every time we got a chance. Shucks, we'd want to get up before breakfast and start our music." Cora's father, Boone Reid, played everything—banjo, guitar, french harp, fiddle; and his wife, Sallie, played the Jew's harp and sang. All of the eight children played, and sometimes they'd be joined by neighbors on wash boards and tubs, and Dulatown would ring with their music. Boone might put down his instrument and take a turn on the dance floor in a wild buckdance or a reel or the Short Dog. Then both black and white neighbors would join in, just the way the music was a mixture of black and white traditions. In the family they listened to what Cora calls "roller records" played on an Edison cylinder machine, and the first one she remembers was "St. Louis Blues," published in 1914 by W. C. Handy and played by every jazz musician in the twenties. Between learning the new tunes they heard on records bought in Lenoir and the old tunes handed down in the family, Boone and Sallie Reid and their children were making the small community of Dulatown in North Carolina a music capital, although mostly unknown except in their immediate region. Although they couldn't read music and now can't remember the names, they were picking up the traditions of musicians like Blind Lemon Jefferson, Lonnie Johnson, and Texas Alexander, and learning "Travis picking" and "Cotton picking," the latter a basic guitar style named for Elizabeth Cotton, another black woman in North Carolina—over in Chapel Hill—who was making music in the twenties. Cora, Etta, and Babe do not have any formal knowledge of the blues tradition, but the "home tradition," which they call theirs, has provided them with the skills and the music associated with some of the best-known blues musicians.

Cora Phillips, like Babe, lets her music talk for her, mostly. She says very plainly, "I love music. It was music in the home and just when I began to hear music, I loved it. We had a happy home. We'd have music, dances, and plenty to eat. My husband, The, he played, and his daddy, Lewis Phillips, he made good music. He'd play 'The Cowboy's Feeling Blue' on the fiddle. He learned it at home like we did. When we played the neighbors couldn't sit still." Then her nimble fingers are dancing along the strings. Between tunes she continues the story, "I think I bought my first banjo from the money I made selling garden seeds." And later she observes, "Clear and windy weather makes good music."

Now she sets aside her guitar and takes us all into the kitchen around the hot Birmingham wood stove (next to a cold Hotpoint electric). At last, the apple pie! While we stand around, Cora takes it out, covers the crust ("Roll it thin") with a generous smattering of butter, and we sit down at the table and she passes around big slices. Fred finishes first and he's ready to go back up on the mountain. As we walk together out the back door, Cora tells us that last night she shot off her gun over the heads of a pack of dogs "and next time I'll shoot lower." No one doubts her. We leave her taking in the washing she's done for the grandchildren and her only child, Marie, who lives with her now. Cora Phillips is a wisp of a lady, her long white hair tied back in neat plaits, her small gold heart earrings shining. She can shoot straight, tune a guitar, and bake apple pie. As we leave we hear—do we?—the music of Dulatown come back again.

On another visit, we drive to Morganton to see Etta Baker, Cora's younger sister. She's been out in the garden since daylight, but if we had arrived sooner, we'd have heard her begin her day with a tune.

Etta Baker is the most demonstrative of the three women, a warm, loving, sweet-talking grandmother who enjoys fast cars and playing for audiences. She plays a six-string and a twelve-string electric guitar. Her favorite instrument is a gift from one of her nine children. Glenn Hinson of the North Carolina Folklife Division says,

"Etta Baker is without question one of the finest guitarists in the fingerpicked piedmont blues tradition." Hinson has helped rediscover blues musicians in the state, organized them for concerts, and recently took a group, including Cora and Etta, to perform at Wolf Trap Farm Park outside Washington.

Etta is an easy talker, her words as soft as a C note plucked on her guitar. "I was so tiny when I started playing," she remembers, "that I would stand between my Daddy's knees, and I would beg him to get my guitar. So he would lay it on the bed for me, and then I would stand up by the bed and play about three frets down on the guitar. Oh, I would look at Daddy, and he had such a smile! I can see it now, the smile he had on his face when I would make a good chord. He would holler, 'That's my girl!'

"When I was three we moved to Virginia. We first went to Chase City, and this bunch of people was serenading us for being newcomers to that part, and they came down and they went around the house playing and Daddy said, 'Be quiet, children. I hear music!' You know it just thrilled him to death to hear music of any kind. They marched around the house, and Daddy asked them to come in and when they did, there was one of the men in the group taught Daddy this 'Carolina breakdown' and then he set down then and taught it to me. It's kind of a blues. Daddy was a real, real sweet father. He was good, real good to the whole family. He was good to my mother, Sallie, Sallie Reid. My daddy was a farmer, a hunter. We worked on a big tobacco plantation in Virginia, and the whole family was together. Mama was real, real sweet, with a high temper. She was Indian, and she was small, with a huge temper. A lot of people say they can see a lot of my mother in me. Seems like I don't really recall it ever being too hard. Only I would hear my mother say, 'Well, we've made it so far, we can make it on.' The greatest thing was everybody would be out working during the day and at night we would have music and we'd always have plenty to eat. Eat a huge supper and then everybody was ready to sit down and enjoy each other with the music. It was a big, happy family. And I felt that this music held everybody together longer maybe than we would have been. I think it was just great. A lot of cousins played, and an aunt, and Daddy's brother. Uncle Monroe, he could play the fiddle left-handed. And a lot of times we wouldn't go to bed until three o'clock. Mama played a Jew's harp real good, and she could play a harmonica, too. We played 'Careless Love,' 'Red River Valley,' 'Railroad Bill,' and 'Bully of the Town.' Then me and Cora played together all the time."

Etta married when she was twenty-three and Lee Baker was about fifteen years older. In 1936 they started housekeeping in a two-room cabin on Johns River near Collettsville; then they moved to Morganton. There was a child coming about every two years. "Even right today," she confesses, "when I meet somebody with a tiny baby, I feel like it ought to be mine!" Tragedy came to their family when Mr. Baker died after a long paralysis, and soon after, their seventeen-year-old son was killed in Viet Nam. The remaining family grew closer together and suffered again together when a grandchild was killed in a car which Mrs. Baker was driving. Her anguish was only partially relieved by the knowledge that she was not at fault. Perhaps it was her religious faith which sustained her, perhaps she drew strength and comfort from a music which has long expressed for her and her people both grief and joy. In her life and her tunes Etta Baker expresses an abiding love of life.

Lee Baker was also a musician, a pianist, and he was a popular dancer. While his wife played, he danced, "And every time I would tell myself, 'Now I know I'm not going to act ugly this time; I'm going to take it and be brave,' and then he would just look so pretty up there and somebody else enjoying him, and no, I couldn't take that. And true enough, when I stopped all the music stopped. So I set my guitar in the corner and that broke it up. I couldn't stand to see him dancing with somebody else!"

Etta and Lee's children started playing instruments when they were young, and two of their boys (one of two sets of twins) started a band when they were about twelve years old and played in nearby towns and as far away as Vermont. Now several of the girls play the piano, and one daughter, Dorothy, sings, picking up every song she hears.

In recent years, since retiring from a factory job, Etta has returned to her music with the same sort of passion which engaged her as a young girl, and she has been invited to perform in folk festivals in the state. She is recognized as an outstanding performer by many guitarists who study her style, which has been written about in publications for guitar students.

Etta Baker loves family, gardening, chickens, cars, and music. She loves home. "And I love people. I love black people, I love Indian people, I love white people, because I have in me all those races. My grandmother was full-blooded Irish. Cora, she taken back after her, I took back after my Indian grandmother. I don't meet anybody that I could say I dislike due to whatever they may be, black, white, or Indian, or whatever, because if I dislike them, I would dislike a lot of my people because I have people of several different races.

"I relax upon my music," she concludes. "When I work in the yard, get tired doing things out there, I come in and have a tune and forget all about being tired."

Our visits are over now, but the stories go on. The music goes on. Up on the mountain as darkness comes Babe Reid sits alone, playing for herself. Cora comes to Etta's house and they play. As we say goodbye to this family, pack up again, and start back to the city, the sun shines on a silver line of a spider's web, going from our car aerial to the door handle. It seems a good sign, and we get in the other side so as not to break it. We drive back down from the mountain, and miles away, the thread holds.

# Green Animals around the Moon

## Minnie Jones Evans

### Wilmington

"Paint, or die!" the voice instructed her in a vision, and she took up an old board which had been discarded in a trash pile and began to draw. "I never did nothing as hard and as terrible as that in all of my life. For hours I worked. Oh, what a terrible condition I was in. My husband said, 'Minnie, how you feel? What's the matter? I want to know, what ails you?' The children say they didn't know I was their mother. I had changed in looks of some kind of thing." Her voice drops to a whimper, her words trail off in unrecognizable sounds; she raises her eyes toward heaven.

Minnie Evans, age ninety, is describing how she made her first drawing, begun on Good Friday in 1935. More than forty years later, her pictures have been exhibited in the Whitney Museum of American Art, the Museum of American Folk Art, Portal Gallery in London, and in other galleries and museums, including St. John's Art Gallery in her own city of Wilmington, North Carolina. Art critics studying her work have called her a "surrealist" and "mystic" and "primitive" and have written about the paintings for academic journals and national news magazines. Her life was made the subject of a PBS documentary, and she has been included in a half-dozen books on American artists.

Minnie Evans was born in 1892 in rural Pender County on the coast of North Carolina, and like many southerners, learned her Bible "by heart." The books of Ezekiel, Samuel, and Revelation in particular have influenced her visions, translated into figures of angels, prophets, and emperors. Fixed eyes appear among the vines and tangles of lush foliage. Green animals with wings, serpents and birds, and sun and stars, make up the symmetrical designs of her bright pictures. These compelling images have the same kind of allegorical power as those of William Blake's drawings and engravings. Indeed, some of the same Biblical stories which inspired Blake inspired Minnie Evans—Ezekiel's vision of the Chariot of God and the New Jerusalem. She has often dreamed that she was in a chariot pulled by lions and driven by a man in a white robe, like the white raiment mentioned so often in Revelation. In the dream she is taken down the street to a pool of water, "but it was water and it wasn't water." In it swims a "great long white fish," perhaps a fish like Blake's in "Images of Mortality," engraved for *America, A Prophecy.*

A passage from Revelation seems particularly to have influenced her visions:

*And the four beasts had each of them six wings about him; And they were full of eyes within; and they rest not day and night, saying, Holy, holy, holy, Lord God Almighty, which was, and is, and is to come. Revelation 4:8.*

The chariots in her dreams and Ezekiel's wheel seem to have merged in her imagination, and she repeats the circular design again and again in her paintings. "What would the world be today without wheels?" she asks.

*The appearance of the wheels and their work was like unto the colour of a beryl: and the four had one likeness; and their work was as it were a wheel in the middle of a wheel. Ezekiel 1:16.*

*As for their rings they were so high that they were dreadful; and their rings were full of eyes round about them four. And when the living creatures went, the wheels went by them; and when the living creatures were lifted up from the earth, the wheels were lifted up.* Ezekiel 1:18–19.

The figures in her paintings are indeed "lifted up from the earth" and float against a brilliant blue background over the earth's red and gold foliage. And the canvas is "full of eyes," eyes in human faces, eyes amidst bands of leaf and scroll, eyes at the center of things. Sometimes the eyes are menacing, sometimes they are blankly indifferent, sometimes they are wide with curiosity or pleasure. Eyes like the eyes of Minnie Evans.

The art of Minnie Evans was first recognized in 1960 when Nina Howell Starr, a New York photographer and art critic, saw her work. For most of her life, Minnie Evans had worked in other trades, as a "sounder" selling fish from the Wrightsville Sound, as a housekeeper, and from 1948 until 1974 as the gatekeeper on an estate known as Airlie Gardens. After Mrs. Starr became her representative and arranged for her first showing in New York in 1966, the pictures of Minnie Evans—in pencil, crayon, watercolor, and oil—began to be studied by art critics. Some have probed her life for sources—one suggests that we understand the imagery in terms of an African and Caribbean heritage—but it seems more likely that her influences are from the gardens of her own locale in North Carolina, especially from Airlie. She would have seen year after year the azaleas in brilliant bloom against a background of dense vines, boxwoods, oak trees, from which stretched, like tentacles, the hanging Spanish moss. In Airlie she must have been impressed with the quiet beauty of the small chapel, the blue ceiling like the blue of her drawings, the windows which later may have framed her entranced faces. A few yards behind the chapel lies an old graveyard, like so many she has mentioned from her dreams, filled with headstones, perhaps later emerging in her drawings. When Minnie Evans looks at her pictures, she talks about her dreams and about Airlie; she seems to have no interest in what critics have written about her. In her presence visitors are filled with a sense of mystery, and it is a mystery which ultimately is revealed in the paintings and drawings.

Until recently, Minnie Evans has lived with her son, George, and his wife in a small apartment filled sometimes with five generations. Her mother died in 1980 at the age of one hundred and one. Grandchildren and young great-grandchildren come in and out of the room during our visit. Then, she has a way of removing herself from this immediate world, transfixing her gaze into another place. Almost totally deaf, she does not hear questions but speaks in a loud voice which rises and falls like a wave. She has said, "I love people to a certain extent, but sometimes I want to get off in the garden to talk with God." Today she lives in a home for older people, but her life is in the past and in her dreams. Seated with her pictures around her, she begins a soliloquy which is as commanding as her paintings.

"I didn't sleep when I was a child. I couldn't sleep for dreams. We were living on Seventh Street between Church and Castle. There were some old prophets. As soon as I lay down and dropped off to sleep, they would grab me, take me, throw me up, wouldn't try to hurt me, and they would laugh and play with me. I remember one night they tossed me so much, they carried me down Seventh Street till I got to Seventh and Market, and when I was at Market Street, to the Soldiers Cemetery, that's where I woke up. Three or four times I have woke up out there. They take me and carry me out there in a dream. And I get up in the morning, I'd be tired, I was but a child. Once, I was in such a terrible state when I went to school; this was when I was in my last grade, six grade. Oh dear me! There I was, so sleepy that I had dropped off to sleep and my teacher come there, say, 'Minnie, why are you sleeping so?' 'I'm tired, I can't rest.'

"I remember another thing. We were living on Green Street with the cemetery, the white cemetery, we could see all those tombstones over there. Then people, somebody, went to calling me. Kept me running backwards and forwards. 'M'am?' 'I didn't call you.' I went in there two or three times and said to my mother, 'M'am?' She said, 'Why do you keep running to me?' I say, 'Somebody keep calling me.' Mama say it ain't her. A long time, the voice would call me, 'Minnie.' And I had to remember not to answer.

"What I'm telling you now is not a dream; it was not a dream. I can't even tell you my age because I was not old enough to go to school. I and some more little children—this is not a dream, this is natural—were out on the street playing. The moon was shining very bright. I don't think I've ever seen a moon like it since. The night the ring around the moon, the circle, I haven't ever imagined or seen another circle like it. I was but a little child, not old enough to start to school. I and these children were out there playing. And my attention somehow was drawed up at the moon, the ring around the moon.

"I thought everybody seen it, but no. The animals was going around the ring of

that moon. I thought it was elephants, great big tall animals, and some different sizes and some big white horses. And I stood there looking at it, and the little boys said to me, 'Minnie, what you looking at?' I said, 'I'm looking at them elephants up there.' 'Elephants?' Then the other children come there and they went to looking. 'We don't see no elephants, don't see no rings around the moon.' But it was a parade, going around that moon. I stood there and looked. My mother was sitting on the porch. I don't know whether she was looking at them or not. But the children was a'laughing at me because I saw those things, going round the ring. She scold me. Say, 'You come in the house and sit down, talking bout you seeing elephants going round!' So I come in and sit down, and there was this old lady right next door to us, said, 'Let that child alone. Leave her off.' Said, 'Maybe you don't see them but God has showed her something that He hasn't showed you.' Now when I close my eyes I can see them.

"Art is a mystery. I didn't have no idea it was like it is. It is so particular. It's a great mystery. When I start a picture, I don't know no more what I'm going to do than you do. When I make a picture the time comes for me to put an eye, and I look and say, 'Oh, I got to go.' I have a granddaughter. She's a good copier. But I tried to get her to *make* some pictures, *make* them, not copy, not after nobody else but start to making, that's the way I get mine. I can't copy after nobody, what somebody else done done. I can't even copy my own. I tried, no. I can't even copy my own pictures. I have *made* pictures, nobody's else's pictures. I'm without a teacher. I've had some of my friends tell me, 'Well, Minnie, if you had been able to go to college or to a university' 'I say, 'Where 'bout? What university? What college? No college in the world, no university in the world can teach Minnie Evans, cause they don't know what to teach me.' Am I right or not? I'm without a teacher. I have never taken no lessons. I went and got the book out of the library that the horses was in to look at to see after I had started a horse did I need it, but I couldn't do nothing with it. I had to put the book back. My mind was telling me how a horse looked and just go ahead. Oh, my, my. I erased a picture once. I had made, got it finished, I thought, and it worried me—that picture's not right. So I had to go over it the next day, two days before I could finish that picture. I say, 'Well, it's done. Who cares?'

"Dream pictures. I have one there. I was all night long, doing this picture in my dream. All night! I got up the next morning, early, said, 'George, bring me some board! Another board.' That picture stayed with me. That twin unicorns. Green unicorns. The white horses is named Angel Wings. Oh, my. So I keep it to remind me, a green picture. The first pictures I did, the paper was so old, till they broke up, just broke. I got a big envelope and I went to gathering them up, I gathered up all that I could see. So I had them things in there, lay down in the dark room, say, 'Lord, what can I do with those pictures?' God spoke to me plain as I am speaking to you, 'Paste them on a board!' I said, 'Oh,' I had to smile, and I looked up and said, 'Thank you, thank you.'

"This big picture is The Ark of the Covenant. Moses. That's it! This is Ezekiel saw the wheel, in the middle of the air. God told Moses to make the covenant and paint it with gold. The Tree of Life, the Tree of Life, my! Is in the Garden of Eden, it's there! See, there are two trees. Eve went got the fruit off of the Tree of Knowledge. But He put them out the Garden before she went to the Tree of Life.

"My whole life is nothing but a dream. All night long I was dreaming, making that picture, all night! God showed me about painting that picture. So I started on it. I was all day long. I didn't finish it that day. I dreamed I was standing on the corner of Front and Orange Street. I didn't know anything at St. John's Art Galley. There was some prophets, I called them, up in the air. They wasn't angels, but they were floating in the air like balloons. And I sit there and watched them, and they were singing some of the most prettiest songs. I dream about so much music, but I never see it. I just hear it. They were singing the beautifullest songs, up there in the air, floating around up there. Right up above St. John's Art Gallery, and I didn't know a thing about St. John's Art Gallery. And the last one waved his hand at me and was gone. But the most funniest dream is the antses wedding. That's when my husband [Julius Caesar Evans] thought I was going crazy. Peoples was telling him that I was losing my mind. He tried to stop me, my mother, too. I felt sorry for him feeling, but I couldn't make him understand. He didn't see no need of me doing that. I said, 'But I've got it to do.' Now you know well, I couldn't do that if it wasn't given to me. So I woke up and I told him about that dream. Antses getting married. This old tree had fell and was laying on the ground, rotten, one end of it. And there was a little hole went into that tree. And in that tree was full of antses. And I went in that little hole, I don't know how big I was. When I got in there it was lit up, the most beautifullest pretty lights. The antses strutting around there, those men with the tails. The women all dressed up in their beautiful dresses. And the bride, she was all nervous, all upset. The women were standing around her, petting her, talking to her. When I come in this little hole on that side, that's where I was. I don't know how big I was cause when they were in they all would stop and look at me. And there was beautiful music. My, my, my. That was the most funniest dream in the world. Dream of antses getting married.

"I had a dream one night. I was going down near about to the bridge; over on that side was an old tank they had towed away and had built a new one. Standing beside that tank was a tall, beautiful angel, beautiful. He said, 'Tell Julius to let you alone. If he don't, he going to die.' I got out. I say, 'Julius, don't say anymore to me.'

"So many dreams have come to me. Big birds flying in the air and lot of people was dropping bombs in the street, and they was saying, 'War, war.' A big crowd in the street. The first airplane I ever saw brought back that dream. It sounds foolish. My Bible tells me, forget the past. Look forward to a higher calling. The world is filled with darkness. Because we are so unkind, so many gods, so many creeds, so many paths that wind and wind. While just the art of being kind is all the sad world needs. That's right. All the sad world needs.

"I'm looking for Jesus. He's coming back soon. So I will tell you a mystery. We're not all sleep. We're not all going to be dead when He comes. He says we'll be changed in the twinkling of an eye! I'm looking for it! I'm expecting it! We will be changed in the twinkling of an eye, Jesus is going to change us. He's going to call the righteous out of the dust of the ground. We are near the end of human history." Minnie Evans pauses in her long narrative and fixes her eyes directly on her visitors. Her voice booms with the authority of a prophet, "Don't let the Devil get your soul!"

# mid·wife
## [ME *midwif*; OE *mid* with (c.G *mit*, Icel *meth*, Gk *metá*)+WIFE]

### Carrie McDonnell Stewart

Franklin

### Maude Lee Bryant

Moncure

The midwife was one of the best-known members of a North Carolina rural community, and her skills, often learned from her mother, were as essential as a man's knowing how to plant and to plow. Carrie McDonnell Stewart in the mountains of the western part of the state and Maude Lee Bryant in the Piedmont were midwives to their relatives and neighbors.* Payment for their services was as remote as the lighted rooms of a hospital. They went quickly and willingly, as if hearing in their dreams the call of a woman in her need. Their stories echo with authenticity.

"I've seen quite a few things very interesting," Mrs. Stewart begins, in her one hundred and fourth year. "I remember them very well." Her narrative claims for its own both what was told to her and what she now has to tell to others.

"They tell me I was born over across the river here. November twenty-eighth, eighteen and seventy-eight. There was ten of us. I have three names, Minnie Carrie Ann. I don't know why they gave me three because I was the oldest, and they didn't know what was behind. My mother was Mary Jane Luvenia, and my daddy was James Marion McDonnell. My mother was born here in North Carolina, too. I knew my grandmother Martha Smith. She died on Christmas Day. She had her burying suit, and she wanted to be buried just like she was going to church, white suit, and black shoes and black stockings. She said if she was going to church she would be dressed from her feet to her head. And, you know, they buried her in everything, just like she was going to church. I remember it very well. She said she wanted to fold her own arms in death, and so she told my mother, said, 'Now, straighten me out. Now smooth the cover and make it all

plain.' And they did that and then she folded her arms like that and that was the last of it. I've had to pull out a many a stitch that I'd sewed; it wasn't sewed to suit her. My grandmother, she could weave, and we kept sheep, and they'd shear the sheep, you know, and then card the wool and make rolls. And then they had a spinning wheel and she'd get that and put those rolls up there and spin and have thread. Then she had what you called a reel. You'd put that thread on there and double it and twist it. Then you had thread ready for knitting. I've saw her weave many a yard of cloth, and then she'd take that cloth and make wee petticoats and make Daddy's undershirts and things like that. They started us when we were children with two pieces of cloth. So I learned to do quilt work and now I, so far as putting quilts together and quilting, I can do that as good as I ever did.

"My daddy did farm work, when he was able. He had rheumatism. Now like it'd be a sunny day and all he'd say, "It's gonna rain, for my legs and knees pains me,' and he's weather propheteering. He farmed and plowed and he hoed corn. I knew all about farm work. I hoed corn; hoed corn and thin it and replant, three times, then the last time they called it 'laying by the corn.' Then we'd sow peas, these clay peas they call them now. We used to call them cowpeas. Sow peas, and then in the fall of the year, why those peas would be ripe to pick. Then we'd go and take our sheets and go to the field and pick peas, put out a sheet and put those peas on there, and we'd pick peas, and then in the afternoon we'd have the sticks, flail them out, put the peas in sacks and the hulls in another sack and carry them home. We'd feed the hulls to the cattle in the winter, and we'd have those peas to eat. I knew how to plow right enough. I remember Mr. Matt Ray owned a place round where I lived, and my husband had a little patch of corn he wanted plowed out, and so I kept telling him, well, I wanted it plowed out so I could hoe it, and he was so busy on the farm, he didn't have time. So I said, 'Well, if I had a mule to go in there, I could plow it out.' That tickled Mr. Ray. He said he had two mules. He had one he called Mary. He said, 'I'm going to bring Mary down here this evening, and I'm going to see if you know how to plow. You don't know gee from haw,' and I said, 'All right.' He brought her down there. So he put her in the row. I plowed up that patch of corn. He said he was surprised. When you wanted them to go gee, you'd pull them right. If you wanted them to go haw, you'd pull them left. Yes, indeed, I knew all about farm work. Yes, indeed.

"I went to school regularly till I married when I was eighteen years old [in 1896]. We had first reader, second reader, third reader, fourth reader, and fifth reader. I went through all those books. And we had primary arithmetic, intermediate arithmetic. And we had spelling books. I have one of those old timey spelling books that rhymed. I have one now—old, old blueback speller. I think it's lying in here on the table."

As Mrs. Stewart hops up (her husband called her "Toad") to get her speller, there is the first pause in her narrative, and we realize that we have been talking for almost an hour. Her hands have been busy making another rag rug for the house she shares with her daughter, Gertrude Conley. When she returns with her school book, she shows us sentences which her teacher at St. Cyprian's Episcopal Church school, the

Reverend J. A. Kennedy, required students to memorize almost a century ago.

*Good men obey the laws of God.*
*I love to survey the starry heavens.*
*Careless girls mislay their things.*
*The adroit ropedancer can leap and jump and*
*    perform as many exploits as a monkey.*
*Kings are men of high renown.*
*God created the heavens and the earth in six*
*    days and all that was made was very good.*

Carrie Stewart sits listening, a centenarian in a fishing cap, time is spun around, and we imagine her as a girl reciting the english sentences with the seriousness required of her by her teacher. As she picks up her narrative in all the southern rural vernacular of gee and haw, we are again aware of a quick mind still faithful to detail.

"I married Joseph Elexander Stewart, and he never would have the Alexander spelled with the a. I met him right here in Franklin, North Carolina; he lived here all his life, and I did, too. The first night after we married I stayed at home. Then the next night I stayed at my husband's brother's home. And the third night, he had rented a little log cabin and had a bed in it. He had a bed of his own and things at his home moved in that little house. We had one bed and pillows and three plates and a dish for the meat and gravy and just little things like that. It was just playing because I'd been used to a big family. As we lived there and grew older, we got a few more rooms added to it. We had ten children. I had twin babies, but the little girl didn't live but a few minutes. Had three boys and seven girls. All of them born at home, every one of them. I had a doctor with the first one, well, then I think I had a doctor with about two more, but then I had midwives with the rest of them. My husband died in '51, nineteen and fifty-one. That's been a long time."

Mrs. Stewart, who now with the recollection of midwifery jumps up again to find her midwife's white hat, started keeping records of her delivery of babies in a little black notebook, the first date 1934, the last entry in 1950 when she was seventy-two years old. She also has kept a certificate, "Midwife Permit Grade A from the North Carolina State Board of Health" dated 1947. She continues her story, remembering the midwifery classes offered in Franklin.

"They taught me everything," she remembers, "from the time the child was conceived until it was born, all about it, every way, shape, form, and fashion. And the doctor, I think it was Dr. McCoy, kind of overseen the thing. I learned how a woman is put together here and about the baby being born breech, that is, feet foremost, or born double sitting down. And he tried to teach us how to turn them, but I said, 'No, I don't want to learn that. I'll just let the doctors come to do that.' I had one funny birth. I saw one time a baby born in the afterbirth. It was a great big bowl with the baby sitting in there in water with his hands up here and his elbows on his knees. I never saw nothing like that before. When it came, I didn't know. And there was a little tore place right up there on his head [pointing to the high spot on the top of her forehead], and I just done like that [drawing her finger across the spot] and he just [here she makes a swimming motion with her hands]. That just started it, and then, of course, the child's pressure. Dr. Siler, he came, cause I sent for him when I saw what it was, but he didn't get there in time to see it. He said he

wished he'd a'got there before so he'd have seen it. But it was all right, wasn't anything wrong with it, but I didn't know this sitting in water. I didn't know. But I saw that.

"Some of the mothers were so contrary you couldn't hardly help them. I went and sit down one time. I said, 'Just go ahead. I shall not touch you until you get to where you can abide by what I tell you.' Some of them prefer sitting up on a chair frame with no bottom. I said, 'No, I'd rather you be in the bed, flat on the back.' Some women are slower than others. Some, they slow along and shrink back from pain as long as they possibly can, and some just know it's going to happen, and they just get down to it and get through with it. I said it looked like they'd a'knowed it wouldn't come just so and have to be some stretching done somewhere. The baby comes head foremost with its hands up here [putting her hands folded over her head] and its knees up against its chest, and as it comes, why it straightens out. After the baby's head and shoulders are born, why that's all over then. After the baby was born, why you cut the navel cord. I'd always tied mine twice and then cut between the ties, and then they used to scorch cloths and put on it. The scorched cloth would heal it up quick, then you put a band on it. If I went took care of a woman like at night and her baby was born, why then the next day I'd go back and see how she was doing. Now a woman with her first child, why she doesn't have any pains or anything hardly ever after her baby is born, but after the first child, they have pains. You know, the menses will start again, and then they have those stomach pains, so I'd go back and see how they was making out. I also carried a bandage for the mother to put on after the baby was born. Put it on and wrap it around her and tight, and stay in bed two weeks. Then get up and don't lift anything. If you have to move it, drag it. And don't take no walks or anything until the baby's three weeks old. I guess they thought I was a pretty binding one, but I don't know, I was just going by what I was taught. If they couldn't do that, why don't bother with me because I'd be to blame for this happening or the other happening. So I never did have any trouble. I delivered two white babies. The father of one of them passed by here some time this last summer. He called him my boy, said I ought to see my boy now. He's married and has a little boy of his own. The father's father-in-law knew of me, and I had waited on somebody of his people, and he told him about it, so he come ask me would I go, and I said, 'I don't know.' He said what doctor told him that I would answer just the same as him. And so I went on."

Carrie Stewart consents to have a last photograph taken on the porch of her house, and we move on, going now to Moncure in the center of the state to visit with another midwife, Maude Lee Bryant.

Mrs. Bryant, born in 1897, is eighty-five years old and lives on a farm which she and her husband, Gade, own in Chatham County. She has already put on lunch for her son and others who work the farm and is out helping a neighbor grind his cane when we arrive. She lives at the end of a quiet stretch of recently paved road where logging trucks take new timber to the markets. In sight of the old farmhouse where she and Mr. Bryant have lived for more than sixty years are the homes of a grandson and three of their children. During the course of our visit, we will sit on the porch visiting, the pigs rooting under us in a loud cacophony of grunts, we will stay for lunch, and we will sit by the fire, though the day is not cold, and listen to Mr. Bryant sing his favorite song, "If I Could Hear My Mother Pray Again." Between stirring the greens cooking on the stove and showing us various kinds of medicinal herbs in her garden, Maude Bryant tells her story, as quietly composed, her hands folded in her lap, as Carrie Stewart is constantly in motion.

"If I had it to do over," Mrs. Bryant explains, "I would just as soon have the days of back yonder as today. I had. But I'm sure the children can have so much more and so much more easier till this is better days for living but not the kind of living we was brought up with. We had time to visit each other, and had time to go see the sick and didn't have no thoughts of putting nobody in the rest home. Maybe if there was four or five working on the farm, one could stay at the house and wait on that sick person. And it didn't put no bigger strain on them. Now it seems like they have keyed up themselves for fine houses, fine furniture, fine cars, fine everything until it takes them both to work [the wife and the husband]. But used to if the man had to be sick, the woman with the neighbor's aid could carry on. Or if the woman had to be sick, the neighbors would help do the chopping or do whatever she had been doing till she could get well. Now there's no way that no one hardly, the way they've got themselves stretched out for wanting so much, that they can carry on as well as we did. When mother stays at home with the children and works with them, like I did, you near about know them. No way hardly they can fool you or nothing. I'm not giving myself no pat, but nobody worked more hours than I did."

As Maude Bryant thinks of her life with her own children, her memory goes back to her parents, Liza Seymour Lee and Tom Lee, both born in the same area where Maude and her children were born. Mr. and Mrs. Lee had nine children, three of whom survive.

"My mother was very kind, we thought, and loving. Of course, I hope that all children mostly that have nice mothers think that, but we just don't think we could have had a nicer mother. I think of her many days, and I can't find one fault of her. People just couldn't be sick in her neighborhood but what she wouldn't walk for miles. She wouldn't wait for Poppa to have time to carry her; she'd just walk. Anything she had in the house when she started, she'd have it in her arms or on her back, whichever size it was, carrying it to help them. She was what I'd call a good neighbor. It's just been a special neighborhood. All when my mama and daddy was living, they got along well together. They [the white children] went to a church just a little this side of ours, and we'd walk to and fro to church to get together. They'd go to their church, and we'd go to ours, and sometimes their parents would let them come home and have dinner with us, and in a little while Mama would let the boys go home with them and have dinner. That's just how close. And the grown folks some days would come to our house about ten o'clock—we didn't go to church that Sunday—and they would stay just the same as a colored family. They'd stay and have dinner with us and stay till time to go home and do up the night's chores. It's not as

close as it used to be way back then. I don't know what got us sort of at a distance.

"My mother went to St. Augustine's [an Episcopal school in Raleigh]. I don't think she went but two years. Her parents were in pretty good shape, I'd guess you'd call it. I heard her say a'many a time when she was married, her daddy had ninety hogs and ninety head of sheep, and I don't know how many cows. And chickens and duck and geese, so they must have been in pretty good shape. And she taught us by her nice daily good living, and of course on Sundays and rainy days she would read nice literature to us and would always read the Bible. After dinner she would entertain us by reading. Papa read books, lots and lots of them. Mostly what he read and I enjoyed most was books of good manners, good behavior. Papa hadn't gone to school, but he could read and write. He was a better student than Mama. I guess he was just real good. He used to, years back, do the posting for storekeepers and people with advertisements; you know they didn't have stencils and typing like they do now, and he would do the lettering. He would do this big printing. He taught himself. He said he and whoever his plowmate was (and that was one of his cousins), they got some books from somewhere. And when they would be plowing and in certain fields it was smooth ground, and they would hurry up and get the mules tied so they could rest them the day at a certain field. Then they would smooth it off, and then they would begin to write with just a stick or straw or whatever they'd get in the field where they were. They'd take these books and copy after them till they wrote—I just wish you could see Papa's handwriting. Just as pretty as anybody's of today."

Maude Lee and Gade Bryant, a member of another large prominent family in the Moncure area, were married in 1914 when she was seventeen, and the next year they moved onto the land where they still live today.

"When we first married, we rented on halves from a man, and whatever we made, well, half of it was his. Well, that year we made five bales of cotton, and nobody but Gade and I, it didn't take much for us to eat, and after he laid by the crop he went to work out at the brickyard, just a few weeks, but we saved out a hundred dollars then had a little money left. Soon that winter we bought a mule, paid cash. The next year we was able to buy this land and begin farming without on halves, straight on ourselves. And in about forty years we added to our land. Me and my husband, we own about five hundred and thirty acres, I believe. We have nine living children. Four live in Philadelphia, and the other five all live in Chatham County, right around us. And would you believe it, every morning, except for less than half a dozen mornings a year, they all come out and have coffee or tea with us before they go out to work."

As soon as the children were large enough to help with the farm work, they joined their parents in the field, where Mrs. Bryant herself "just made a regular hand." She worked in the house during the early morning hours before going out to the field, and would return mid-morning to prepare dinner for the family; following dinner, she returned to the field and at night, after supper, would do more of her household chores. "I'd chop cotton, wheat, tobacco, and we'd plant the corn, just whatever was to do, I did, except to plow. Always come in about ten o'clock and get dinner ready. We had dinner together every day while they were growing up. Every day. I'd do the dishes and go back to the field and work till time to have supper, just before sundown. And then I would bathe the children and get them ready whenever they got ready to go to bed. Then I would begin to churn or wash my dishes, whatever had to be done; there was always something. I worked many hours after they was in bed. I'd scrub my floors, wash by lantern light many a'night. And after they'd all gone to bed I'd patch, wash, iron, starch. Plenty of times I've been to bed at three and four o'clock and get up at five the first one in the morning. Just with the Lord's help, that's all. I enjoyed every year. I've looked back—the children fresh and clean and had clean things to put on. I was just as happy as a woman who hadn't done nothing; she couldn't have been happier really. My main object of working was wanting the children to have a better way of living, that the world might be just a little better because the Lord had me here for something, and I tried to make good out of it, that was my aim. And I always looked down on nothing being hard, really."

When Maude Bryant was about twenty-one years old, tending several children of her own, sharing the farm work, and doing the chores in the house, she began to serve as a midwife in the community: her mother, who had been delivering babies for many years, was ill and could not go to a woman in labor. Mrs. Lee described to her daughter how she was to care for her.

Mrs. Bryant remembers her instructions, "How the first thing was to fix her bed. We would pad her bed, get a stiff board and have it covered so it would be soft and put it right where her bottom would be laying, so it would sorta push up instead of down in a sink of a mattress. Let her lay on that.

Whenever they would get to hurting, she would tell us what to do. One of the main things she'd have us to do was prop up her feet, have her feet where she could press against the foot of the bed, and take her hands and whenever she'd have a pain, you'd just pull and have her to press down and hold her chin down to her neck. Have her to press down as hard as she could and then whenever she'd stop having the pain, of course, you'd let her loose and let her relax. Sometimes if it looked like she was slow she had me to take a hand on each side of her stomach, and when she was having pains, just press down. Just keep on doing that until often you could feel the baby slip. And I'd gave her catnip tea, and I would repeat that if it didn't look like this cupful done her much good. I had one birth I'd call real difficult. We didn't lose it. Looked like she was so slow I had them to send for the doctor. And he come and examined her—she was a healthy, fine-looking woman. We sent and got him, and he come and he examined her and he looked around to the mother and said, 'Maude (that's what he called me), Maude's just scared; she's getting along all right. She's just one of the slow ones.' But I knew that she won't making a bit of time in having the baby so when he got ready to go, I went out. Instead of he taking his bag, I carried it out with him. I didn't know, just along then folks said what they pleased to us. And I didn't want to be embarrassed before the crowd, and I didn't want to embarrass him, either. I took the bag and went on out with him, and he said, 'Maude, didn't you know it was impolite for ladies to carry men's bags?' I told him, 'Well, not in this case.' And then I told him that this girl was sick. I said, 'She's very sick and she's got to have a doctor.' He

said, 'Oh, she's not.' And I said, yes she was. 'Well, how do you know?' 'I have had so many children till I know she has suffered and suffered and not making no headway at all. And something must be done, and I want you to go back in there.' When I convinced him, he said all right. 'I want you to look around at them people,' I said, 'and tell them just as sincere as you told them that she's getting along all right—because she's not—tell them that I was right.' So he went in there and he did. He said, 'I guess we'll have to send her to the hospital. Which one do you want her to go to?' And they told him. But they didn't get her ready. She begin to have convulsions. I knew she was sick. But they had to take the baby, and she had to stay in the hospital, I don't know how long. [The white doctors] would always come if you sent for them. I delivered many more for blacks [mothers], but I had delivered some, quite a few with white. But they mostly were just the real poor white ones; the middle class, of course, I'd be caught with them sometimes when the doctor couldn't get there in time. Some paid, in pigs or in chickens. A lot of them didn't pay me nothing, but love, of course. They would bring the children after they'd get up any size all along for me to see. Then they'd bring me aprons after then just to let me know that they loved me.

"I went to see one white woman. It wasn't scary or nothing, but it was the pitifullest sight I have ever seen. One morning a man come for me. His daughter won't married. The ground was covered with sleet and snow, it had been hardening. You'd walk a step or two and slip back one. We done that for at least five miles. We had to do that climbing this high hill over here. When we got there, the baby was born, and she was born in a pile of straw, just like little calves or hogs. That's how the baby was, and the straw had dried on it. They didn't have not a sheet in the house, not even a quilt, except on the mama's bed. But this girl, she didn't have nothing except this straw raked up, and the baby was born in it. I didn't know how in the world I could clean it. And I happened to think I had vaseline in my bag, and I greased it real good with this vaseline and took the rag (and I had to wash the rag—the daddy's shirt tail—to bathe it in), bathed the baby in that and wrapped it up in some old things that I had. It was cold, sleet on the ground, snow. Fixed the baby before I could leave it, just like that. They just knowed I was a midwife, they hadn't said nothing to me about coming, but they knowed that in a case like that if you got the word you'd try to go. I don't think I ever turned nobody down."

After the delivery of her own grandson in 1944, Mrs. Bryant, then forty-seven,

was unable to continue working as hard and she had to give up being a midwife. In recent years she has been invited to several meetings to talk about her experiences. At a conference for doctors at the University of North Carolina in Chapel Hill, she described a woman's giving birth to a baby as being as natural as the births of farm animals. One of the doctors objected to her comparing women to farm animals, and she responded, "I told them there was a few things they didn't have to learn by reading. If you read it, some of us might misunderstand it. But I knew this by experience. I said, 'I know every stage a woman's in because I've been there so many times myself.' The doctor didn't see how it was so. I said, 'I could tell you but I can't make you exactly know.' And one real old white man come up and shook hands, said, 'I appreciate that statement. I didn't doubt it a'tall.' I told him I had no other choice because it was so to me."

The narratives of Carrie Stewart and Maude Bryant are representative of the experiences of a large number of black women who were practicing midwives in North Carolina. (In 1920, for example, 4,000 midwives conducted approximately 34,000 deliveries, of which 80 percent were black.) Standard medical histories have generally disregarded the contributions made by midwives; a doctor at one of the North Carolina medical schools has written that they were "anathema" to the competent practice of medicine in the South. Midwives themselves, like Carrie Stewart and Maude Bryant, however, are accepting of "professional" medicine, and as these narratives have demonstrated, the midwives themselves asked for the services of a doctor. In recent years, largely because of the women's movement, midwifery has come into its own as a professional part of total health care. There are hospitals specializing in midwifery training. In 1981, the General Assembly of North Carolina enacted new provisions for the licensing of nurse-midwives to aid home births. Such recognition of the services of midwives is, in part, an unspoken tribute to women like Carrie Stewart and Maude Bryant, who more than a half-century ago walked the country roads and performed services essential to human life.

# Cool Buttermilk, Brown Gravy, and No Chickens under the House: A Dream

## Anita Stroud

### Charlotte

Anita Stroud ministers to the needs of children, "the little ones nobody sees." Born a foundling, shifted from one cabin to another on a South Carolina plantation at the turn of the century, she knows how it feels not to be loved. For the first thirteen years of her life, she felt as much an outcast as any orphan in the world. But because of two older black women, she did not give up. She nourished a dream someday to have a farm where she could care for children.

Today the dream is partially realized in a small trailer in a housing project in Charlotte where she lives. At the end of the day after being with many children, she seems old and tired and discouraged. Arthritis and diabetes have weakened her health. But as she locks the door and watches the last child run off through the dirt paths of the project, she brightens, she raises her head, she goes on. The story of Anita Stroud is one of confronting hard reality with a child's dream.

Her work with children began almost fifty years ago when she invited them to her small apartment for after-school instruction, financing her program out of the meager wages she made doing domestic work. St. John's Baptist Church and Myers Park Baptist Church, two of the largest white churches in Charlotte, became involved in supporting her programs; later joined by leadership from the local Sertoma Club, they formed the Anita Stroud Foundation and began to receive contributions from individuals and organizations. During the first year, 1974, the Foundation raised thirteen thousand dollars; in 1978 the amount had risen to over twenty-one thousand dollars. Today the Anita Stroud Foundation has a solid reputation among many churches and organizations, and certain individuals

send checks annually. One of the largest contributions, a check for one thousand dollars, was recently given by a Charlotte black social club, particularly gratifying to Miss Stroud, who blames the black community for its failure to support her ambition to buy a camp.

Her activities include afternoon programs of Bible readings and crafts, special celebrations at Thanksgiving, Christmas, Valentine's Day, and Easter. At Christmas out of the fund she has provided clothing, toys, fruit, and candy for over four hundred children, and food boxes and clothing for twenty-five or thirty-five families and shut-ins, doing much of the planning and gathering herself. Her Christmas dinner feeds over 400 people. Funds are also used to send some seventy children to summer camp at William Umstead Park near Raleigh, children who would otherwise never have such an experience. At the end of each summer, she directs the closing of the camp and the packing up until she seems almost exhausted. But several days later she is back at the trailer, the children flocking to her.

Anita Stroud was born in 1900 on a plantation near Chester, South Carolina. She has no recollection of her parents, does not believe that she ever even saw them or knew their names. She was passed from one cabin to another among the black women who worked on the place. Her only schooling was lessons from an old black woman who invited the children over to her farm. Despite her lack of any formal education, Anita Stroud tells about herself with a dramatic and engaging sense of narrative, a gift born perhaps of her need to tell stories to children. She never falters, as if she has practiced it even in her dreams.

"My interest in children started when I

was a child. Nobody cared nothing about me. As for love, I knew nothing about that. And I had such a hard time, you know, coming on like that, and nobody loves you, nobody even likes you. And then you have one or two little friends and they're treated just as bad as you are treated. I wanted to get gone. That was my whole heart's desire—to grow up. Where we stayed out on the farm, me and the few little friends I had, we'd go down to the spring, way down from the house a piece (we used water from a spring), and we'd go and fill our buckets with water and we'd come on up the bank and set them down. There was a great big sycamore tree, and we had taken the hatchet there and hacked marks on the tree. I was measuring myself to see how fast I was growing. I was going to buy a farm, buy me a big farm, just like what they had there. We were going to have all kinds of things on the farm, for I was going to build them a house that didn't have tin on the top, a house that had rooms to it. I wasn't going to have the pigpen in the backyard, and I wasn't going to have the chickens roosting under the house. Besides the odor in damp weather, in the morning about four o'clock that rooster would start, all of the roosters up under the house, start slapping their wings. You know, they'd slap up against the floor and then they'd start crowing, and they'd crow from then till daylight. I wasn't going to have no chickens under the house. I wasn't even going to let the dogs stay under the house. We were going to have good shortening corn bread, which we didn't have, and we were going to have fried chicken. And I was going to be sure I threw away the neck and the head. I wasn't even going to give those to the dogs. I was going to have brown gravy, and I was *not* going to have that white

gravy we had. And I was certainly going to make it myself so I wasn't going to let no flies get in. And we were going to go out and sit down, spread a cotton sheet, now that's how silly we were—a cotton sheet that you pick cotton with—we were going to spread it out and put our food there, and we were all going to sit down all around it, and everybody was going to eat just what they wanted. We were going to have nice, cool buttermilk, plenty of it, and corn bread and fried chicken. And we were going to have cabbage, too, but it was going to have some shortening in it, and the tough leaves on the cabbage, we were going to give them to the pigs. Now I was going to buy this plantation. I done planned all I was going to have on the plantation, all what kind of building I was going to have, and I didn't have one penny, and I didn't know how I was going to get it. I was going to go round and get all the children, *all* that I knew, everywhere, and we were coming there to that farm to live.

"I got the children, but no farm. I decided I was going to work to help other children who had to come up hard like I come up, children who were unloved, children who were shoved around and didn't get the benefits of the good things that were going on. That's the reason I'm still working with them now.

"There were so many places I stayed. Sometimes I think I was in the big house, but I didn't sleep in the bed . . . well, at times, you know, we'd all get to playing and everything, we'd go to sleep right there in the bed, with the white children. I remember sometimes sleeping out with Granny Ann. Now Granny Ann, she was an old slave down there, and I thought nobody in the world was like Granny Ann. Granny Ann was so old she wasn't working, and the people kept her. You know, most of the slaves, they always told me, when they were free, they had nowhere to go and they stayed on where they were. They took care of Granny Ann. The Boyds and the Johnsons and the Hemphills. They were the plantation owners. We were under the Boyds. Granny Ann was a Johnson. Granny Ann was just sweet and kind. She had been a nursemaid to take care of the children. She worked in slavery. In fact, she was the midwife when the babies were born on the plantation, and she was midwife to a whole lot of other black people, too. Everybody respected Granny Ann. She loved children, and she loved people. And this little house, they had her a nice place out there. And I remember they never would let her cook for herself. They sent food from the big house out there to her, for once she'd fallen into the fire. Her elbow on this side was burned, and her arm was burned. She lived alone, but they had a walk from the kitchen right on into where she was. We'd go out there and sit down on her little porch, and any of our old troubles, we'd go crying to Granny Ann, and she'd always say, 'You're going to be free one of these days, and you're going to be proud of yourself one of these days if you live the life.' And she said, 'Whatever you do in this world, try to be somebody.' She'd always tell us that good manners and good behavior would take you farther than any money you had. And she always said that instead of running after money and trying to be rich, try to richen your life. Try to live a good life. When she died [about 1908], she was 109. I must have been eight or nine years old, if that old, when Granny Ann died. I thought the world had ended right there and then. And after Granny Ann died, I remember staying

a while with Miss Bollier, she was a worker on the plantation, and then I stayed with Miss Poll. Part of the time I have been hungry. I mean I've been *hungry*, no food. I got my food wherever I could.

"And then Aunt Rhoda Strong. She stayed a good ways off the road, I'd say about seven or eight miles from where the plantation was. And Aunt Rhoda had a little place of her own, four acres of ground. I don't know how she come by it, but she had four acres of ground. Aunt Rhoda, she wanted everybody to have some education. I think she'd gone to a school somewhere for a little bit. She wasn't educated, just went to school—learned to read and write. On Sunday Aunt Rhoda would have Sunday School and she'd come over there on that farm. They told her, you know, any time she wanted to have Sunday School. And this old house set up on the hill among some cedars, and that's where she'd go and have Sunday School. The house looked like the chimney was leaning back this way from it, and it looked like the house was swagged a little, but she would go over there and we loved to go over there. She had a little mule and wagon she'd hook up, and she'd cook good things on Saturday, such as ginger cakes and molasses cakes, and she'd even cook little vegetables and things like that, and she'd even bring along milk. And we'd all go over there and stay all day long, and I learned to spell coffee.

"The house had been papered with newspapers, and we'd lie down there on the floor and we'd talk and everything, and I remember somebody made some benches to put over there. They were like logs with legs on them. Some would be sitting on the floor, some would be sitting on the bench. On the floor, instead of rugs we had this straw matting. And up on the wall, Aunt

Rhoda taught us our alphabet, and up there was c-o-f-f-e-e, coffee. That was the first thing I learned to spell. The next thing I learned to spell was Jello. There was a picture upside the wall of this bowl of Jello. We thought it was jelly. We didn't know Jello from jelly. And I learned to spell that J-e-l-l-o. Whooo! I was getting somewhere. The next thing we learned to spell was Blackstop. That was the next station. There was Cornwell, Chester, Evans, and Blackstop. Those were train stops, and we were closer to Blackstop than we were to Evans and we were closer to Blackstop than we were to Chester. We learned to spell Blackstop. Now you couldn't tell us we weren't learning something.

"Then I remember Aunt Rhoda use to read the story about Uncle Wiggily and the Tar Baby. And you know, I got a book out there has that yet, and I wouldn't take nothing for it because it has that one story, *The Tar Baby*. Aunt Rhoda used to read that. And I quite naturally knew she made up a lot of things and put to it, but she used to read that book and she used to read her Bible. Her Bible was a big old thick Bible. She used to read the Bible to us, and we'd all sit down and listen to Aunt Rhoda read. And then Aunt Rhoda would pray. And we always said we didn't like to hear anybody pray but Aunt Rhoda, for Aunt Rhoda looked like she was looking right at God when she prayed.

"She'd get around the fire. In the summer, she'd make us get some chips and wood and put some fire in there and then she'd put potatoes and things like that and roast them in the ashes. Then she'd get this table and she'd say, 'Come around children, and let's eat. Let's eat these vittles.' And we'd get around there, and she'd have

tin cups and little pans and she'd give us something.

"In the summer we'd go out and sit under the trees, and Law! we thought that was the best thing. One of the main things Aunt Rhoda would do, she'd make this molasses bread, and she'd make ice cream. And how happy we were! She didn't make ice cream very often for she'd only make ice cream when they had ice up at Cornwell Station, and that wouldn't be often they had ice there. She'd get that ice and she'd make whipped cream and she'd wrap it up and she'd bring that little churn of cream and give us a little spoonful of cream.

"All of us would get round and go together, walking, it wasn't too very far, and Aunt Rhoda would always tell me, 'Now you be sure and tell all those children around there where you are to come on out.' And we would get round and tell all the children. Some of the parents were mean and wouldn't let them go—'You got to take care of them cows!' 'get out and mind them cows!' Oh, brother!"

Most of the time Anita was working on the plantation, picking cotton, hoeing cotton, cutting briars, cleaning out ditches, carrying in wood, carrying in water, sweeping the kitchen. There weren't any special days. "They gave you what you ate, and you took your pan and you went and sat down there in the kitchen in the big house. There was always a fireplace in those kitchens down there. Now if there was something left over, like somebody have something on their plate and didn't eat all of it, you know they didn't believe in throwing things away, they might put that on your plate. We used to hear when it was Christmas. I didn't see any celebration. They gave you an orange and one apple. We'd go up to the big house. Any morning we could get up there we'd hang around. We'd hang around for some cold bread or whatever they had. They had their corn shuckings and quiltings and things, and you'd get a little stew beef and rice. We didn't see it. It was just a lot of grownups having fun. There was dancing and singing, but it was with them, not us. Before the dancing and singing, we had to get home and get to bed.

"I didn't attend a church until I was almost ten years old, and when I went to that church, the very first day I went there, I said, 'I don't want to go to this place any more.' How would you like when you go in and sit down places, people get all over like this moving away or else get up and change seats? This was a church under an arbor. They were people just like me. You know, we still have that feeling that I am big and you are little. They want to single out somebody out of that crowd so they can beat on and turn their nose up at and treat terrible. They moved away, and I said, 'Oh, what did I have to go there for?' The last time I went back, Aunt Keziah Bollier said, 'Well, you're not going back any more unless you want to. Them persnickety niggers over there ought to go somewhere and drop dead.' I never will forget that word 'persnickety.' She said, 'I don't like them myself.' Never bothered going back to that place. And I used to look at that church and *swear* I was going to burn it down.

"I didn't hear music much around there. The only singing you heard was when the people got into the field and went to work, and then it sounded like a choir with a thousand voices. I used to sit down and listen to those people as they were on the farm working, some of them half sick or

half dead they were so sick, but they would always raise their voices when they'd get in the field and go to singing. I remember a whole lot of the songs, 'A Charge to Keep, I Have' and another was 'Amazing Grace' and 'Did Christ O'er Sinners Weep.' I would join in and try to help to sing for everybody was joining in, and that's where you forgot your misery; there's where you forgot your hunger; there's where you forgot how you were treated. You were all wrapped up in that song, and you didn't think about anything but that song.

"When I first got on to loving God and knowing there was a God—Granny Ann started it. After she died it was Aunt Rhoda Strong. She always told us it didn't matter how things were, how bad it was, God would always fix the way and you would come out. God took care of you. I remember one time she told one boy, forget what his name was, that we were all God's children, and he said, 'Hmf! I don't know what you're talking about, we're all God's children. We must be God's step-children.' And Aunt Rhoda slapped him in the mouth. I don't know what I felt like. I felt like I was *nobody's* child, not even a step-child. And not only me. There were others round there the same way."

When Anita was about ten years old, she and other children on the place walked into Chester to see the Hagenbeck-Wallace and Barnum and Bailey circus come to town. The events that followed that occasion represent the first change in her life from the plantation where she was born.

"They would parade the streets from— they must have started from Southern Station. And from there all the way round to the Fair Grounds or Show Grounds they called them, round there where they had the rural County Fair and the shows and everything like that. And when they lined the streets, we came from everywhere to see the circus, see the animals, and oh! how happy we were! And I got lost from the group. When the last wagon passed and it was going on toward the show ground, everybody noticed crowds were following, and I was in the crowd. Never thought about it. In fact, I didn't think I was lost until Miss Lightner asked me wasn't it time for me to go home and where did I live. And that's when I thought about it. I said, 'Oh! they've gone and left me now.'

"And I was just wandering around from place to place looking into everything I could see. I had been down looking at the horses. I just loved the horses, for we had horses and mules and everything on the farm. So there was a stand over there and this man had a pit of snakes, and he was selling snake oil, a little bottle about that size, fifteen cents. And that was for your corns and your bunions, which *everybody* had, and he would guarantee that it was so good that you could pour it on the *shoe* and it would cool the toe. He'd pick up a snake and tell about the snake and how he got the oil and everything, then he'd drop him back down in the pit. Well, I wanted to see, and I climbed up on the side. When I got up on the side, he said, 'Don't you lean too far over there. If you fall on where those snakes are, they'll eat you up.' I wasn't about to fall over in there. So here comes this woman, this white lady, coming around there, and she had two children. And she stopped to look and listen. When he'd hold up the snakes, Rosa couldn't see. Rosa was the baby girl. She was a little bitty thing, and she and Jean hollered, 'Mama, Mama, I can't see!' And I said, 'Oh, I'll take her up here. She can see up

here.' And I just reached down and got Jean. There we sat and looked at all those awful snakes down in there. And then we got down, started walking round, looking at different things. I wanted to take the children down to see the horses, and she said 'No! They weren't going down to see those horses.' Well, you see—those great big horses—I was used to horses and things, but I don't know whether those horses were used to children. Some of those big horses stomp you. But I wanted to go down where the horses were. She told the children they weren't going down there; she was going to take them into the big arena. Far as I knew, I didn't know they had an arena. So when we got there, Rosa had me by one hand and Jean had the other. And she says, 'I'm not taking her!' I just stopped.

"Then Jean started hollering, she hollered and she kicked and she just lay down on the ground. Miss Lightner told her she was going to spank her. Jean says, 'I'm going to leave you and never come back for I just hate you! She says, 'Jean, Jean!' She says, 'I hate you, I hate you, I hate you!' She said, 'Come on you,' that's what she said to me. She didn't know my name, and I didn't know hers. I was just so happy with the children. So she took us into the big arena and we saw the circus. Come out. Nowhere to go. And Jean, she was still yelling, and I was still with them, so Miss Lightner asked me where I came from, and I told her. And what was I going to do? I told her I didn't know. I'd go out there and sit out there in one of those circus wagons till daylight. I wasn't scared. I never will forget: 'You're not going to sit out there! Those wagons are going to leave here before daylight.' So Rosie and Jeanie started to hollering, wanting me to go home with them. Then her two boys came up, Jack and J. D., and Jack wanted to know what was all the carrying on about, and J. D. just stood there and looked. And he started looking at me and laughing. And she said, 'If you look at her and laugh again, I'll slap your face!' That's what Miss Lightner said to J. D. I didn't pay any attention. I'd been laughed at so many times. Miss Lightner asked me did they have a phone. Well, they did have a phone, had one of those, you know, that you take it off and wind, wind, wind, crank it. Well, she had one, too, same way. Well, she says, 'I'll call in the morning. You come on out here and stay out here.'

"So I went on home with Miss Lightner, and Jean had a bed, and Rosa had a bed, and there was another kind of cot bed in the room. She told me to stay there. And I never will forget, she came and brought me a—I don't know whether it was a gown or a housecoat—a great big something to sleep in. And I put it on over all the clothes I had on and got into bed. And that next morning, we waked up before day, and when she came in all of us were sitting in Jean's bed.

"She called out to the farm and they hadn't even missed me. She told them she was bringing me back out there. They said she could bring me back if she wanted; if she didn't want it, it was all right. She carried me back out to the farm. She talked to them out there and she said, 'Well, if that's the way you all feel, I'll take her on back.' And she told me to get my clothes, and I went in and when she saw what I got, she said, 'Don't you bring those rags out here to me!' And we went on back. She bought me some real nice ones, and I stayed with Miss Lightner."

Anita was happy to be in a new home, especially happy to be with the children, and she felt that the family was kind to her. Although she was only two or three years older than Rosa and Jean, she had some responsibility for looking after them, and she remembers with great pleasure how they played in the streets and yards of Chester, and she got to know most of the families and businessmen. The girls' father was a pharmacist, and their mother apparently was active in civic work. When it was time for the children to go to school, Anita stayed at home, sweeping the porch, helping to feed the chickens, apparently never asking if school was a place she could go. She was, however, still harboring the dream of having her farm. Taking her meals alone in the kitchen or eating with "Bessie," an older black woman who did the cooking, she doubtless talked with her about the farm, or with Rosa and Jean when they slipped away from the dining room table and came to join her in the kitchen. This happy life continued for about five years, long enough for Anita to know the family and the town and residents very well. Then she became ill and was taken to the hospital where she was operated on for appendicitis.

The family came to see her every day in the hospital, but when her recovery was complete, they did not pay the bill. She was required to remain there and to work off her account, washing dishes, setting up trays, washing the trays, setting the table for the nurses. She does not remember how much money she owed the doctor and the hospital and nobody told her when she had completed her work. Later a doctor saw her and exclaimed, "Is she still working on that bill? Good God! That bill's paid!" Anita was free to go, but like the old slaves she was told about, she had no place to go. She continued to work at the hospital until two or three years later when she was asked to live with another white family in Chester and help care for their baby. This arrangement ended dramatically and tragically for the family when the husband, who "stayed drunk all the time and was one of the meanest husbands," shot and killed his wife, scattering pellets over Anita and the baby she held in her arms. Confronted with the instability of this family, she reacted with all the horror of a child witnessing a murder, and after the husband was jailed, she looked for a chance to leave. When some friends she knew went to Charlotte to find jobs, she followed.

Charlotte is the largest city in North Carolina, and to a young woman not quite twenty years old, with no money and no place to live, it must have seemed particularly frightening. She began to find jobs working in white homes, housekeeping and looking after children. She remembers two families with affection. Through them she began to develop her dream to do something for children and began to have groups in her small apartment after school, in much the same way as Aunt Rhoda had done in the old farm house with the crooked walls and chimneys. She has lived some sixty years in Charlotte now, but still it does not seem to have the place in her life which she has given the small town of Chester, South Carolina.

"Now we knew in Chester where we were supposed to go, and we went there. We knew we could not eat in the cafes, and it didn't bother us. There were other cafes we could go to that black people had. If we met on the street, we spoke to each other. And the homes that you went in down there, you knew you were supposed to go in the back door, and if you were out with the white children, they all played together.

And there was a section there in Chester where blacks stood on one side of the street and whites on the other, and the children all played together. Many times I went into the homes of white children. If I was by myself I went in the back door, but if I was with the child that belonged in the home, she carried you in the front. Sometimes you'd meet people and they'd call you black niggers or something like that, but that was mostly the ones from the mill hill. People around there in Chester did not allow their children to have anything to do with those children on the mill hill. And I tell you one thing, the police kept things *straight* there.

"When we got to Charlotte here, the things were altogether different. To ride the streetcar was horrible. If the streetcar was full and any whites got on, we had to get up and give the seats and stand. And if you sat down beside one, you went to jail. And the motorman was just as nasty as he could be! I wasn't used to that. I wasn't used to that at all. The cafes and things like that, the same way in Chester, we knew we weren't to go in them. And there was no toilet facilities nowhere uptown for black people. Why that beat Chester! On Gadsden Street in Chester, on one side there were two cafes and a barber shop, and they always had toilet facilities. Back in the alley, what they called, there were toilet facilities. Of course, there were nothing *but* black people in the alley. I felt for a while I didn't know what in the world I would do. I was altogether in another world."

The new world which Miss Stroud had entered was, in part, an adult world. It was large and crowded, a long way from Aunt Rhoda's Sunday School and Miss Lightner's kitchen. Though she had certainly faced hardships unknown to many adults, especially to whites in the growing middle-class in Charlotte, she had miraculously been taken in by a few people who had cared about her. In Charlotte she had to start over finding her own way. She found it by directing her energies to "the little ones nobody sees."

In 1982 Anita Stroud, facing the effects of age and poor health, was required to say a final goodbye to all her children and to close up her trailer. Already ahead of her, however, were the hundreds of young men and women out in the world, fortified by her teaching. After her retirement, the University of North Carolina at Charlotte awarded her the honorary degree of Doctor of Humanities in recognition of her service to children. The tears she shed when addressed as "Dr. Stroud" must have come from the deep recesses of memory. She alone knew how far she'd come from the fears of a motherless child to the strength to keep a dream.

One afternoon standing in her trailer, she summed up her philosophy: "I feel like if we were all in a ditch and I happened to crawl out, I'd want to reach back and get somebody, if not but one, and pull him out, too. Let's all come out, if possible. If you're walking up to heaven on a road, it would be a grand road and you'd enjoy it a little more if you'd get just one child and carry him along with you. That would keep you company."

# *Esse Quam Videri*

## Susie Williams Jones

### Greensboro

Susie Jones invites visitors to come in, opening the door of her comfortable white clapboard home, which served as the President's residence on the Bennett College campus in Greensboro. Mrs. Jones extends her hand, and, if there is a certain formality in the gesture, it is relieved by her smile.

The house is muted in shadows across drapery and chairs, across the ridges of many books, falling on the keys of the piano. Over the mantel there is a large abstract painting; beneath, logs are laid for use in the fireplace. Carved ivory statues rest on shelves and tables. Everywhere there are books of poetry, art, and history. There is music, but not from the piano; it comes from Mrs. Jones's high, flute-like voice. She comes to her guests with freshly made orange juice on a china plate, with a linen napkin. She turns the conversation to ask about our families. The hour passes until the room seems to be filled with sunlight.

Here is the home to which Bennett girls came for breakfast with her husband, David D. Jones, who served the school from 1926 until his death in 1956. Here there were teas, parties, and dinners presided over by a woman who is widely regarded as one of the most gracious hostesses in Greensboro. Here there were the activities of their four children, encouraged to participate in the life of Bennett College. Here there was good sense, good manners, and good will.

Susie Jones, now in her ninetieth year, is one of the best-known and best loved women in North Carolina. Her years of service with her husband during his presidency of Bennett College and with the YWCA, the Methodist Church, and the United Council of Church Women have given her unique opportunities to advance humanitarian concerns and the progress of what she, in an old-fashioned way, refers to as "our group." By this she means, of course, all black Americans. Born into a family where education was more extensive than that of many southerners and where attitudes were broadly democratic, she grew up with an informed understanding of human rights. From this kind of environment, she developed a deep resourcefulness which sustains her now.

Her lifetime of involvement in schools and organizations, her travels, and her contacts with people of national importance have not separated her from other lives unlike her own. Whether her concern is for the black children who were thrust into integrated schools or the first black contestants in the Miss America pageant, or the numbers of blacks in jails, she is especially sensitive to the lives of members of her own race, particularly those who have had a less protected environment than her own. Although she is comfortable in the college home on the Bennett campus, Susie Jones will never be satisfied until her own comforts are shared by a larger number of black Americans. Thus, she lives both with the serenity which a long life of family success has brought her and with the quiet insistence that other black families come to experience a better day.

To begin her story, we go back from Greensboro, the center for the first civil rights sit-ins which changed the nation, to Kentucky, where her family was perhaps already preparing for a new America.

"I was born in Danville, Kentucky, April 30, 1892. This was my grandmother's home. It was our custom every year, as soon as school was dismissed, to go to Danville and spend the summer. We always went on the train from Cincinnati, Ohio, because my mother insisted that we were interstate travelers, and this meant we did not have to use the segregated coaches. I did not understand this at that time, but I can remember that she would often have arguments with the conductor as to where we would sit. We all looked forward to going to visit Grandmother, because my mother was a very practical woman, and she had many interests in the community as well as the responsibilities of her home. We lived a very simple life; we had a very simple upbringing. But Grandmother did not feel that way about it. She felt that all of our underskirts should have lace sewed on them and that it was important for children to have a party every summer. She brought lots of glamour into our lives. I think I have heard my sisters say, and I know I have said often to myself, 'I do hope I can grow old gracefully as Grandmother did.' I have my grandmother's cups and saucers. They are old Haviland, and during our summers in Danville, one of the things Grandmother did always was to entertain her club of friends. And for this club, my uncle, my mother's brother who was a very sought-after caterer, would send her either pastries or strawberries from Cincinnati. He would send them by porters on the train, and we would go down and pick them up. He and his wife added a great deal to our lives. They thought it was important for us to have kid gloves and simple jewelry that every girl appreciates. He had great love for his family and was mindful of them. My grandmother was also a very good seamstress, and she did beautiful handiwork. Every year during the winter months, she would make her mother a cap to wear, a cap made of lace and fine material. One of our jobs when we came in

the summer was to 'go out to the hill,' as we called it, where my great-grandmother lived, to carry her this cap.

"My grandmother had great influence on my life and on the lives of my sisters and brother. She was the slave of a Presbyterian minister, and it was his custom to read to his wife every evening. He always insisted on my grandmother sitting there, listening to him, and so she learned to read and was a great reader all her life. When my two oldest children were about three and four, I took them to see her, and she recited for us, sitting in her rocking chair on the front porch, all of Byron's *Prisoner of Chillon.* She had a great love for English and Irish literature. I think you can understand why she felt it was important for her daughter to go to college. My mother started her college work at Allegheny, where she had an uncle living, and then transferred to Berea, and there she met my father. She had been the favorite in her own home and family. Her college education was rare for a woman at that time. She made a brilliant record, and she would stand no interference with her plans. It was she who decided that my sister, Frances, must go to Mt. Holyoke College. They had not enrolled a colored student at Holyoke for years, and when she applied for admission for Frances, they wrote her that Frances would probably be happier in an environment where she was more at home, and she answered, 'Frances's happiness is none of your business; that's my business. I want to know if you will admit her.' And they did. When my youngest son went to Andover, his teacher said to him, 'You are the best prepared Latin student that I have had in years. Where did you study your Latin?' His reply was, 'My grandmother.' He had studied with his grandmother while in high school.

She was on the advisory committee for the national YWCA before Negroes were on the board. At seventy, she resigned all the clubs she belonged to and became a member of the recently organized League of Women Voters. At her death we found that she had adopted a child under CARE.

"My mother and father graduated from Berea College, receiving their bachelor's degrees. My first experience in race [discrimination] was when the Negro students, because of the Day Law that was passed by the legislature in Kentucky, were put out of Berea.* Lincoln Institute was established for them. Some of the Negro graduates of Berea protested this. My father was leader of the group that protested, so my first racial experience was hearing very heated discussions on this matter. The president at that time was Dr. Foust. He came to our house several times to meet with this group to try to work out a satisfactory arrangement, but this never was realized. Although in these later years, under Dr. Hutchins, Berea opened again her doors to Negro students, my mother never forgave them, and so she never made a contribution to the college. My father did give, but she did not. Because, you would probably remember, Berea was founded for Negroes and mountain whites, and she felt that they had in such a large way betrayed their heritage.

"My father was a great teacher. As I was growing up, he was a teacher in Louisville, Kentucky. Later, he became principal of the high school in Covington, Kentucky. This was a very significant event in our lives, because he immediately enrolled in the University of Cincinnati for advanced work. He was the only Negro principal of a

*The Kentucky Day Law 71904 prohibited co-racial education in the state.

high school in St. Louis for years. We saw him take demotions and new assignments. He had made Sumner High School one of the first high schools in the country, and he was moved to a downtown high school that had a very bad image, the Vashon High School. It was located in the inner city, and the majority of the students came from deprived homes. One of the first things he did, which to me was fascinating, he sat on a stool in the hall, and as the children came into the building, he would say, 'Good morning' to each of them. He believed clearly in certain principles. One of the marked ones of these was thrift, and he thought our group would never make the kind of progress they should make until they were adequate economically. And so one of his first activities in the St. Louis community was to organize the New Age Building and Loan Association. Another thing he deplored was the housing of Negroes in St. Louis. Those of you who know St. Louis know that there were many very large houses there, and St. Louis was something like Brooklyn in that these houses were grouped around. As people moved to the west, and Negroes went into these large houses, the only way they could sustain themselves was to sublet. And so there was a feeling in St. Louis that property would do down when Negroes moved into the area. And my father was greatly concerned about this. We had all at this time graduated from college, and out of his earnings, he had saved enough money to build an apartment building for Negroes. This building was built by one of the leading construction firms of St. Louis, and the building was very adequate, very impressive looking outside. And so there happened one of these strange phenomena of how people that you're trying to help turn on you, and my father faced a severe school fight. Interestingly enough, a friend, who came by one day as he sat on his porch, said to him, since there was his own home, the apartment next door, and a housing unit next, 'Mr. Williams, this is your trouble. You are looking too prosperous.' But he did live to see all the leaders in the school fight come to him for some favor. I can well remember one time being there when a teacher came to him with his monthly check, and I said to my father, 'What does this mean?' He said, naming the teacher, 'He does not seem to be able to handle his finances, and the Board of Education is continuing his employment if he will come to me every month with his check, and we will sit down and make a budget, and he will keep out of the hand of vendors and people accusing him of not paying his bills.''

A grandmother who recited poetry, a mother who read Latin, a father who was a community leader—these were the earliest influences in the life of Susie Williams Jones. Her future looked bright, indeed. She entered kindergarten when she was three years old and continued through elementary and high schools in Kentucky. After graduation, she took an additional year at Woodward High School in Cincinnati, the alma mater of William Howard Taft, to qualify for entrance to the University of Cincinnati. "At Woodward High School," she remembers, "there was quite a tradition not only for a certain type of education, but for relationships of students and faculty. I remember our Latin teacher, a Mr. Peabody from Boston Latin School, had been teacher there for years. The days at Woodward, you can understand, had certain adjustments that had to be made

because I was entering the senior class. Most of the students had been with each other through all of their high school experiences. But I was reasonably happy. I did not feel that I had any particular problems. I think our parents had been successful in bringing us up with an acceptance of people as people, and this was the important thing. We had certain normal situations with people of the white race, but I never was particularly impressed with what color they were, or whether they were Negroes or whites. In the yearbook, the comment under my picture read: Susie believes in our class motto, *Esse quam videri*, To be rather than to seem. Our parents were very anxious, as far as their means allowed, to give us experiences of enrichment that were wider in scope than life in this small Kentucky town. One of our Christmas presents was always a season ticket to lectures given in Cincinnati on Sunday afternoons during the fall and winter. We heard prominent leaders in the country. Through this kind of an experience and attending political meetings in Cincinnati involving national politics, we had a feeling of world outreach.

"The matter of race did not really hit me until I went to college. Although there were just a very few Negroes who attended the University of Cincinnati at that time, it was largely a municipal college. It had no dormitories, and so the students came from the Cincinnati area, and if not immediately from Cincinnati, from some of the smaller Kentucky towns. One of the most outstanding irritations that I suffered was that an English teacher, who was from the North, left a vacant seat on both sides of me. I went to the head of the department and complained about this. After our initial conversation, he sent for me to come back.

Dr. Miller did not want me to transfer; he wanted me to stay in the class. This was a very difficult experience for me, but not difficult enough to deter me in any way. When it was necessary to use the same material, or if I wanted to see somebody else's notebook, or they wanted to see mine, we would just move in the seats of our own accord, and so it did not deter me, but it really was my most unpleasant experience in college. When I graduated, I had persuaded my father, who was not easy to persuade, to let me go to the University of Chicago for a summer session, so that I could graduate early. He granted this request. There, too, I found discrimination of a different kind, people not willing to even answer simple questions. I later found out that there were a great many Southerners who came for the summer session, and I am sure unfriendliness was more or less common because there were a great many Negroes attending the summer sessions. So my racial experiences came along at the time of life that I was mature. I must have taken them in stride as most Negroes do, and worked with them when I could. I always had enough pleasant experiences to outbalance those that were difficult. I never felt persecuted, and I really never felt that I couldn't do anything I wanted to do because of race. Those of us who grew up in a more or less protected environment, where we did not have to use public transportation, where we did not have to—now, I can remember my mother on this, you just never bought anything at a store where the clerks were in any way rude to you. You go to another store because there were plenty of stores where they were kind and gracious to you. And my grandmother's home, although it was right in the heart of the bluegrass, she had a horse and buggy and so you know you weren't up against a lot of things that some people had to contend with. I think that—I don't quite know how to say this—but I think that as I grew older and began to understand more of the system and what was happening in the world, I began to feel that I must do whatever I could to work on this matter. I was able to work in the Methodist Church and in the United Council of Church Women, where there are both white and Negro women working together for solutions. This was a most exciting experience. I also was here for the first sit-ins and marched and participated in all of the activities that were a part of this movement in Greensboro, North Carolina.

"Just as race was not emphasized in my family, neither was the matter of sex. My father had both men and women as faculty members, and so I never felt there was any question about my identity as a woman. I never grew up feeling that there should be preferences. Just as I acquired a deeper knowledge of the race issue as I grew older, so I became conscious of the problem of women. In my married life, I was always interested in the YWCA, and I inherited this from my mother. But the women's movements, except the League of Women Voters, were not as clearly defined in focus or in activities as they are today. And so I have a mixed feeling about the women's movement, not that I am specifically against it, but I feel that there are some strategies that are questionable. I feel strongly that the struggle for racial equality and the struggle for women's rights have been two parallel struggles in American life. I feel that it is important, since women are moving out into the mainstream of life, and our home responsibilities have become less, I do think it is important that they be supported by non-discrimination of all kinds. In many ways I am very grateful for the movement, but at the same time as I have seen some of it from the sideline, which is quite different from being responsible for things, I have felt that there were certain things in our struggle for rights that we did not want to lose out on. Just as Mr. Hooks, present director of the NAACP, was saying in his 'Face the Nation' interview, that he was dedicated, he wanted liberty for everybody, but he was committed to seeking it out for people who had been deprived. I think that what we do in these movements is so dependent upon the kinds of people that we are, and I don't think that I have been over-aggressive in the area of race because that's just not my nature. I can remember a man came in my house one day; I can't remember just why he was there, but he had his hat on, and I asked him to take off his hat, please, and so I dropped my voice and he took it off. Then I can remember when we lived in Atlanta, I volunteered to take nursery school children to the clinic at Grady Hospital. Registration cards had to be made out for each child, and the woman who was head of this part of the work asked me one day, what was my name, and I said, 'My name is Mrs. Jones.' She replied, 'We do not call Negroes by titles.' I suggested that she not use my name because I would be uncomfortable if she attempted to use my first name. Her reply was, 'I will call you what you wish. I can't let you be more polite than I.'"

After marriage to David Jones in 1915, when she was twenty-three, Mrs. Jones settled down to a life in which the family and home were of primary importance. When Mr. Jones, a graduate of Wesleyan College and the University of Chicago, was interviewed by Edward R. Murrow for *This I Believe*, he said, "From the outset my wife and I have had the feeling that no matter what else we did in life, we had to devote our best thinking and our best living to our children." After Mr. Jones became president of Bennett College in 1926, Susie Jones and their four young children became part of the campus family. The children were included in receptions and dinners in the home which were given for distinguished visitors. And "there were chores to be done, the grass was to be weeded, and the trips to the post office and banks were made daily. This was a priceless heritage. The children learned to work, and they knew when work was well done. There was a far greater blessing that came to them and came to me as their mother. We were starting a new enterprise and there were people who were willing to help; and so in and out of the home there were visitors who greatly enriched all of our lives. I can remember one Sunday evening, the youngest boy was with us as we were taking Mrs. Mary McLeod Bethune to the station. And he said in the car going down, 'Daddy, you know this is the first time I ever heard a speech where I understood all the speaker said.' And Mrs. Bethune laughed in her characteristic way and said, 'Well, Dave, I really put the cookies on the lower shelf today, didn't I?'

"I would like to say a deep word of gratitude for the opportunities that were ours on the college campus. Mr. Jones's illness in the 1950s stopped all of my outside activities. At his death, the trustees were kind enough to elect me vice-president of the college. I felt that I should not accept this. I wanted to be sure not to presume on the college in any way, and whatever I did, I wanted people to understand that it would be something that was important for the on-going of the college. And so I asked that instead of being elected vice-president, I should be elected registrar, work which I had done voluntarily in the early days of the college and an office where I had started the college records. And so I worked in this office until I was seventy-two years of age."

The four children of Susie and David Jones attended public schools in Greensboro, the boys finishing their secondary training in northern preparatory schools. Later, they studied at some of the most distinguished colleges and universities in America—Wesleyan, Harvard, Boston University. Their daughter, now on the staff of Harvard University Medical School, is still proud of the training she received at Bennett College.

"I hope as I have talked," Mrs. Jones concludes, "I have not made it seem that life was without struggle, because my life has been filled with ups and down. [One of the tragedies of her life was the death of her oldest son in 1976.] My father was wont to say that the good life does not necessarily mean that you do not have trouble, but it does mean that you get the breaks. My husband used to say to the Bennett girls, 'The next most certain thing to death is that effort counts.'

For Susie Jones the "good life" has meant a legacy of education, manners, and opportunity received from her parents, which she, in turn, has passed on to her children and grandchildren.

Acknowledgment is made to the Black Women Oral History Project, sponsored by the Arthur and Elizabeth Schlesinger Library on the History of Women in America of Radcliffe College, for permission to quote from an interview conducted with Mrs. Jones by Dr. Merze Tate.

# In This Dark World and Wide

## Lyda Moore Merrick

### Durham

Lyda Moore Merrick is by birth and by marriage a member of two of North Carolina's most prominent families. An understanding of the contributions of those two families explains the tradition which has directed Mrs. Merrick's life. John Merrick, her father-in-law, and Dr. A. M. Moore, her father, were among the founders of the North Carolina Mutual and Provident Association in 1898, later to become the North Carolina Mutual Life Insurance Company, the largest black-owned business in the United States, and one of the oldest.* Merrick, Moore, and C. C. Spaulding, Moore's nephew, were the ruling triumvirate of the company and the black community, and their leadership in the insurance field as well as in a half-dozen other business enterprises sparked the rise of black capitalism in Durham. In 1910 Booker T. Washington, whose philosophy of self-help the Durham leaders emulated, called the North Carolina city "a city of Negro enterprise." Durham has enjoyed that reputation on into the present, bolstered not only by the Mutual, its building dominating the skyline (on the former site of the mansion of Benjamin Duke of the American Tobacco Company), but also by North Carolina Central University, founded in 1910 as the first state-supported black liberal arts college in the South. Churches, particularly the White Rock Baptist Church which several prominent Mutual officers attended, have had an important role in the development of black leadership in Durham. Socially, many of Durham's black families formed a prestigious middle and upper class. Their fine homes lined Fayetteville Street and often served as "hotels" for distinguished visitors to Durham, many of whom were giving programs at the Mutual's Forum (W. E. B. Du Bois,

Philip Randolph, Robert Moton, James Weldon Johnson, and Adam Clayton Powell) or at the college, under the leadership of James Shepard, one of the founders of the Mutual and a close friend of the Mutual officers.

Dr. Aaron McDuffie Moore, Lyda's father, was born in the eastern part of North Carolina (three of the first five presidents of the Mutual came from this area). After graduating from the newly opened Leonard Medical School of Shaw University in Raleigh, he became the first black physician in Durham in 1888. He married Sarah McCotta Dancy, the daughter of an important political leader in eastern North Carolina. Dr. Moore founded Lincoln Hospital in 1901 and the Colored Library in 1913, and led the movement for the improvement of rural schools for black children in North Carolina. "Cottie" Moore was well known and well loved in Durham, "a friendly person, full of fun," her daughter remembers, who played the accordion and sang and kept a cheerful household full of kin from Columbus County. Dr. and Mrs. Moore sent their two daughters, Lyda and Mattie Louise, to Scotia Seminary in Concord, North Carolina, and then to Fisk University, from which they graduated magna cum laude in 1911. To complete their educations, Dr. Moore encouraged them to continue at Columbia University, after which they returned home to Durham. Lyda then began teaching private piano students, devoted herself to making portraits and other drawings, and was courted by Ed Merrick, a son of the Mutual founder. Their marriage in 1916 marked an even closer alliance between two of the most powerful black families in the state; the local newspaper called the wedding "a social event of state-wide importance," attended by Du Bois, Charlotte Hawkins Brown, director of Palmer Memorial Institute; the president of Wilberforce University, and the mayor of Durham and his wife. Mr. and Mrs. Merrick easily settled into the Mutual family. In addition to raising their two daughters, Lyda Merrick sang with the Mutual's glee club and quartet, became active in the Federation of Negro Women's Clubs, book clubs, and church circles, and served on the board of the Durham Colored Library.

In 1952 Lyda Merrick realized, in her work for the blind, the single greatest challenge of her life, founding *The Negro Braille Magazine* (Now *The Merrick/Washington Magazine for the Blind*), the only national publication directed towards the needs of black people who are sightless. She served as editor for the next eighteen years. "My father passed a torch to me," she explains, "which I have never let go out. We are blessed to serve." In her ninety-second year, Mrs. Merrick is the oldest member of a family which before the turn of the century began a significant chapter in southern black history.

Mrs. Merrick, who makes her home with her daughter and son-in-law in Durham across the street from North Carolina Central University, turns spontaneously to her father's beginnings in eastern North Carolina to tell the story of her own life. "My father tried to teach there down in the country where he was born," she begins, "but he realized its inadequacy and kept trying to take a step where he could to further his education. He was aiming to be a teacher, and he went to Shaw, where the Department of Medicine had just opened the year before. The president persuaded him to join the medical class. He awakened to the importance of it. You know, you can learn but you'll die before you get to learn [everything]. It seemed very important that we have physicians. And he was a student all his life. He would go to his room nights; we weren't allowed in there. He had to have quiet, and he would study his books. I see him there reading. He was still learning. And he had an office on Kemper Street, now where the courthouse stands. That's where the North Carolina Mutual was born, in that building. In one of the back rooms of Kemper's Corner. But really, Lincoln Hospital was born in our house. Papa had built a twelve-room house next to White Rock Baptist Church. Our back porch was screened in, and that was his operating room. Mama would sterilize instruments. He pulled teeth; he would sew up wounds. Saturday night was a busy time for coming in, cut, bleeding. When I'd see them coming in, I'd run across the street to my cousin's because I didn't want to see the blood. And Mr. John Merrick had been here three years before my father, and he was the private barber of Washington Duke. He owned three barber shops, all white. Mr. Duke told Mr. Merrick, 'I want to erect a monument of some kind to the black mammy who took care of our families while we were trying to keep you slaves.' Papa and Merrick, my father-in-law, talked it over, and my father said, 'The best monument you could make would be to give us a hospital.' Duke said, 'Well, why not put an annex on Watts [Hospital] for the blacks?' And Papa said, 'We don't want that. We want a place where our blacks can practice and our nurses can be trained. We want our own.' And that's what happened. And so they built that hospital on Proctor Street, a two-story wooden structure. Most of the money was contributed by Washington Duke, but my father put on a campaign among black people to help raise money. And it opened in 1901. And that's where Papa lived. He slept and ate at home!

"My father was superintendent at White Rock twenty-five years until he died, and it was the biggest Sunday School in Durham. He taught Sunday School all the time. Riding that horse, he'd tap somebody, 'I didn't see you Sunday.' We had a closet with clothes for those that needed shoes. Papa said, in the summer, 'Wash your feet and come on to Sunday School.' And the missionaries would fix them up, whatever they needed to be decent, and they came. My mother was behind my father in everything he did. She nursed and tended to him and raised us, the two girls, and all these folks from down in the country. I said, 'It was an underground railroad!' They all came up here to stay in our house. We had a spare room. Papa was always bringing somebody in that house. He'd bring them from the country and fix them up city-like, and we had a very happy home. They were so grateful for what he was doing for them, and Papa saw that they got their schooling. So many of the men died early, and the widows were left with these children. And they were Papa's cousins so he just brought them up here one by one. My mother was raised in Tarboro, and then she went to St. Augustine's. She was very smart, artistic; all our clothes were made in our house until we were grown. Mama could sew, crochet, knit, tat, everything, busy all the time. She was a great church worker, and she was a club woman, federated clubs, and anywhere she saw she could lead.

"I was thinking about after we finished school [Lyda and her sister]. Papa took us to the World's Fair in California [in 1915 in San Francisco]. He got this geography book, and every night he would say where we were going to stop. It took us thirteen days to make the trip by train. And he'd say we're going to stop here and what this town is noted for. We went to Salt Lake City, Pike's Peak, Chicago. We went by the northern route and came back the southern route by New Orleans. And Mama didn't go—she didn't think Papa was able to do it! I guess we got along better without Mama, too. But that's the way it happened. My father was fairer than I am, and my sister, too. They tried to make us white, you know. But Papa would hunt for the colored people's section. He'd go to a town and say, 'Show me where the colored people live.' There's always a colored section, you know. And it became so difficult till he just gave up and said we'll just go to white hotels. I wouldn't leave my room because I was too brown. Papa would walk around. And I've had so many experiences like that. I was coming from Fisk once. I tried to look nice enough. I went to the diner, and this porter spoke to the waiter there. I don't know exactly what he said, his back was to us, but the waiter shook his head. He didn't know what I was, I reckon. This white porter perked up, took my fur, pulled out my seat. He was just as courteous as he could be like he was apologetic for doubting. It just tickled me. Looks like he would learn some day that people are people. And then one time we were going to Fredericksburg, and we stopped. My husband just loved Cadillacs, and we had a chauffeur. So the chauffeur went in and ordered our dinner, and the manager came out and apologized for not inviting us in. 'Yes,' we said, 'we'd rather eat out here. And you brought this tray out here. This is all right.' And the man stayed as long as we took to eat, apologizing, saying, 'I know this is wrong, but I have to feed my family.' Oh, things like that happened often. One time we were coming from Fisk. John Hope Franklin and those Ph.D.'s and all like that, Fiskites, and we were sitting down here talking, and so this conductor came in. The white people were in the rear with glass in front of them so I could see their faces and expressions. This conductor had one of us get up. He got up on the seat and tied a string from rack to rack—it was one of the most asinine things I ever saw—and hung a paper over it to divide us. I said, 'I wonder how he felt doing that.' I'm telling you, that was a select group of black people who had achieved, had gone back to the President's inauguration at Fisk. You just read what happens to us, discrimination, and those of our people in jails. Innocent, innocent. And they're not able to hire good lawyers. Oh, you see it on television and in papers. But the unfairness of it! The jails are crowded with innocent black people. It's a maddening thing. These school children are mad. They're tired of it. You just feel discrimination. I remember when Papa, when I was a little thing, old enough to get the meaning, he told a white man, 'If you waked up one morning colored, you'd commit suicide.' He said, 'You meet it the minute you leave your door. Discrimination hits you on every side.' And when Papa came here, the white people, the white doctors had to tell our people that he wasn't a quack doctor, wasn't a root doctor. They never heard of black doctors."

Lyda Merrick finishes her narrative as she began it, with the role of her father. She recalls having heard him say, 'If only my people had something to read!' That simple wish provided his incentive to establish a library. His words came back to her almost fifty years later when she began

the Braille magazine. "I was destined to do this," she concludes. "It was in my heart and in my lap, and I did the best I could do day by day."

If the North Carolina Mutual is the successful child of Mr. Merrick and Dr. Moore, *The Merrick/Washington Magazine for the Blind* is the child of Lyda Merrick. Revenue from the sale of the Durham Colored Library property (after the library became part of the city-county system) supports the magazine, which is also endowed by gifts from the North Carolina Federation of Negro Women's Clubs and individual donors. In the early years of its growth, Mrs. Merrick often paid costs out of the gifts of her husband, and whenever they traveled on business or vacations, she took every opportunity to make appointments with individuals and foundations, asking for funds for the magazine. While editing the magazine, she began the practice of excerpting from national publications news of particular interest to blind readers, fulfilling the stated purpose, "to give the Negro blind a bridge between themselves and the sighted world." It is published quarterly at the American Printing House for the Blind in Louisville, Kentucky, where it is set in Braille and mailed free to more than six hundred blind readers, including white readers who request it. The steady increase in printing costs from 72¢ to $2.31 a copy threatens to limit the publication to a biannual. But Mrs. Merrick believes in "answered prayer," and her daily prayer is for help for the magazine. She is known to the readers through her annual Christmas column, which she continues to write. "I've studied the world of the blind. I know them. They are the same as sighted people; some are lazy, some are hardworking. Those with drive seem to have an extra amount. Their senses are sharpened. With some of our people, suffering has made finer souls, coming out pure gold. They have created for themselves a beautiful world. When I ask John [her blind friend] if things seem to him light or dark, white or black, he says, 'That's out of my experience.' He doesn't know about that dividing line of color in America. There is no reason for blind people to have race prejudice."

Inspiration was provided Lyda Merrick by John Carter Washington, born blind and deaf. He began life as a foundling, under the care of nurses at Lincoln Hospital. When the hospital burned (around 1922), Dr. Moore brought the baby to Lyda's home until a foster family could be found for him. As she watched the child crawl about her home, she was impressed with his alert mind and his responsiveness to her directions. Their close friendship has lasted for sixty years. It was at John's insistence that Lyda Merrick began to think about ways of helping their people who are blind, starting with the Library's Corner for the Blind, and he influenced her decision to begin the Braille magazine.

John Washington and Lyda Merrick often visit back and forth, recalling their long association and speaking of present fund-raising efforts for the magazine. Mr. Washington, a well-known masseur at the Durham YMCA, is the father of three children and four grandchildren, one of whom is a grandson who is blind. Mrs. Merrick ends a recent visit by asking about the grandson, speaking to John through sign language. The boy, Mrs. Merrick explains, "is just like John." "He's bright!" she exclaims, and snaps her fingers for emphasis. Although John Washington does not hear the sounds, he smiles, perceiving by his own means joy in this "dark world and wide."

I am indebted to Walter Weare's history of the Mutual, *Black Business in the New South*, for my understanding of its importance in Durham.

# Sisters

## Annie Jones Burke / Sally Jones Jones / Alice Jones Nickens

### Winton

Winton, North Carolina, with its population of fewer than a thousand residents, is a quiet place. The center of public activity is the county courthouse; traffic is slow on Main Street. One can stand at certain times of the day and night at the crossroads and never be disturbed, taking long looks up and down at the rows of old houses, their ornamented eaves, broad front porches, gables, and turrets from another century. A few people gather in front of a cafe. On the south side of town, the Chowan River meanders with a lazy motion. Winton appears as undisturbed as it might have been in 1766 when it was first laid out and incorporated in Hertford County. The ferry, which operated as early as 1720, is gone; gone, also, are the Chowanoc Indian settlements.

If history seems asleep in Winton, however, it is only time's illusion. Like many of North Carolina's villages and hamlets which nest far from the madding crowd, Winton has its own pace, determined largely by family and church and, for its black population especially, by a sense of the historic past. Three sisters, born in the large Victorian house in sight of the Winton crossroads, are keeping that history alive.

The sisters are Sally Jones Jones, age seventy-nine, who moved back home to her birthplace in 1960 after a teaching career in New York City; Alice Jones Nickens, who is seventy-eight, a retired teacher and a native who never left home; and Annie Jones Burke, age seventy-one, also a retired teacher. Their combined years of teaching total one hundred and twenty-six: thirty-seven for Mrs. Jones, fifty for Mrs. Nickens, and thirty-nine for Mrs. Burke. The sisters are accustomed to taking a long look

through history; their ancestors in Hertford County go back to the 1790's.

The town is their home. The school building built in 1886 for the newly established Chowan Academy; the Pleasant Plains Baptist Church, which their grandparents helped establish in 1851 for free blacks; the family homeplace, built around the turn of the century; and the mercantile store, operated by their father from 1886 until 1916: all are visible reminders of their past.

Obvious changes have occurred in Winton over the years. Young people have left the town. Many of the elders have died. Young families with husbands who work during the day in Newport News, Virginia, have settled there to take advantage of the comfortable and less costly life. (In 1939 E. Franklin Frazier analyzed patterns of black family life in Hertford County in *The Negro Family in the United States*. Frazier, whose wife was the daughter of C. S. Brown, the first principal of Chowan Academy, discovered a higher proportion of black landowners than the average for the state as a whole.) The Jones sisters, daughters of landowners, have changed with the times also. Yet their pride in the present-day community is as deep as it must have been among the founders of the Chowan Academy, where their mother, Annie Walden Jones, was the first graduate in 1890. If they regret the passing of traditional manners and customs, they do not dwell on it. In all ways, they continue to reflect what in the South has been called "good breeding."

Although their voices and their faces are remarkably similar, the sisters are quite different from one another. Mrs. Sally Jones talks rapidly, accuses herself of being "as foolish as a beetle bug" and, despite an earlier heart attack, is sometimes almost frenetic with activities, including her paid job with the local Title V program to find employment for people over sixty. A widow and childless, she lives in the family home. Mrs. Alice Nickens is divorced and also lives alone, within sight of her birthplace. She continues to work in public schools as a substitute teacher, serves as a notary, and "begs" from door to door to raise money for community services. Mrs. Jones and Mrs. Nickens do most of the talking. Mrs. Annie Burke, the youngest of the thirteen children—her sisters tease her as having been "made from the scraps"—often sits quietly, her hands folded in her lap, and says nothing as she listens to Sally and Alice. She is married and has four children; she lives in neighboring Gates County. Perhaps as the youngest of a large family, it was useful for her to remove herself from their domination and make her own life elsewhere. Ironically, she has been probably the most outspoken of the sisters in public affairs, notably in her leadership for the Center for Alternative Learning in her county, established to provide day-care services for the children of working mothers. Only her quiet insistence and her alliance with one or two liberal white leaders persuaded the commissioners to fund a program in which most of the children are black.

In the parlors and kitchens of their three homes, Mrs. Jones, Mrs. Nickens, and Mrs. Burke now speak for themselves.

Mrs. Jones begins. "In our early childhood, we were pampered children in a sense. Our father was quite a few years older than our mother. He was already a merchant with a huge mercantile business. It was at a county crossroads as well as one of the largest stores in town. He was the only person with the School Book Depository franchise. In those days many people did not pay for things they bought but two or three times a year. So when they married [in 1890], my mother worked in the store as his bookkeeper. By the time there were children, there was a housekeeper, cook and maid, and two men that worked around the yard and such. We had a surrey, the only one in town. All the townspeople used it for weddings." Mrs. Nickens continues. "Our father sold everything imaginable: molasses, flour, sugar, cookies in the big wooden boxes, and apples by the barrel, corn, herrings and meal, and dress material, ten cents a yard. And spool cotton. I still have the O&T cabinet that thread was in. Our father used to be a fisherman. They fished in the Chowan River, and he was the captain or the manager, and they sold herring right there by the thousands. He had these horses that went around in a circle with nets, and in the spring of the year—" Mrs. Jones interrupts. "It was called a windlass. They used mules that went around in a circle and the rope that they had the corks on pulled the nets back to shore." "But anyway," Mrs. Nickens resumes, "They gave everybody who came to buy fish, corn bread and cooked herring. He had a cook who cooked them there, and this was free, when we were little. Some were packed in hogsheads in salt and some were sold and shipped away." "The Chowan River," Mrs. Jones adds, "is where our father did the fishing. All of us were baptized in the river."

"Our mother was a Walden, Annie Walden Jones," Mrs. Nickens says. "She was born in this county. My mother was a little better educated than the average person around here. Our mother had a very good elementary education. Because she was one of five sisters and because her mother and father had so many children, a couple in Enfield, North Carolina, asked them to let them keep her as a little girl. Now, they didn't really adopt her and she wasn't given away, but this couple took her. They were educated, and we feel that this had a great influence on her early education, so when she started she moved right along. There were others in her high school but she was the first and only graduate. And the man who kept her until she was twelve, I believe, he was sent to Washington as a representative and they had to let her come home. She went to Shaw one or two years after she graduated here. At that time they took tests in order to teach, and it was said she made the highest score of any teacher during that time, black or white. She was an excellent teacher and she did things for people. We'd come home and we couldn't find Mama and after awhile here she'd come walking up and we'd say, 'Where have you been?' 'Well, so-and-so had company, and she needed a chicken for dinner, and I went down there and fried the chicken for her.' She did it all her life. She even wrote love letters for people. I've often heard her laugh about this.

"After our father's death [in 1916], six children were still at home and dependent on our mother. You know what our sister in New York tells us, that she was born with a silver spoon in her mouth but by the time we were coming along, the spoon fell out because our Daddy died. I remember our mother saying a'many a time when we were eating, 'All right, remember so-and-so hasn't had anything.' You had to share. We pushed white children [in strollers] up and down the street to make money." Mrs. Burke speaks. "My home-life so far as I remember was happy, even

though it was a struggle. We came up very poor and all of us had to work at very young ages. I took care of white babies for twenty-five cents a week when I was ten or twelve years old, just a baby myself, and my brothers were handy boys around white homes in Winton. The families were very kind, very lovely people."

Mrs. Nickens picks up the narrative again. "My mother and father had so many children they could not send all of us to school, especially at the same time. So when I graduated from high school—I graduated with honors—the first year the principal's wife was ill and they gave me her job, I taught that year in her place, taught history. Then the next year they hired me for thirty dollars a month, and I began teaching. It took me about twenty years going to summer school, taking extension work in every way I could to get my B.S. from Hampton Institute. (It was the trend to send the boys to school and the girls got their education any way they could.) I'd go to Norfolk or Virginia Beach and work in between. I gave ten dollars to my mother and ten to my brother at Howard, and I had ten dollars to save for my own use. I was living here with my mother. She was teaching also. I kept on until I got my master's degree from the University of Pennsylvania."

Mrs. Burke continues. "I graduated from C. S. Brown in 1929 and entered Elizabeth City State Normal School, which had two years. I wanted to be a social service worker, but mother had two sons in college and wasn't able to send me where I could get what I wanted. I got a Primary B certificate at Elizabeth City and took summer courses and extension courses. By that time, they were making the school a college, about 1936, and I took more residential hours and finished my degree in 1949. I worked at the school sweeping rooms, and I wore hand-me-downs and anything I could get to wear. My mother did what she could for all of us. Now one of my brothers is a doctor in Williamsburg, Virginia, one is the retired president of Fayetteville State, one is a dentist from Howard, and one is a mortician. My sister in New York is also a retired teacher. There are eight children living now."

Mrs. Jones takes up the narrative. "I graduated from Waters in 1920 and left there and went to Shaw for a semester. I stopped and went to work. I stayed out of school twenty years. My mother wanted me to go back to Shaw because I went there before, but I told her the children there had more money and they had more of everything. I decided to go to Elizabeth City where I could be among the best. I finished at Elizabeth City and later taught in Hertford County. I left North Carolina and went to New York City and taught school and got my master's degree at Columbia University. I came back to North Carolina in 1960 and taught two years and had a heart attack in the classroom."

One thread running through the narratives is the school which opened in 1886 as the Chowan Academy (the Academy later went through various name changes, including Waters Normal Institute and now the C. S. Brown public school). Mrs. Nickens explains. "When the school was first founded in 1886 it was Chowan Academy. A few of the older citizens in the community had been given the land by Levi Brown, who owned almost all of this end of town, and he gave the land for the school, and the trees had been cut when Dr. Brown came to preach at Pleasant Plains Church. The people were cutting the tim-

ber and getting ready to build, and they were doing most of the work of the building themselves, some of the outstanding Negro citizens were doing this at that time. They found out that Dr. Brown had a pretty good education and they asked that he come back and be principal of the school." Mrs. Jones adds, "He was recommended by our mother's sister's husband, who was a medical doctor here, Dr. Manassas Pope. He asked Dr. Tucker, President of Shaw University, to recommend somebody, and since he and Dr. Brown were friends, he sent him." Mrs. Nickens explains, "I'm the one who knows him because I taught with him twelve years before he died. I went to teach there 1922–23 and I retired in 1970. He was intelligent, he could play the organ and most any kind of instrument. He was kind, he was a lawyer to the people in the community. He was very religious; he preached at every church in the county and all over this state. He traveled abroad. He was an outstanding person, and he was just a joy to work with.

"The doors opened October 1, 1886. We had thirty-five boarding students in 1886 and eighty-five town students who were able to walk to school. The only way that the school could survive was through freewill giving and there were many philanthropists in the North at that time would help any group of blacks that were trying to do something. There was a Mr. Waters that Dr. Brown had met at Shaw, and he was very interested in Dr. Brown's career, and he gave the school at one time eight thousand dollars. He was a piano manufacturer so they named the school Waters Normal Institute, and that was the name when Sally and I attended school. The children came from all over Hertford County, Bertie County, Virginia; Chuckatuck, Hampton.

And we didn't even have any electricity. No indoor plumbing. They had little outdoor toilets. The boarding students at one time when it first opened were just paying a dollar and seventy-five cents a month. But you could bring potatoes and meat to help pay for your board. There was a lot of competition between the boarding students and the town students. We played basketball, tennis, we played baseball. It was the town against the boarders, and you would be surprised at the competition. It was the school that started it all. Negroes have assumed the leadership for everything in Winton because of the school."

Warming to her memories, Mrs Nickens continues. "In the spring of the year the coal pile was getting low. We would take pails and Dr. Brown would give us one penny to pick up a bucket of coal. Sally says she doesn't remember it. Annie doesn't remember it either. The coal was brought to Cofield by train or else it was brought up the river by boat. Where the children had gone out to get a pail of coal, it would spill all over the campus, and we would pick it up. We took our pennies and went across the street—there was a store there—and I think it was about six vanilla wafers we could get for a penny. Some of the children bought sour pickles."

In 1923 Waters Normal School was taken over by the county system of public education: a transfer of control which eventually brought about many changes opposed by the black community. "We have through the fifth grade now," Mrs. Nickens explains, "but they took the high school away about two years after the integration law passed and took our children and sent half to Ahoskie High, which was white, and half to Murfreesboro High, which was colored. We resented this very much because we had more land, better buildings, but there was nothing, of course, we could do about it. After they took the high school, then they took the seventh and eighth grades and then another year they took the sixth and at present we have from kindergarten through fifth. This winter we have had several mass meetings, and Sally and I have written newsletters, and graduates from away have sent the Board of Education all kinds of letters because we really feel that they should not do away with our school, but there is talk about it closing completely. Our nephew is principal of the high school in Murfreesboro where half of our students go. But this is because he applied for the job as superintendent because he did have the education, and it came to the place where they had to give him something."

With the discussion of the changes at the C. S. Brown school the sisters talk about race relations. Mrs. Nickens begins. "I really do not think that the black children nor the white that go to public schools are getting the same attention that they did in the days when we were not integrated. I see too many children standing out in the hallway. This is a form of punishment, now, you stand in the hall. And I don't think the teachers are as dedicated." Mrs. Jones adds, "I think it's a decline of standards." Mrs. Nickens: "And you have some black people that still have it in their hearts that they are mad about something, and the same way you have some whites that feel the same way about black children." Mrs. Burke, who started teaching in a two-teacher school where Sally was her principal, recalls that she made fifty dollars a month in a Rosenwald school, "the best in the county. Teachers were really teachers at that time. People really thought we were the cream of the crop. We had more invitations to dinner than we could fill. We were respected, and the parents cooperated with you. You spank now, if you dare." Her experiences after school desegregation did not change her love for teaching. "I loved every minute of it," she says. "I felt like a child was a child, and I was going to do the best that I could for the child. Integration didn't bother me at all, and I haven't had any problems."

Mrs. Nickens picks up the story. "To tell you the truth, we've always had integration because in this particular section there are so many mixed families of white and black. I have taught children that were just white, and we have even had families to prove themselves white, not Indian. We really have had very good race relations in Winton and always have. All our neighbors were white up until a very short time ago. Because we were here actually when there wasn't anything here but woodlands." Mrs. Burke adds, "I've been associated with whites all my life. All of our neighbors were white, and there were only two Negro families who lived where we did. My daddy's sister lived across the street. The Secretary of State's wife was born across the street—Mina Banks married Thad Eure."

As the conversation turns to racial discrimination, Mrs. Jones insists, "Never, never, I don't feel it." "Sure I have," Mrs. Nickens interrupts. Mrs. Jones responds, "As far as the beach is concerned, because I couldn't be going anyway, but that was segregated. Now the only thing about that that I disliked was that we used to have a showboat that came here every summer and when they made that into a beach the showboat wanted to go there, and because they wouldn't let Negroes come down there

then, they wouldn't come. So we didn't get the showboat anymore." "Well, I'll say this," Mrs. Nickens continues. "We always had good race relations, but you still knew that when you went to their house, you still were supposed to go to the back door." "Well, see that's where we differ," Mrs. Jones argues. "I don't ever remember going to anybody's back door, and I've never felt that I needed to go to anybody's back door. I think that is definitely a personal thing, and I'll tell you something else, I think that the people that live up the other end of town have an altogether different attitude towards white people than we do. Because all of our lives we lived around them." Mrs. Burke then speaks up, "Gates County is one of the rabid counties. Hard to give up. They don't want the Negroes to do anything or be on anything or to get ahead. We feel that we can't get any help in Gates County for day care because there aren't many whites who will send their children to it. It's what I've been living with. They promise you things and they don't do it, and I guess really we should do more fighting against that than we have done."

"There were a lot of free born Negroes in this section," Mrs. Nickens explains. "In fact, our church is known I think all over the United States because they have joked about if you go there and see that choir you would think you were in a white church there are so many light-skinned people. There have been brothers and sisters that went to school right here in town, since I've been here. And everybody knew it. It would be a white man that had gotten a child by a black woman, but maybe he had his own family, you understand. And his child by his white wife would be going to the white school, and the child by the black wife would be going to the black school."

"Everybody in our family was free-born," Mrs. Jones adds. "Our grandfather's father voted before 1835. Mr. Walden [Annie Walden Jones's father] was in the Union Army, and he was a staff sergeant. He was the ministerial treasurer of the Pleasant Plains Church in 1873." Mrs. Nickens continues the discussion of her mother's family. "Mr. Walden was a carpenter and a real estate person. He gave land on the Ahoskie-Cofield Road for a school that was named for him, the Walden School. My grandfather owned a large farm, and he and his wife are buried there. Their tall tombstones are there. Most of the land here in Hertford County he acquired after coming

to Hertford County from Northampton County, but he was from a family that did have some money, so he could have brought some money with him." "There is property ownership on my mother's family side as far back as 1845. That was the Weaver side," Mrs. Jones concludes.

Time has stopped momentarily for Sally Jones, Alice Nickens, and Annie Burke as they have looked back into the past. Holding a picture of their mother, they pose on the front porch of the family home. Traffic goes by now and then on the Main Street of a small southern town. In another moment, they will move with it. Gracefully and purposefully they live in the past and the present.

# Taking Low to No One

Beatrice Garrett Burnett

Tarboro

"My father often said, 'You're as good as anybody else. I'm as good as the President. The President has one vote, and I have one vote.' And that's the philosophy we were brought up under. I'm telling you," Beatrice Garrett Burnett says, looking straight at her visitors, "and I have never taken low either."

Mrs. Burnett stands in the shoes of her father, "a politician from the sole of his feet to the top of his head." She, more than any other person, is responsible for the establishment and growth of the NAACP in eastern North Carolina. She urged blacks in Edgecombe County to register and vote, giving strong encouragement to women after passage of the 19th Amendment. Between 1940 and 1970 while the number of registered, voting age blacks jumped from ten percent to fifty-five percent, Beatrice Burnett was at work, calling, visiting, and encouraging. She has made her own voice heard and she has helped to amplify the voices of others.

Mrs. Burnett had two professions: politics and physical education. During fifty years of teaching in Tarboro public schools, she introduced children to games, old and new, and after school she organized recreation and team sports in vacant fields. Today in her eighty-ninth year (she was born in 1893), Mrs. Burnett expresses herself as forcefully as her father taught her to do.

"That is a good starting point," she says. "What I have done, I have done because of the inspiration my father gave me. He was born in slavery time, but he was not quite six when the Civil War ended. My father's father was the shoemaker of the plantation. His work was to do all the shoes on that plantation and then his master would hire him out to another plantation to make the shoes there, and to another. And my grand-

mother said when my father was born—he was the third child—his father came home, and his father was hired [out] some place at that time. My father was just crawling, and he never did see his father anymore. They don't know what happened. Whether he attempted to escape like so many of them did, or what, but he just didn't ever come back. So his mother just reared the children. She was one of those like my father that didn't take anything from anybody.

"So my father was reared on a farm, and when he came to town, when he became twenty-one, he went right into politics. He was born in Princeville, [one of] the oldest incorporated colored towns in the United States, February 12, 1885. There's always been some whites over there, but principally, it has been a colored town. It was first called Freedom Hill because most of those people were born in slavery time. The school my father went to and the school John C. Dancy went to [he later became Register of Deeds in Washington, D.C.] was four blocks from where I lived. The first principal that they had was a man who had finished Lincoln, out from Philadelphia. He finished Lincoln before the war. He was from down at Wilmington, so he set up the first private school. Now my father often liked to tell, 'I didn't have but five years of formal education,' but you wouldn't know it. He was as well read, as well everything as anybody. When he came to Tarboro [adjacent to Princeville] at twenty-one, he only held two jobs under anybody for the first four years. He worked first for one man who was a Captain in the Civil War. He worked for him one year doing the same thing he ended doing, running a store. Then he worked for another man doing the same thing, and after that man went west, the store got into my father's hands, and he had it from there on, a big grocery business, and it was where the biggest white business is located in Tarboro now. He was in business on Main Street from 1895 till he died in 1928. His leadership encouraged at least ten other blacks to go into business on Main Street. He reared seven children. Everything that we have, all the education that we have, came through that business. The house I live in now in Tarboro was the fourth family home he built. And my brother started a drug store in Tarboro, which my sister ran when he moved to Durham to start another one. All of us worked in the grocery store. I remember now, the circus coming to town. Poppa would say, 'Well, you all come down and see the parade in front of the store.' And he would let us, my brother and me, sell apples and candy while we were waiting for the parade. Then, when the parade came, he saw the circus, and he always employed my older brother to take us to the circus. We had practically every benefit, everything anybody else had.

"The county was sixty-six percent black till about twenty years ago. My father went right through the Reconstruction period, and Edgecombe had one of the largest number of blacks in the General Assembly. My father was elected to the General Assembly, and he wasn't seated. When the votes were counted for him, they wouldn't count any of the vote that blacks had. But I tell you what, he was the [elected] magistrate in our county and served as magistrate two terms. He was in everything, and he voted. There were twenty-five or thirty more just like him. My mother said she'd let my father do the politicking. But she'd stick right behind him in anything he wanted to do. He also worked through fraternal organizations—Masons, Oddfellows,

Pythians, Gideons, Elks. They were really long before the NAACP because it wasn't organized until 1909 and they were working back there in those 1800's.

"Tarboro is a town that has always been educationally oriented. Let me give you a true illustration. A situation arose in 1921 [when Mrs. Burnett was twenty-eight]. Edgecombe County was a big cotton county, and the school board said they weren't going to open—I say Negro schools because that's what we were saying back then—until the cotton was gotten out. And so they had a meeting in the auditorium of the white school, and one of the biggest men in Tarboro happened to be Superintendent of the schools. So he called us together, and we were there in big numbers. I was there with my father and brother. So he put it before us why they would have to close the school. My brother said, 'I have a suggestion. I know what cotton means to the economy of Edgecombe County, but if it is necessary to get the cotton out, my suggestion is that we close *all* of the schools, and then possibly in two weeks, we can get *all* of the cotton out.' Judge Howard said, 'No, no, no, no—we can't do that!' We had a principal who wasn't scared either, so when Judge Howard said, 'There's a law in North Carolina that children can be kept out if it's necessary to harvest the crop,' my principal was sitting right on the stage with the Superintendent. He said, 'Mr. Howard, I have a school law, and I have a section here I would like to read.' Mr. Howard didn't have any idea what it was. So Mr. Howard said, 'All right, all right, go ahead, go ahead.' He said, 'The law says a farmer could keep his *own* children out to harvest the crops, but he could not hire any children of people who were *not* farmers to harvest the crop. So you can see, Mr. Howard, sir, that takes care of that!' So then Mr. Howard said, 'Well, it looks like there's nothing to do but put it to a vote. All in favor of closing the schools, let it be known by standing up.' Four people stood up. He said, 'Well, that's to have the thing closed.'

"And the county has been like that from way back. Then another instance happened. They were building a high school; by the way, Tarboro was one of the first four black high schools that were set up east of Raleigh, and there were at least five towns east of Raleigh that were bigger than Tarboro. We had our high school a year before whites got theirs, and we were accredited. They could build the building, but they couldn't build an auditorium. So they called a meeting in the Courthouse that time, and *we* were there, women and men and everybody. The question was asked by a friend of my brother's 'Why is it you can't build our auditorium?' They said, 'We'll have to borrow some money, and the interest would be so much.' So this young man said, 'How much would the interest be?' They said, 'About fifteen hundred dollars.' So the young man said, 'Suppose fifteen of us sign to pay one hundred dollars apiece. Can you do it then?' They answered, 'Oh, yes, the only thing that was bothering us was the interest.' So those men signed *then*. I know when that class. graduated, *that* building was built with *that* auditorium. Now it was in the fall when they said they couldn't do it. And the first class marched down that aisle in May, 1924, in the morning. Not all towns went that way. Tarboro has been a town that has been forward-looking ever since before I was born." As Beatrice Burnett pauses in her narrative, looking back to the influences of her father and forward to her life

as a teacher and a political activist, she defines her philosophy: "Nothing is going to stop me, especially where my folks are concerned. I am not afraid of anything."

She graduated from Elizabeth City State Normal School and began teaching in Tarboro in 1912 at the age of nineteen. Mrs. Burnett continued to teach and learn for the next fifty years, taking advanced courses at Hampton Institute and other colleges and universities almost every summer. "I hadn't had any particular training for physical education," she says, "but they called me a tomboy, because everything my brother did, I did. And we were fortunate to have an old principal who loved to see us play ball. Sometimes he'd give an extra long recess while we were out there. We had a real big ground, and he'd go across the road and sit to see us play. I was interested in all kinds of sports, but mostly baseball. And when I began working, I began teaching basketball. And there wasn't another woman down there that could teach basketball. Now, you know it was long before we had any gym or anything like that, but I didn't have to have a gym to teach physical education. I had the outdoors. We got our gym in '52, and I coached the only county girls' team that ever won the tournament. And because at that time there wasn't a man hired on the seventh grade level, the only way boys could get basketball was I had to teach them. And they talk about it now. They come back home and come a-running to me and hug me and say, 'If it hadn't been for you, we couldn't have made the high school team!' And I had some girls could do anything the boys could do.

"Anything I'd come back from Hampton and say I wanted to do, my principal stuck right with me. He said, 'Okay. Give me your book.' He meant the book I taught it from. 'And send me four of your seventh grade boys.' And he'd just go up to the Superintendent and tell him what he wanted to do, and he said, 'Well, tell her just buy the material.' And I bought the soccer ball myself. My mother said it was silly, it was my money. But the ball didn't cost that much. I went to Hampton, learned soccer, came back and put it over with my seventh grade class in 1929. And that was the only time that soccer had ever been taught in North Carolina until the last fifteen years. I'd just go on out and go to summer school so I could pass on something new to my children. I'd have fifty girls on the gym floor at one time and everybody doing the same wand drill. And I told them, I said, 'Now, listen, I'm not going to have you buying the wands. Go home and find a broom that your mama has gotten rid of and cut that broomstick off. Be sure it's a yard long.' And they could go through those wand drills, you know, turning them this way and over their heads. I went down to Hampton and took aesthetic and folk dancing. I believe I was thirty-two. And I loved it to death! Aesthetic is really the part that deals with ballet. My father said before I was four every few weeks he had to have my shoes half-soled because there would be a long hole where I had danced them out, as early as that. And we called it buck dancing. It's similar to clogging. I taught all these children clogging. I clogged right up to '62 when I came out of there. In fact, I did actual ballroom dancing till I was seventy-seven. So you see, it was just in me.

"When I first began following the Olympics, Jesse Owens won the decathlon. So I told my children, I said, 'Now, listen, you don't know any more about the Olympics than I do, so you go look it up." I said, 'Let's go back to the beginning and see how it started and where it started and all of that. Then, hereafter, when you see the games and when we hear this expression or that expression, we'll know just what's happening.' Then, when I was teaching eighth grade, Wilma Rudolph won three gold medals. That was interesting because at one time she couldn't walk. I said, 'So see, children, there's no point in giving up. Don't ever give up. If she could overcome that physical handicap,' I said, 'you can do anything. You can overcome anything.'"

For her lifetime of leadership in physical education and recreation (including helping to organize the Little League teams), Beatrice Burnett was honored by the community, which named the gymnasium of the city recreation center for her. And for her success in raising money for the NAACP, she was named to the Association's Million Dollar Club and proudly wears the NAACP medal.

During the time she was teaching and coaching, Mrs. Burnett was active in the NAACP, serving as president of the Tarboro chapter for seventeen years and holding state and national offices. It was her organization of the first Youth Council in 1948, however, which gives her the greatest satisfaction. "And it has gone without stopping," she says. "I'd take them to the State Conference or take them to the national conference, or they'd take themselves because the children would raise their own money. And we carried the voter registration program almost entirely since '58. There had never been more than four hundred blacks registered and now there are over two thousand. [In 1981 records show there are 6,139 registered black voters in Edgecombe County.] These kids are largely responsible. They sat down and mapped the whole town out, every street in our section. We had set up for the election in '48 when Truman, Dewey, and Henry Wallace ran. We assigned the children to represent the Democratic Party, the Republican Party, and the Progressive Party. And they did research on it, and they gave a town discussion. The Mayor came—of course he didn't stay but a hot minute—he said he just came to express his appreciation that we had young people interested.

"You know when women were first allowed to vote in '20 [Mrs. Burnett was then twenty-eight], my sister and I and a doctor's wife were the first women, I don't mean just black women, that registered in the town of Tarboro. And the man who was registrar said, 'I know you were coming because I know your father won't let you live in that house [without registering] after this law went through.' I'm registered Democrat, I vote independently. After I hear all the issues and I go behind that curtain there's only one thing in my mind and that's the blacks that I have been working for all these years. My point is, which one of these men is going to do most for my people?

"The first man that I really became deeply interested in was Truman. Now I wasn't interested in Truman because of Truman, but I knew what Truman meant to us. Anything Franklin Roosevelt would have done would have been all right because he brought us through. We were in the midst of having nothing, this country. I was sitting out in front of the Lincoln Memorial when Truman made that speech that electrified the world. We didn't have any idea what he was going to say although I knew about the inside because I was supposed to check with Walter White and Roy

Wilkins and we knew how this thing got started. This was one statement Truman made—he wasn't an orator by any means, but he could get over what he wanted to—he said, 'No longer,' now these are his words, 'can we wait to have the federal or state government to right some of these wrongs that are going on. No longer can we wait for this. So—and he had had Walter White and Roy Wilkins to tell him what were some of the worst things that were going through—as of tomorrow, I as head of the federal government of the United States will see to it that many of those wrongs will be righted.' People didn't think anyone from Independence, Missouri, had the sense.

"My children had a program on presidents. A lot of blacks said Lincoln just freed the slaves to save the Union. I said, 'Uh, huh, that's all you know, cause I knew history, from back there when he was carrying that raft of logs down the Mississippi River.' He said he was going down the river, and he saw an auction block of blacks, people selling children from their fathers and mothers. He said, then, 'If I ever get the chance to hit that, I'm going to hit it hard.' This happened to be an opportunity. So I planned the program on presidents, and we knew we were going to take Lincoln. And we had Lincoln, Truman, FDR, Kennedy, and Johnson. I selected the program, and they went up there saying just what I wanted them to say. That's the type of thing I've done all these years. My teaching and my work have been much broader than just standing up in the classroom.

"I have followed the union since Samuel Gompers down to John L. Lewis. I had to teach the ups and the downs, the whys and the why-nots. I said to the man hired for the purpose of bringing industry to the town, 'You can say all you want but I was out there working, and if we hadn't got a particular industry into a union, my folks still wouldn't have a job.' And Black & Decker invited some of us out, and I spoke. And I opened my speech by saying, 'As I look all over this building, I see at least fifty of my own children who sat in my seventh grade. I want the same thing for East Tarboro that I have wanted for every other Negro boy and girl that sat in my seventh grade, and I want the same things for them that I want for my own family. Why should I expect less?'"

On the afternoon of the second day of talking with Mrs. Burnett, she stops her narrative, and pauses for a long time. "This is one point I started to tell you yesterday, and then I didn't know whether to tell you or not," she begins. "How our men—the same night I told you about closing the schools—about three days later, how our men just stood up. One of the deacons of my church and the superintendent of my Sunday school got a message to be out of town at such-and-such a time if he valued his life. When my father and the

people in his age group heard about the message, they met and said, 'We've got to do something about it.' They first called for a meeting—I'll put it this way—of the rich, the rector of the Episcopal Church and others. They explained what the message was. They said, 'What are you going to do about it?' The whites said, 'There is nothing that we can do about it.' The colored folks said, 'Well, that's all we wanted to know. He isn't going anywhere. His house will be protected twenty-four hours a day by one set of us or the other. He'll be surrounded and we want to warn you that no white face should be seen anywhere around it. You say you can't do anything about it. We will.' My father said, 'I don't even have a gun but I'm sending to get one.' It was right after World War I. 'You understand that the young men who have just come back from France have brought their guns. We're just warning you. If any white man is seen anywhere in our area, we won't be responsible for what happens.'

"I wanted to tell these three stories," Beatrice Burnett concludes. "About not building the auditorium, about closing the school, and this."

# Ivory Towers and No Sidewalks

## Gatha Horton Lassiter

### Chapel Hill

In the university community of Chapel Hill, North Carolina, Gatha Lassiter is better known than many professors. And with good reason. While they work in the isolation of classrooms and libraries on problems of the intellect, Mrs. Lassiter is out in public meetings confronting the ways poor people live. The distance between their intellectual exercises and her social involvement is often great, yet the University of North Carolina campus and the Multi-Purpose Center where Mrs. Lassiter is in charge of the meals program for elderly citizens are only a few blocks apart.

Chapel Hill is widely known and loved in North Carolina as "the southern part of heaven." Mrs. Lassiter first heard the description in 1954 after moving here from rural Chatham County next door, and when an opportunity came to speak in a public meeting, she responded, "Now those of you all that know where the southern part of heaven's line stops, I live a block on the other side. I have to tell you my view of the southern part of heaven, what I can see. I don't live in it." Until school desegregation came to Chapel Hill in the sixties, neighborhood schools for black children did not have sidewalks. Mrs. Lassiter immediately became involved in the needs of school children, families who lived in low-rent housing, and the elderly. Today she is known and admired by the people of Chapel Hill, including many university professors, as the conscience of the community.

"I grew up on a farm in Chatham County," she begins, "and I'd see how people treated people, how people treated me when I would work for them. After I married, this lady wanted me to stay with her one night when her people were gone away. We were sitting down there, and she said,

'Let me draw the curtains. I wouldn't want people to pass here and see you in my living room.' Well, she'd just as soon as spit in my face as to say that! I was there trying to do for her although she didn't want people to pass by and see a black person in her living room. And I always said that if I ever got to the place where I could help get justice, I was going to do it. This is from a child up. I saw things.

"My father was a teacher, but he died when I was ten years old [Mrs. Lassiter was born in 1910]. My mother was very strong. My mother was a working person. She just believed in a good day's work. She was humble, but of course, her parents were slavery time. Her parents were slaves under the Wilsons. My grandmother stayed there on that plantation in Chatham County as long as she could keep house. She died in 1932, and she was in her eighties. And my father's mother was a slave. I don't think his father was. I heard them talk about slavery. I was raised about fifteen miles from where my mother was born and so I knew the people. My grandmother's brothers, they had different slave masters and they went under different names, but they all knew they were brothers and sisters. One set of children had three sets of names. And I always thought it was so cruel. Everybody should be a person. That's what I always wanted to see.

"The education of our family was very important. The boys all went to school. There were ten of us, five boys and five girls. They didn't even have a high school for black children in Chatham County, and you'd have to go off to boarding school. My brothers had to go up to Henderson. Then after they attended Henderson Institute, they went to North Carolina A&T. My two brothers went there. Then my other brother that's a minister, when he finished elementary school, he went to Winston-Salem. There was a high school there; I think at that time it was called Slater. I completed the seventh grade early, and then I just repeated the seventh grade. I never had a chance to go to high school. When I came to Chapel Hill, I took up night school and got the equivalent of a high school diploma. I was forty-some.

"I was always concerned about people. I know that one time when I was a child, I heard about a boy that they were going to lynch because he had walked across a field. A white girl had run across the field, and this boy, they said, he looked at her, and they were trying to catch him to lynch him. It got me so nervous that I thought that I would just have to go to bed. But it just worried me so bad to think about people that didn't have that privilege to even walk and anybody could look at anybody. I felt like justice wasn't done.

"So I'm forever sticking my nose into something. When I was in Chatham, there was nothing which I could not be involved in—the school and the church activities and the community activities. I guess it was born in me, and the more I see and the more things I get into, the more things I see need to be done. I didn't vote until '52 [at the age of forty-two] and that was in Chatham County. I had always wanted to be in the political life, and Chatham was one of the worst places that you could try to get in. Everybody knew everybody, but I was willing to get out and try. This man that was a registrar, he and my mother grew up together. My grandmother belonged to his granddaddy in slavery. So he knew me when I walked in and they teased me so much about it because my husband had said, 'Okay, but I'm expecting to catch

you hung to a tree.' I said, 'Well, that's all right. If it takes it, I'll do it.' I went on in that morning, and the registrar thought that I was going to the store because it was then a store building. I came on back and he said, 'What do you want?' And I said, 'I came on down here to register to vote.' He said, 'You ain't Minnie's daughter?' That's what he called my mother. I said, 'Yes, I am Gatha Horton Lassiter.' And he looked around the store and he said, 'Well, there's nothing I can do. She can read and write. I have to register her.' So he registered me, that was all. 'Well,' he said, 'Tell your brothers to come down here and register.' And I went back and told my brothers. That fall [1952] when there was a presidential election, they said they had heard that the man at New Hope Township said he wasn't going to register a black person. They asked if I knew anyone who lived in New Hope Township. They said they would like them to go to register. I told them I would try. So I went on back home, and I called a school teacher because I knew that we'd have to get the best we had to go down there. I asked her if she would go to New Hope this coming Saturday and register. I said, 'If he asks you to read, you can read, but don't answer any questions he asks you.' So she went on there to register, and he said, 'No, we don't register niggers.' That evening late, I saw the lady coming, and I thought, 'Oh———oh! He sure didn't register her!' So she came. And I called my brother, Reverend Horton, and he called a representative of the NAACP in North Carolina. He came to Pittsboro that Saturday night. On Tuesday, the headlines of the papers were FORMER SCHOOL TEACHER OF CHATHAM COUNTY REFUSED REGISTRATION. They sent me word. They confirmed at Pittsboro that it wouldn't happen any more. They sent me word to go tell the lady to come back. So I did. I said, 'Will you go back next Saturday?' She said, 'Yes, I'll go back any time you tell me to go back.' This man told her when she came in and said she came to register, 'Why didn't you tell me you were a former school teacher?' She said, 'I didn't know that's what people had to tell you to get on the books. I just came in to register because I am a resident of New Hope District.' So he registered her and the rest of them.

"I've always been outspoken. I feel that black women have courage to go on where the men are so, 'Oh, well, it's going to be,' and they'd wait anyway. And the women saw that they balked and if they'd get out and fight for it, there might be a change. I always wanted to go to Africa. I wanted to do missionary work. This is what came to me one time, that was after I was married. 'You talking about going to Africa! You can do the work right around you.' And I said, 'Well, yes I can.' So then I started helping people. Now since I've been in Chapel Hill, I've been allied with the League of Women Voters and the volunteer service. I joined the League of Women Voters when I came to Chapel Hill, and they asked me, 'What led you to join the League of Women Voters?' And I told them, and they used to quote me as saying, I was going to get into anything I could get in because staying on the outside you wouldn't find out what was going on on the inside. When I moved here I had this big house, and I started keeping teachers or either students. This was in '56. I had six teachers staying here. We were sitting around the table and one of them said, '*Porgy and Bess* is going to be showing downtown, and we would like to go.' And I said, 'Well, I don't ever go to shows' but I said, 'If you all want to go,' I said, 'I'll do

the best that I can.' At that time I had lots of white friends that was liberal, white friends, cause I was going to meetings nearly every night doing something. I turned then and called my friend and asked her about it, and she said, 'Well, we'll see.' She called some friends of hers and asked them about it. They said, 'We don't know.' So we turned it over to the Ministers' Alliance. The Ministers' Alliance was integrated. In the process, they asked the pastor of the Methodist church, of which the man that ran the Carolina Theatre was a member. He said, 'Don't you all go to him. Let me go to see him,' I understand they talked to him for two hours, but this man said it would hurt his business. That night the young people had a meeting and decided that they would picket. I said, 'What do you want me to do? I can't walk.' I always had arthritis. 'But,' I said, 'I can do telephone [calls] or have the lunch vans there and do things like that.' So we started from there. As for the picketing, I did never picket, but like we would go march, or vigil, yes, I stood on a vigil. We were going to march like from the church to the Town Hall. I got in a car and rode that day down to the Town Hall, and I was down there when they got there. I was with them. And I never shall forget the drug store up there. He was determined. He was a really nice person. And he was a great druggist because he would let you have medicine that was over the counter. You could tell him your complaint, and he would prescribe you medicine for it. But anyway, he refused to integrate, so we had a time with him. At last they took up the seats because blacks would go in there and sit down and wouldn't move. He like to went out of business. And after that, I mailed him his check for what I owed him, and I never been in his store but once since. I had heard talk of picketing, but I had never known what the method of picketing was that much. But I know that anything that you disapprove of, you could just picket it. I believed in that then. Now, I think there is more of another way that you can do. That [picketing] has been tried, and it proved out successful. Each day done its due, and that day has passed on. You can do more at the ballot box now. I don't believe in violence, but I believe in something to draw the focus of the attention of people to say that this thing has been going on a good bit, and we're tired of it, and we'd like for the public to know it. Now we got lots of names on the voting books that weren't on the book. Everywhere that we had a black person to run, even if they didn't win, it would help to get names on the book. That helped a lot. When Howard Lee ran for mayor, it meant everything to Chapel Hill. First thing about it, I guess, lots of people in Chapel Hill didn't think a black person could win but the way that he went round about it with his campaign managers and everything like that, that really surprised Chapel Hill. See, they got all the black votes out plus the white ones that were for him, and his overwhelming election was a surprise to Chapel Hill, I think. And after he won the first time, he won all the rest of times. He was a good mayor. He was the cause of a lot of things getting done, like the nutrition program or the senior citizens being looked at.

"I started in '58 doing volunteer work at Memorial Hospital, and I did that for eight years. In everything I did, I tried to integrate. Now when I was doing volunteer work at Memorial Hospital, there was a job coming up, and they did let you know when jobs were coming up, I knew that I could hold the job, but I knew someone else who had the training, and I'd recommend them. That was in the fifties, but they never did hire them. There were lots of things that I saw that were going on. There's progress, but there's lots needs to be done. I've seen what people are doing. I counsel people, and people come and tell me things, the ups and the downs, like people who've been on jobs for a long time and there's no advance for them. But another person comes who's being trained in sales, he's being trained to be a boss. These are the things I can't understand. It worries me. And those are the things I'm going to continue fighting for. I wrote an article in the paper back here this summer about how at this Multi-Purpose Center we had been doing without anything and going along and people come and pat you on the back and say, 'Oh, you're doing good,' making out with what I could. So we started here from scratch, but I'm wondering when we get a new building would they put somebody who had never been here, somebody haven't suffered and tried to make this thing anything, and my work in it make somebody else happy. I guess because I'm getting so old I have a one-track mind. I work with senior citizens all the time. That keeps me fighting."

The continuing fight for human rights in Chapel Hill in the eighties is quite different in many ways from the fight to end racial discrimination in the sixties. One of the few ties that bind the two decades is Gatha Lassiter. Always, she is here. The young men and women who led the first protests in 1963 and the hundreds of other students in Chapel Hill and Durham who joined them have gone on to other places. The university professors and their wives who stood with Mrs. Lassiter on the vigils have gone back to their studies; some have moved away. The Board of Aldermen, which resisted endorsing integration in Chapel Hill during the racial protests, has changed. The effect of Howard Lee's election as mayor of Chapel Hill in 1969 and 1971 was to open up the old traditional avenues of power in the community and to help shine the tarnished image of Chapel Hill as a liberal place. (Students had marched in 1964 with placards which said, "Black is not a vice, segregation is not a virtue; Chapel Hill's image is a fraud.") If the sixties were a time of protest, the seventies a time of change, then the eighties are emerging as a time of complacency. The University of North Carolina students, like university students everywhere, aren't protesting much more than their ticket chances at the new multi-million dollar sports complex. Protest has lost its place on the streets and in the headlines, and only the most committed and the most selfless are still in the fight. Gatha Lassiter is one who remains. In her seventy-second year, weakened by heart trouble, she works on. She appears, energetic, to start the day for her elderly friends at the Multi-Purpose Center. At home, her phone rings; somebody needs help or advice. There are still large numbers of people who need an advocate, and Gatha Lassiter speaks for the neediest. "My house," she concludes, "was a meeting house for the people."

# Seeing a Thing Through

Nelle Artis Coley

Greensboro

February 1, 1960, was a historic day for America and for Nelle Coley. On that day four black students sat down at a Woolworth's lunch counter in Greensboro, North Carolina, and, by their actions, initiated a means of non-violent challenge to racial injustices.

The role of students has been documented by journalists, but there is another story which has not been told. It is the story of black women—mothers, grandmothers, and teachers—who first taught their children love and pride and courage. Only a few, like Rosa Parks of Montgomery, have been widely known. Yet without the guidance which other older women provided in homes and schools, perhaps young people would not have been prepared to act. One of these women was Nelle Artis Coley, who taught English at Dudley High School in Greensboro, attended by two of the original four Woolworth protesters and by numbers of other students who later joined the marches.

"They weren't doing a thing but what we had taught them to do," she explains. "We had taught them not to accept; you know, you're going to be the victim of segregation, but don't accept it. Don't go saying this is all I can do because they have me here. You are going to soar above all kinds of limitations put on you by anybody else. There are no limitations unless you put them on yourself. So when those youngsters began the sit-ins, we just commended them. I thought it was a forthright thing to do. I remember the day, it was a Saturday, and the kids were going back and forth. By this time, there were long counters full of youngsters who were sitting there, and I know they weren't studying anything, but they had their books there. I'm pretty sure they were thinking about what was happening to them. But I was going to the hairdresser's, and I said, 'I'm not going down there because I don't want to get mixed up.' And then something told me, you'd better go down there because you are not going to see this kind of history again. And so I went on down into the main street, and I went into Woolworth, and I saw—I'll never forget it—I saw those youngsters. The blacks were sitting, and I saw the whites in those blue jeans with those Confederate flags standing up over those blacks. It was just about to explode. It wasn't too long after I got in there that they closed the door so nobody else could get in. And that closed the store that day. And then these blacks went on back to A&T's campus because that's what they wanted— to close it up or open it up. So by this time some had spilled over down to Kress's— they had two ten-cent stores on that street. After that, all during the interim, we had these mass meetings. All the community went to those mass meetings. That's when the marches began around town. My husband came to me one day and said, 'I want to show you something.' And so he took me over on Market Street. There were all these youngsters lined up. There was a youngster who is a minister in Washington now who was working at A&T, and another man who was a preacher, and they had on their clerical garb. I never will forget that. They had their cross over their shoulder, and they were in the front marching. And there wasn't a word! They were just two abreast, and there wasn't a word spoken. You could just hear the shuffle of their feet. It scared the living daylights out of the whites of Greensboro. And after that, the people in the community joined in. So I marched with them. And that very same summer following the sit-ins in February was one of the summers that I motored with a group to California; we were going out to Los Angeles to the National Education Association meeting. And the first thing we saw when we got into the suburbs of Los Angeles were some Orientals picketing the Woolworth store, and I just grew twenty feet because I knew that these youngsters had started that thing."

It was no accident of history that the sit-ins which spread across America in the sixties began in Greensboro, North Carolina. Greensboro has outstanding black leadership, centered around North Carolina A&T State University and Bennett College, which flourished under President David Jones, the first black member of the Board of Education. In addition to these institutions, the community is also influenced by the presence of the University of North Carolina at Greensboro (until the sixties known as Woman's College) and Guilford College, established and maintained by Quakers, an old and humanizing influence in the state since before the Civil War. Although the chancellor of Woman's College instructed his students to stay away from the demonstrations, a handful of women went anyway, joining the students from A&T, Bennett, and Dudley High School, which had long had a reputation for excellence comparable to that of Dunbar High School in Washington, D.C. The Greensboro School Board had been the first in the South to agree to comply with the 1954 Supreme Court ruling, although it was one of the last to satisfy federal desegregation orders completely. Considering the explosiveness of the issues and the energy and courage of young demonstrators, the mediation of the Greensboro protests was generally moderate and level-headed, but some groups impatient with delay organized dur-

ing the months after the sit-ins and made Greensboro a home for the Black Power movement. Leaders like Nelle Coley, however, disassociated themselves from the "extremists" and continued to use their influence to persuade students toward a more moderate, non-violent course.

"I remember during the fights, I didn't go," she explains. "I didn't believe in what they were doing, you see. I remember very definitely one morning it was raining cats and little fish and they had a rally, and I remember a little girl came in after it; she looked like a little mouse, she was just so wet. And she said, 'Mrs. Coley, why weren't you out there?' And I said, 'Because I don't believe in what you're doing. And I thought I had taught you better.' I didn't believe in violence. You see, the same man who is now a Communist who led that grew up at Morningside Homes, the same man came and just took over. He just went down to the gym at the end of that main building, and he had his bull-horn going, and he and his cohorts with him, and they just staged a meeting down there. Well, of course, the kids would gather round to hear what they were going to say, and this just disrupted the school. It just proliferated after that and there were scuffles and fights. And I remember there was a division; there were some faculty members in favor of what the kids were doing. I remember one girl who prevailed [upon the principal] to call the policemen off, and so they called the policemen off and as soon as they did I heard the tinkle of glass. You see the English building is the first building in that complex [Dudley High School] that you come to when you come off Lee Street. I remember that afternoon I was teaching; my classroom was on the back of the building, so they're hurling bricks at the front of the building, and I'm on the back. That came because the policemen weren't there, you see. And these kids are tearing up things, and I'm not for that because I don't think that does anything. It's just not my way of operating."

Nelle Coley believes in the rights of her people, protected not only by the law but by the insistence of each individual that his or her rights must not be violated. It is an attitude she acquired through her study of history and literature and, much earlier, from the influences of her home.

"My father had a profound influence on me," she says. "First of all, he was a little man. I don't believe my father ever weighed more than one hundred and twenty pounds. But I have a whole lot of his personality. He was scrappy. He had an excellent mind and was very much interested in everything, but particularly civic things. Around him, things always happened. The community would need things, and it was my pop that went and got them for us. He was a tough disciplinarian. One of the things he would always say was, 'Have some system to it. Organize it, whatever it is.' And that just got to me! If I cannot see it through in the planning stage mentally, then I just forget it, but I am an organizer. He insisted upon education for us. It was more his insistence than my mother's. My mother was strong, and I think our value system comes primarily from our mother. I remember a lot of little sayings from her. For instance, she would say, 'Your word is your bond.' And I wouldn't know what she was talking about, but I found out. My father had more training than my mother, and I think she became less and less comfortable with us as we progressed beyond her ability to understand what we were learning. My father

was on an equal base with everybody. But they were a very good team. The truth of the matter is, my father taught me to read because I didn't learn how to read in school. I think I was a slow starter, as I look back on it. Of course, the schools were just abominable here. We were blacks, and schools just hadn't been developed for us. There were little church schools that my father found better than public schools. I went to the Episcopal school, and then I went for a while to a Lutheran school, and then I went to the public schools. And after my father taught me to read, I just went fast. There were seven children. Everybody went to college but the first brother. Everybody was doing little jobs. I know we worked in summers. When we were in college, after the first year, I believe, some of us [from Bennett] went to New Jersey to work. We would wait tables in the little hotels along the Jersey shore. I remember particularly one night when we were down in Point Pleasant, New Jersey, and we went to a little theater to see Dreiser's *American Tragedy*. Came close to being a tragedy for us cause we didn't want to sit in the segregated seats there. There were some seats closer to the front that we wanted, and we insisted on sitting in those seats, and they came to get us, and I thought the police were going to take us, but we saw they were getting very angry, and then we just came on out and left. New Jersey's very, very prejudiced.

"For us there was a theater here in Greensboro, the Grand Theater, and shows would come. When these shows would come through, out of his mere pittance, my father would roll us up and take us to those shows, musical shows that were here. And I have a basic appreciation for music. I went to Bennett College in 1926. I finished high school there in 1927, and then I just kept right on to college. Dr. David Jones had come in '26. I don't know whether what impressed me about Bennett was what was there, as much as what Dr. Jones did with what was there. That's the impressive thing to me. And coming through Bennett you had top people, not just blacks, but you had top people. One of the persons that I remember was a Dr. Henry Hitt Crane, who was a very, very outstanding Methodist minister. As a matter of fact, he spoke when I finished college, and his speech was on the Wise and Foolish Virgins. And he was just so dramatic! And he would come back again and again, because the girls just loved him. And then, of course, there was Howard Thurman, who was a great theologian of the world, and he was very dramatic. But more than that, it was the deep philosophical things they would impart to us. Women came through there. In later years, Mrs. Roosevelt was right there, and outstanding black women like Mary McLeod Bethune were there, also, time and time again. She was as ugly a woman as you ever want to look at, but when she opened her mouth, you didn't know what she looked like. You just forgot. She was absolutely charming. The Fisk Singers would come, but we were more interested in singers like the Morehouse Men. There was a sort of bond, there is still a bond, between Morehouse and Bennett, and there still is a concert by the Morehouse Men in the fall at Bennett. I could talk forever about Dr. Jones. First of all, he was a strong father figure, too, you know. He was just that. And Mrs. Jones was a mother figure to that campus, and they knew each one of us as individuals. They couldn't just call names, they just knew us. But what I liked about him was his forth-rightness, his strong character. Of course, he had a brilliant mind, and he looked after all aspects of our being. I suppose he was a superb planner because he envisioned a whole lot of the campus as it looks now. It was a blueprint in his mind. He knew where he wanted to take us, and he seemed to know how to get there. He emphasized, for example, character education. You know, a lot of times when we come away from home, and especially when we grow, we tend to want to kick away the aspects of home that we don't like because we've outgrown it, because the people at home are likely to be cruder than we are now. Isn't he sitting there polishing us to the nth degree by exposure to all kinds of things and people on campus who are looking after our appearance and our grooming and all of the things that make for a balanced human being that can relate to the body politic regardless of where you run into it? You can relate to the whole in America. And he was going to see to it that you were going to be ready for that. And of course, that kind of growth is going to make sometimes where you came from a bit crude, but always there was no gap. He prepared the whole person, and if you are whole, you are going to be aware of what you bring from wherever you came. He was going to be certain that you didn't go kicking where you came from out and ending up being warped to that degree.

"And I remember the conversations with my father. We discussed political, national, and international issues. It was a forum, you know, and we just talked across lines, and it was very exhilarating. And I have a feeling that the breadth of my interests is a spin-off of my times with him. I always think about my father when I am doing what, to me, seems the thing to do because

I think my ability to take a stand on things stems from my being with him. And I don't care, really, if I believe a thing, it doesn't make any difference to me who's over here with me. The important thing is that I am over here because this is how I see it now. I don't say that this is how I am going to see it eternally because I think new occasions teach new duties. I think that circumstances and growth alter things so that I have a right to change my mind because it's not a fixed mind. When I first started teaching in 1932, I taught in eastern Carolina in a little place called Beaufort. It was rough down there. It was Depression and nobody had any money. Even up here in Greensboro they were using scrip to pay teachers because they didn't have the money. Because of poor working conditions and scant and irregular pay, I said, 'Well, I'll just quit down here.' But one of the things I did when I was contemplating quitting was to take my argument for quitting and mentally try that on my father and on Dr. Jones. And it wouldn't work with either one of them because they were the most influential men in my life. I couldn't square this with my father because I would be quitting, and he would tell me that he didn't teach me to quit. And I think David Jones would have said the same thing. One of his pet expressions was, 'My God, girl! I thought I taught you to stand when things were tough!' And I knew he would say that, so I didn't quit. I taught at Beaufort and I would go in summers to get my master's degree at Columbia University in New York City. I came to Dudley in the fall of 1935. I remember I had misgivings about Dudley because Dudley was such a school! My word! All over the state it was a famous high school and an excellent one. I said, 'Oh, my! Can I fit in to that place?'

But I wasn't there but two weeks when I knew that it was all right. I could do Dudley. I had confidence that I could do Dudley, and I did. I taught English; it was the reading and the literature and it was also the composition. I was always interested in the students. I was especially interested in them particularly when it was an all black school. I was interested in helping them to see life as a whole, to not accept anyone's estimate of who you are, but accept your own estimate. And your own estimate, of course, would be based on your own interests and the breadth of your own development. I could do that in a lot of different ways. I could do that in subjects posed for compositions. I could do that in oral reports that they were going to give. And especially could I do it through the literature because, of course, literature deals with humanity. Shakespeare says that character is fate. And what you are is going to determine largely what your choices are. That is what's running through all his plays. In other words, Macbeth didn't have to have somebody sit in judgment on him. The fatal flaw was in the man.

"As we would discover any kind of deficit in a child, he would become focal for our removing that deficit. In other words, suppose he got slack in his interest; we'd do all kinds of things to get him back because you can't do anything with a mind if he's not willing to lend it to you. I remember this open classroom bit. I went into the schools in Winston-Salem with an evaluation team, and I saw some open classrooms there. And you see kids selecting what they're interested in. There's a kind of thing about knowing what you're interested in. It's possible that you don't know what you're interested in. And if you find a little black kid over there lying on his belly looking at a funnybook, but you can't say his interest is funnybooks. You could get him off his belly and get him over there to learn some of the things that other exposures would teach him, except you don't care whether he learns or not. And you will have him with his little head folded down out there in the hall, learning nothing. Because you put him out there, he might have become, perhaps, a little belligerent inside because he wasn't being challenged at all. Now I think that our children are suffering. In other words, the prejudice of people hasn't eased a bit. It just takes another form. So when you have these black children put into these classrooms, what are these white teachers doing? Many of them are venting their displeasure with having them there by ignoring them. Now how can you learn if someone's ignoring you? I was better trained than most of the whites that were teaching with me because I had to be. The black teachers were excellent teachers because they didn't have a variety of vocational choices; hence, they concentrated on being good teachers.

"Even though our youngsters were better off with us than they are now, I think their predicament now is part of the price they must pay for being in the mix. In other words, I think it had to get worse before it can get better. I don't know that it will be better than when it was all black. It will at least be equal to what it was; perhaps, it will get better. I think the biggest problem is the problem that always was. It's a change of heart on the part of people, and as long as they don't change their thinking, change their way of looking at things, we aren't going to have any difference. Somewhere, short of eternity, we ought to learn to live with each other."

# As Long as You Give Us the Equal

## Eliza Miles Dudley

New Bern

## Mary Terry Eldridge

Fayetteville

Eliza Miles Dudley was born in 1912 in Selma, North Carolina, the fifth of six children. Her father, who worked for the railroad, died when she was three. She and her brothers and sisters were raised by their mother, who believed in education and saw to it that all the children completed high school. Eliza graduated from Fayetteville State Teachers College, received her master's degree from Hampton Institute, and completed twenty-eight hours of credit toward her Ph.D. at the University of Michigan. (She warns her friends that if they discover she is gone one day, she has returned to school.) As a young woman, she wanted to be a missionary; instead she became a teacher. Her first job was near home, in New Bern, and she taught there for the next thirty years until her retirement in 1977. Her experiences during the initial years of school desegregation have led her to admit, "I didn't like integration. Do you want to know the truth of it? I didn't see any advantages for black children."

Mary Terry Eldridge was born in 1911 in Pittsburgh, Pennsylvania. Her mother and father had come from Danville, Virginia, so that Mr. Terry might find work as a pullman porter. They devoted themselves to the care and education of Mary, their only child. After graduating from high school in Pittsburgh, she went on to study music at Oberlin College, an institution recognized for its policy of admitting women and blacks when most others would not. Later she received a master's degree from Carnegie-Mellon. Her dream was to become an opera singer. Instead, she began a career teaching music, a year at Tuskegee Institute, then thirty years at Fayetteville State Teachers College. Today she is chair-

man of the Board of Education of the Fayetteville City Schools. In reflecting back over the years, Mrs. Eldridge concludes, "I love the segregation. I still am for segregation as long as you give me the equal. I think blacks are suffering in integrated schools; the minorities always suffer in integration."

Mrs. Dudley and Mrs. Eldridge each taught for thirty years in public education (Mrs. Dudley in public elementary schools, Mrs. Eldridge in a state-supported college); each was a candidate for a seat on the school board and ran for public office at the urging of former students and parents of former students (Mrs. Eldridge was elected, Mrs. Dudley was defeated); and each is very outspoken and articulate in her attitudes toward education. If their first reaction to school desegregation was a concern for the black child, subsequent experiences in observing racially mixed classes have given them a concern also for the white child. Although each has passed her seventieth birthday and could enjoy retirement in comfort and leisure, each remains active in her community, bringing together races, social classes, and generations in which deep divisions can surface at any provocation. Each still retains her sense of growing up black in America.

Mary Terry Eldridge had a very favored childhood. As an only child, her father bringing wages and sophistication from his railroad travels to Buffalo, New York, and Detroit, she was the center of a comfortable home in which she had many opportunities. The Terrys and one other black family lived in a residential neighborhood with white families. Mary played with their children from her earliest years, and only when they started school and the white parents told their daughters they could not invite Mary to their birthday parties did she begin to feel any exclusion from society. Then, she ran home to her mother, who explained to Mary that she must accept her friends' feelings without animosity and without bitterness. "When I went to school, they would call me 'nigger,' and I would come home and be heartbroken," she remembers. "And my mother would say, 'Let me tell you this: you are not a nigger. A nigger is a person who has a very black heart. If they say to you, 'You, Mary Terry, you are a nigger,' then you can fight or you can call them a name, but other than that, if they just call the name, you just go on and don't pay any attention to them.' I had friends that would throw their books down and fight. But I never paid any attention so it never bothered me. My mother would always tell me this—and this was interesting—'You know, the South is the best place for the blacks.' She never liked the North because she said the North was superficial. They pretended that they had integration, but they really didn't. She said the North would call you Mrs. Terry or Mrs. Eldridge, and the South would call you Mary or Lizzie, but they give you a better break. And she said, 'That's what I want.' It is true. And when you read about school integration, look at Boston. You wouldn't ever think that would happen there. It exists everywhere. Even though I was in Pittsburgh at the time, we couldn't go to restaurants and eat. We had integration in the schools but they didn't have black teachers. So it wasn't really a true integration."

A high school teacher, recognizing the talent of Mary Terry, one of her best stu-dents, first suggested to her that she try to attend Oberlin College, and with scholarship help she enrolled. While she and the half-dozen other black students at Oberlin, including the daughter of Dr. R. R. Moton, president of Tuskegee Institute, shared the old and liberal tradition of study in the humanities with some of the brightest and most privileged of the daughters of white society, they were not always protected from contrary attitudes. "I've had the house directress say," she explains, "'Now, why in the world do you want a single room?' And I'd say 'Because I'm accustomed to living by myself, and I think I would like it.' And she'd say, 'Well, I don't think you should have a single.' And so at that time I expressed myself a lot; I said, 'Well, my father's dollar is just as good as anybody else's dollar.' And by the time I got through she'd say, 'I want you to have a single!' Even at Oberlin, a very lovely girl from Georgia came to our table, and I was sitting there, and she just got up and walked away. She said, 'You know, whites and blacks just don't eat together.' I've had girls to tell me, 'It's been a pleasure knowing you because I had the idea that blacks would stab you, they carried knives.'" Mary experienced the same kind of exclusion from private parties which she had felt as a child in Pittsburgh, but at Oberlin she had music to occupy her mind, and she began to dream of becoming a singer like Marian Anderson.

The necessity of getting her first job, however, began to turn her dream away from becoming a star and toward a more secure future as a teacher, and after one year teaching music education at Tuskegee Institute, she accepted a position at Fayetteville State. Mary arrived for the job interview with her mother, and the courtly southern manners of the president so affected Mrs. Terry's desire to return to the South after the death of her husband that she persuaded her daughter to accept his offer. They made their home together in Fayetteville, and after Mary's marriage in 1959, Mrs. Terry continued living with Mary and her husband until her death at age eighty-six. At Fayetteville State, founded in 1867 for black students, Mary Eldridge taught voice and music education, directed the choirs, and became chairman of the music department. After her retirement in 1974, she became a candidate for the Board of Education; now in her second term, she is the first black woman to serve as chairperson.

Fayetteville—an old community with the slave market still at the center, preserved as a historic site—is one of the major cities in the eastern part of North Carolina, larger than its official population of 65,000 because of its proximity to Fort Bragg. Fort Bragg children are bused into Fayetteville City Schools after the eighth grade, and the system receives from federal impact aid about half the cost of running its schools. Threats to cut off this aid and to build schools on post are a serious challenge to the support for Fayetteville City Schools, already depleted in numbers by the exodus of families to the suburbs and the county schools. During Mrs. Eldridge's terms on the Board enrollment in city schools has dropped from 11,000 to 9,000 children, whereas the county schools serve 26,000. The city schools have a black majority of about 57 percent. School officials boast that they have the best school system in the state, a reputation Mrs. Eldridge backs up with statistics: 47 percent of the graduates

go on to senior colleges and universities. Only 1.8 percent of the seniors failed the state competency test; all of these students had been previously identified as handicapped. Fayetteville City School students score above the state average, and in some cases above the national average, on standardized tests. And Mrs. Eldridge is proud also of the ethnic mix of students in the schools, including a large number of Hispanics and Asians who come from the army post. She is proud that the school system is resourceful enough to provide courses for non-English speaking students and offers this fact as evidence of concern for children of all cultures.

As the conversation turns to the topic of racial desegregation, Mrs. Eldridge, who is soft-spoken and elegant and politely wary of controversy, admits, "I've gotten into something that I hadn't planned to talk about." Despite the presence of a tape recorder, however, and in subsequent conversations, she seems to welcome a chance to speak of her personal preference for segregation, perhaps a chance which public office does not often afford her. "Now I know the correct thing is integration, the moral thing. But I believe in segregation for the betterment of the young blacks. I feel that black children have to have something to impress them. When I lived in the North, very few black students went to college. In the South, a larger percentage went on to college. Why? Because they were encouraged. The North had problems. I remember when I left Oberlin I had a black friend who was going into music education, and a teacher told her, 'Why are you going into music education? You know you can't do any student teaching here.' Our black leaders in the North came from the South. My mother pointed that out. They came from black institutions. They [these institutions] took bright students from the northern ghetto and from the South who had the nerve and drive to be successful. I'm quite concerned about nowadays. In black schools with black leaders, they [black children] have something to look up to. They don't have it when you have integration. Yes, I think blacks are suffering in integrated schools because there are people that you like and you can't help it and there are people that you don't. Students that you like and students that you don't. I've had teachers say, 'I don't care how good you do, you can't get more than a D out of me.' And that's just because you're black. Any of them will tell you. So yes, I feel that black southern children were getting along better before desegregation. Now we didn't have the facilities. Right here in the city of Fayetteville, Terry Sanford High School [the formerly all white high school] had better equipment, better facilities than E. E. Smith did [the formerly all black high school]. And if white parents have to send their children to a school which originally was black, they want their children to have the very best, and they're going to see that they have it, and that's what happened. E. E. Smith was renovated, enlarged, and got things they didn't have before. When we didn't have the facilities, that's where our innovation came from. Blacks were doing some of the things that people are making a lot of now. They just didn't have it and they made do. The teachers really created things themselves.

"And I think black children are hurt emotionally in an integrated school. Just imagine yourself in a class of entire blacks. See, the thing about it with you all [whites],

you have never experienced that and that's something. Even if nobody has said anything to you, if you go into a place where there is predominantly another group, there is a feeling there until they get to know you and you get to know them and you prove yourself. It's a thing that you're *proving* all the time. And this is the thing I hate to see with the young blacks now. They say, 'Why do I always have to be proving myself?' Right now, if you are in an integrated situation—and this is the way most of the older blacks have felt—you think, I have got to do so much better than someone else. And this is what I am trying to get my son to see while he's going to an integrated school: 'You're going to have to do better than the guy over there.' He was growing up when they had this revolution, and I think he's a little black oriented, too much so, but I tell him you're going to have to work when you get out in the world so you might as well learn to live with people that you have to. People are changing, progress is being made, and eventually integration probably will be better, but this is the way I see it from my experience and background." Mrs. Eldridge pauses, then says, "I haven't expressed myself this way in a *long* time."

During her childhood, Eliza Miles Dudley worried less about being invited to parties and more about how her widowed mother would support six children. When Mr. Miles died in 1915, neighbors urged her mother to "give the children up," but Joanna Miles kept her family together: "No. If I have one biscuit I will divide that one biscuit with all six of them." Excused from school during cotton season, Eliza and her brothers and sisters joined other children, both black and white, to pick the crop, their wages to be used for buying their school clothes. Mrs. Miles worked for a family which owned the hotel across from the railroad station, "friends that we came up with," as Mrs. Dudley remembers them. The Miles children and the children of the hotel owner knew one another on a friendly basis, and Mrs. Miles was encouraged to come home whenever necessary to check on her children. Mrs. Dudley continued to visit the family long after the hotel was sold, the railroad passenger business a ghost of the whistle-stop past, and now they are all gone, including her own brothers and sisters, and Selma is a memory. Next in importance to her family was the church, and early on Eliza sang in the choir and traveled to church meetings. She was diverted from her dream of studying at Shaw University to become a missionary when she followed the crowd to Fayetteville State, and there she was trained to be an elementary school teacher. After graduation, without a job, she went with a friend to work in a white home in Boston, but when she got a telegram offering her a first grade job in New Bern, she told her employer, "Washing dishes ain't my thing," and got on the train for home. Now she had her first opportunity to put to practical good her mother's belief in education.

Beginning in the first grade at the old West Street School in New Bern, she found herself completely at home among young children. New Bern is a pretty town, and by the mid-thirties families were beginning to feel a little relief from hard times, enough so that mothers could think more readily of what their children were learning in school and less obsessively about the next meal. Still, Eliza Miles fulfilled her

earlier hope of doing missionary work by taking an interest in the children's home life; she knew more than their performance in reading and numbers; she knew their families and the back streets where they lived. As New Bern flourished and Tryon Palace, the site of the 1770 home of a royal governor and the first capital of North Carolina, was restored in the fifties, signs of elegance and prosperity directed local community pride toward the show they could put on for visitors. Although Mrs. Dudley took her school children to be led by hostesses in bonnets and wide skirts through the splendors of a royal palace, she well understood that the children's lives were almost as foreign to the life depicted at Tryon as the life of eighteenth-century yeomen was foreign to the life of the royal governor. Perhaps it was the disparity she saw between lives which renewed in her in the sixties a determination to want more for her own people. And the fact that court-ordered school desegregation resulted in what she feels were disadvantages for black children is an ironic twist to history.

A common practice in many southern school systems facing school desegregation was to move the best black teachers to formerly all white schools. Eliza Dudley was required to leave the old West Street School, which she knew as well as she knew her own home, and to move to Central. "Of course, no," she insists, "I didn't want to go." The ensuing weeks and months were difficult. She remembers, "We had a whole lot of confusion by some whites who weren't even intelligent people. They came on the campus during recess and declared that this black boy did this to this little white girl. There was just a lot of ignorance. I didn't want to go to Central because I didn't like integration in the first place. I thought we were getting along all right where we were. Up to this point, we were working and educating our children. They were going to colleges and doing well. A number of them had launched [themselves] and were going to white colleges, and they weren't failures when they got there. If black children had a black teacher, all well and good. But truthfully, white teachers don't understand black boys and girls. They don't know how to cope with them. Now don't you know if I went over here in Duffyfield, and Duffyfield is predominantly black, that I could get along better over there with those people than you could? You see what I'm saying? But when they got those boys and girls, not knowing the background from whence they came, they didn't know where to launch; they didn't know where to latch on. If a child acted as if he were mean and ugly, it was because he was mad in the first place. You see what I'm saying? It was just one of those things where, well, black boys and girls didn't do as well; they aren't doing as well as they could do now. And I'll tell you this, and I tell this to any white teachers—I don't have to bite my tongue—I said it to them when I was over there working with them, if you take a black child who's smart, he can get along with a white teacher, because she'll work with him. If you take a black child who's slow and that teacher doesn't know the background, she doesn't know how to help him. She just hasn't had the experience. On many occasions, when black children could get free lunches, they had to fill out a blank, and the parents would have to sign it. You had to get this blank signed, and many blanks I've had to take way back over in this area.

I don't go over there myself. I'd go [and here she knocks on wood], 'Who is it?' I said. 'Is Mrs. So-and-so in?' 'No! What you want?' I said, 'Well, is so-and-so in?' that was the child. 'Yes, he's here. What you want?' I said, 'Well, I'm his teacher and I want to see his mother!' And that's the only time they'd open the door. They'd say, 'Excuse me for hollering at you but I didn't know who you were.' The white teachers didn't know where to go, they didn't know how to cope with the situation, and I don't blame them for not going.

"Yes, I felt that I, as a black teacher, could relate to white children. Whites have never had to deal with blacks. They lived over there on A Street, and they never lived with these kids. I told a teacher one morning who said, 'So and so comes to school late and doesn't get his work and doesn't do so-and-so,' and about that time my cup had run over. So I said, 'Look, if you had to leave home in the morning without your breakfast, when your mother had gone to a white lady's house to get her children up and wrap up the baby and take it over to a neighbor's house to put the clothes on and feed him if she could until she got back, and the others were left at home to get ready to come to school,' I said, 'How do you think that child felt when he got there that morning? He hadn't had any love from his parents, he hadn't had any food from his parents—if he ate anything it was something cold. She's gone over here to fix the white child's breakfast, and he's had a hot one. And the lady has got somebody in there to do her dishes. You know, when it's all summed up, we're human.'

"Blacks have had it pretty hard. I've seen that in school situations. It's getting different because I think white teachers are trying to understand. I think they are. And what I really think is people who are coming in to really deal with children in a classroom all day long have realized what it takes. It's something you've got to love before you can make it. Only thing you got to do is sit and talk with children, and they'll tell you what the story is. Find one that comes in in tears in the morning, and take time when you can find him by himself. Those children when they leave their parents need somebody they can lean on."

Eliza Dudley still goes to a public school to read to children as a volunteer and serves on the boards of numerous civic groups, including the New Bern Historic Preservation Committee. Although she is widely regarded by whites as a leader, she is realistic about the role of a minority representative. During the run-off for a seat on the school board she was opposed by four white candidates, and lost. "So one black didn't have a ghost of a chance," she concluded.

Perhaps it is the long tradition of white dominance which gives teachers like Mary Eldridge and Eliza Dudley their deepest misgivings about desegregated schools. They realize that courts and laws alone will not right the wrong. What is needed is what Nelle Coley has called a change of heart. Mrs. Eldridge and Mrs. Dudley are both skeptical enough not to count on it and hopeful enough to welcome it when, and if, it comes.

# A Woman on Wall Street

## Viola Mitchell Turner

### Durham

A white woman on Wall Street thirty or forty years ago was probably on her way to a secretarial job. And a black woman on Wall Street was likely to be cleaning offices. But when Viola Turner, female and black, from Durham, North Carolina, arrived in the offices of the New York Stock Exchange and the Securities Exchange Commission, she wasn't there to take dictation, and she wasn't there to clean. Mrs. Turner, who started in 1920 with the North Carolina Mutual Life Insurance Company in its Jackson, Mississippi, office, and moved to the Durham home office in 1924, represented the largest black financial institution in the world, and her knowledge of investments for the Mutual made her one of the best known women on Wall Street. When she retired from the Mutual in 1965, she was financial vice-president and a member of the board of directors, the first woman elected to so high a position in the company. For a black girl born at the turn of the century in Macon, Georgia, Viola Turner has an American success story singularly meaningful to southern women and to black women.

Mrs. Turner's association with the North Carolina Mutual dates back to her childhood in Macon when her parents had as a guest in their home Ed Merrick, the son of the company's founder (and later to be Mrs. Turner's boss in the Durham office). Visiting Macon on Mutual business, Mr. Merrick had been directed to the Mitchell home and had engaged their spare bedroom. During his visit, Viola took her young friends to the room to admire his rows of handsome suits and shoes, her earliest impression of the Mutual's success.

Viola Turner begins her narrative with remembrances of her childhood. "My mother was sent to Macon from a very small place, Clinton, Georgia, to go to school, to live with an older sister. My father had come up from Fort Plains, Georgia, a young boy, really. And somewhere along the way, they met. He was not in school. At the age of fifteen they were married. At the age of sixteen I was born. Wasn't that something? My grandmother must have been thoroughly disgusted at the whole thing. But, at any rate, they were really two children, so to speak, with a daughter. My father was, I suppose, a cotton sampler then. I don't know. But the two things that I knew about him and making a living was that he was a cotton sampler from the early fall to the late spring. Then he was a hotel man, a waiter, from the spring through the summer. My mother was a very smart little lady. She was aggressive, ambitious, determined, and probably because she had a child so early, she came to realize how unfortunate it was not to have continued in school. Because I think she was about the sixth grade when she married my father. But that's all I heard all of my life, 'You've got to go to school. Stay in school. Be a school teacher.' My father was a sweet, loving man. Nobody had a dearer father than I had. He gave me lots of attention, both of them did. I had a lovely childhood: poor—I didn't know it, however—but very lovely. But my father, I'm quite sure, he didn't see the point in all that education my mother was talking about. It was okay. If she wanted me to go to school, it was okay. She was determined that I was going to have things that she wanted me to have. Maybe things that she'd wanted, I don't know. She sewed beautifully. She kept me very well dressed. She took a great deal of pride in that. She only sewed at home. She tried to stay home as much as she could. But when she decided that there was something that she wanted—and when I look back on it, everything she really wanted was something that was for my benefit— she worked out. I think she would have done anything. I remember two jobs out of the home. One was with a doctor, a white doctor. I know now that my mother probably went to work there as a maid. And she worked with him to the point where I feel quite sure she was assisting him in his operations in that office. The other job my mother had out of the home—the doctor had a patient, a baby, and when that child went home, my mother went with that family to take care of this boy. Mother always saw me off to school. And Mother always saw me back home, one way or the other. Then she would work at intervals. For instance, she wanted a piano because she wanted me to take music lessons. My father saw no point in a piano. Now, of course, I can understand. My father was making ten dollars a week. But my mother was determined that I was going to have a piano. So whenever she was determined to have something, she got a job. And then I got the piano, and I took music lessons. My mother was not a well person, she was not a strong woman, and my mother died at thirty-two. I was born when she was sixteen and she died when I was sixteen.

"I lived all my life on Tatenall. Up on the corner of Tatenall and Chestnut, whites lived. Across the street my school teacher, her family, they lived on this corner, and that corner, opposite them, whites. There were white families and white children here, black families and black children. Now, all of the children met out here and they played up and down that street, all but me. Most of the children were boys, and my mother said that little girls shouldn't play with little boys, so I didn't get to go out there and play. But now, most whites there, would just as likely be over talking to my mother, or my mother would be over there talking to them. I don't mean that they went in and sat down to visit, either way. But they'd sit on the porch and meet out in the middle of the street and have conversation. I didn't ever think about them as white people, or black people.

"I never went to public school. All Macon had for blacks was from the first grade to the sixth grade in public schools. No more. They didn't get a high school until I left Macon. I went to the American Missionary Association School, connected with the Congregational Church. They set up schools all over the South, and they were schools that originally started with the first grade and went through twelfth. They were called normal schools. And you had black teachers from the first grade through the eighth. And from the ninth through the twelfth, you had white teachers from the North. They were usually Yankees. Our principal was a German, Von Tobel. And your tuition was a dollar a month. Of course, you had to have that at least to be able to make it. So my mother worked, because I was going to the end.

"I go back to my parents. They were very smart people. We had picnics all the time. As a matter of fact, I guess I had more parties than anybody in the whole world. Because all you had to do was get up in the morning and say, 'Let's have a party.' And my mother would say, 'Okay.' And maybe she'd bake some cookies. Now if there was anybody around to invite, I could invite them over for the cookies. If not, we had the party, my mother and my father and myself. And, of course, they were my brothers and sisters and another day, they may be my cousins. And I would get up in the morning and announce, 'Cousin Fanny, what are we going to do?' And they indulged that. They would be cousins all day. Cousin Philip. And they went along with those fantasies. But the picnics; my mother would fix a basket and we would go down to the city park. Any Sunday that they took a notion, or it was a beautiful day. And we just had a wonderful time.

"My father took me to the opera house. I saw *Ben Hur* there when I was a kid. They had the chariot race with the white horses and the black horses, they were on stage just racing away for all they were worth. I couldn't imagine how that was happening. But I know now there was some stationary thing down there making the motion. But they had the white horses and the black horses. I saw an outstanding minstrel show. I remember the Interlocutor coming down and asking Mr. Bones something, and Mr. So-and-So something. They'd come up and dance and sing. That was at the opera house. I saw Black Patti, [a] great singer, there. The city auditorium was where all the school performances were. And when I was growing up, they would have a combination of schools together for your performance. For instance, the *Mikado* we did. I was among the kids that were in that. One of the things I remember so much, they had a prima donna—I don't know who she was. I believe that lady may have been local. At any rate, she really had the opera voice. And the only thing I remember about that was that she'd stand up and she'd say, 'So-o-o ha-a-appy.' And all

of us would say, 'So-o- ha-a-appy.' How funny it was that the teachers wouldn't stop us. But the lady would come with this 'ha-appy' and we'd come right down with 'So-o ha-appy.' We did all sorts of things at the auditorium.

"Incidentally, I went to Georgia in '65, and the Mutual people who were sending me to this meeting said, 'Do you want to stay at the Holiday Inn, which is brand new, or the old hotel?' I said I wanted to go to the Dempsey. Nobody could understand why the Dempsey. So I go to the Dempsey, and I saw that hotel being built, as a child. It was our skyscraper. And then my father worked in there, when he hoteled in the summer. So then I announced to the folks after I got in to the hotel, I said, 'When I was a kid and I had wanted to see my father on life or death business, I would have had to come down Cherry Street, go around on this side, go through there, and go to the back door, and ask, 'Please, could I speak to Philip Richard. Would you mind telling Philip Richard that his wife is dying?' Or something like that. They said, 'Are you kidding?' And I said, 'No, I'm not kidding.' That's what I would have had to do. You know, I had to come and walk through the front door of the Dempsey Hotel and be served. It really was a thrill, just to know that I was not going to be hampered in any way. Because they were perfectly lovely. As a matter of fact, the hotel was filled with little Boy Scouts, and there were as many little black boys as there were white boys, all up and down the place. This was something to behold. Dear old Macon."

After graduating from the AMA school, Viola enrolled in the business department of Morris Brown College in Atlanta,

Georgia. She was especially impressed by several of the women who taught there, and in the summer when she helped one of her instructors teach single-entry book-keeping, she knew that she had found what she enjoyed. Her training at Morris Brown and the earlier security of her home were the preparation she needed to enter the world of business, and if she needed a model for her life of determination and ambition, she could remember her mother, and perhaps unconsciously, she could fulfill her mother's hopes. After completing her work at Morris Brown, she was employed as a secretary at Tuskegee Institute. Among her memories of the year were her encounters on the streets of the campus with George Washington Carver, who stopped to show her a weed or a flower. From Alabama she went west to Mississippi, where she worked in the State Office of Negro Education and was soon hired by a Mutual officer to work for that company. She helped install a system of records in the Mutual's branch offices in Oklahoma, Mississippi, and Arkansas. Soon she was assigned to the Durham office where she was secretary to the vice-president. As she became more familiar with the company and her successes became more widely known, she received a series of promotions, beginning as assistant to the treasurer, Ed Merrick, then after his retirement treasurer and vice-president. She gives generous credit to Mr. Merrick for her promotions. He seemed never to have felt threatened by the success of his assistant and, in fact, praised her so often in board meetings that it was no surprise he had her in mind as his successor. Her greatest contribution to the growth of the company was in handling investments. From a meager assortment of

bonds and mortgages, she developed a portfolio of stocks and securities which was respected by Wall Street brokers.

"I was just a little stray that came along," she laughs. "I always felt I could improve, and I was always trying to improve. And I think that's an attitude you've got to have. I never had any thought of promotion until well after it started happening. I liked my job, and I enjoyed the things I learned about. Any woman has to work twice as hard as any man to make it in the business world. There's no question about that. You take students in business school. The girl goes in and the first blooming thing she picks up is a notebook and a pencil and starts learning shorthand. Shorthand and then the typewriter. The guy learns about the typewriter, but he goes straight over to business administration. So he's starting off geared for top management. She's geared for somebody's secretary. Now, if you get into a situation where there's something else offered to you, and you find it interesting, you can believe me, you'd better work hard and you've got to learn a whole lot of things about that job. Because if you just learn a part of it, and a young man comes along and he wants it, he doesn't have to be as good as you are; he can be just about half as good as you are. And the very fact that he's male, he's going to get the first consideration. But I timed it perfect. The company didn't know anything about investment itself. When I got there, we had mortgages. We had government bonds. Every time the government had put out bonds, from the first year of war, we bought them. Well, of course, it was a beautiful thing we did. Not only for the government, but they were good bonds for us. At least it was something we could be safe and secure in. But, now, we began to grow. We didn't have sense to know that we needed to know something, and the next best thing for us is to get somebody who knows something to help us, so we immediately made a contact with this investment service. And they asked us to send a list of everything that we had.

After they had gone over everything, we sat down and talked. That's how we got the start. I sat down and wrote a letter [to the adviser], over Mr. Merrick's signature, and told him the facts of life. I told him what we didn't know. And then I asked would he be kind enough to recommend some reading for us. We got us a little library. I was doing most of the reading; I was having a good time. And of course, Mr. Merrick was encouraging me, 'That's fine, honey. You just go right up.' The company was in a learning process. I recall the first letters that we received from [the investments adviser] when they were making recommendations to us for purchasing. And they had something like twenty thousand of this, twenty thousand of this, twenty thousand of this. Maybe altogether—and this may not be exactly accurate, but it gives you an idea—they were recommending a purchase of a hundred thousand dollars of securities. We had a committee meeting. And of course I sat in on all the meetings simply because I was secretary at that time. I was not a member of the committee. I read off these things to them. Oh, you never saw such frowning. We couldn't put that much money out, you know, like that. So it was cut back to ten of this and ten of that. But there came a time when we didn't think of making a purchase of any block of bonds of less than a hundred thousand, you know. But boy, that twenty thou-

sand scared us to death. Any rate, we'd begun to have a portfolio that you could look at. And then, [brokers] made that discovery, a black woman that can talk their language. At least she knows what they're talking about, and in talking to them she uses the same terminology, well, boy, that's more than they can believe. So they fly back to New York and start getting the word around. And it was no time at all before I did nothing but talk on the telephone all day long. Mrs. Turner this, Mrs. Turner that. After I got to the place where I knew the Street pretty well, and there were some people that we became really good friends, and we [would] talk and talk about anything, oh, I found out that they were just as gossipy as they could be. No small town in the South can be more gossipy than Wall Street. This is many years later and we've started having classes in the office, and I decided to take some of the classes. Every little bit that I could learn, that I didn't know, was good for me. So I go downstairs to one of the classes one morning, and I came back and I'm sure I'd had a dozen calls by the time I got there. So I start returning the calls and every blooming person asks, 'Well! Are you out of that class at last?' I had been downstairs in a class and the only way they could know that, one had told the other. I said, 'You're all as gossipy as you can be.' And of course, the other thing that's beautiful about them is this: I could pick up my phone any day in the week and any hour in the day. And if I had any sort of question I wanted to ask, I could call and say, 'Look, what about so-and-so? What do you think? My opinion is that I should do so-and-so. What do you think?' They'd call me back in thirty minutes. They sent it all down to their research department, and when they called me back, I'd have the expertise of everybody in that area to tell me this is the way they see it.

"I could be wrong, but I don't think too many men would call in and ask for something and say, 'Look, I'm stumped. I don't know what the heck to do with this. What do you think?' I don't think most men are going to try to call you up. Even if they want the information, they're not going to ask for it. They're going to talk all around and sound intelligent, and think that maybe in the course of the conversation, they'll get the answer. That didn't make any sense to me either, and still doesn't. If I don't know, I don't know. This may be an unkind observation, but it's one I had then, and I don't think I've changed it at all: our men are not too happy about our being too intelligent. A pretty natural thing. You can be smart as long as you're not obviously smart. You know what I mean? Most of the men I've come in contact with might think, 'Yeah, she's smart.' But they never thought I was smarter than they were. Sometimes they were underestimating me and sometimes they weren't. Because sometimes I was a whole lot smarter than they were. But I was also smart enough not to have acted like I was smarter. There are a lot of obnoxious women, who really aren't as smart as they think they are. And I think men do not like to be the lesser of the two. But really, to tell the truth, I think I had more potential resentment coming from the girls. Girls don't like to work with women. Did you know that? Women sometimes were against women instead of being darn glad to see one woman making it so that meant they might get a chance at it."

As a woman, Mrs. Turner often was able to have her own way in social circumstances which might have been embarrassing for men. Her way had to do with requiring any visitors to the Mutual office to address men and women by their titles. "There wasn't very much difference in the types of the white men who came for many years," Mrs. Turner explains. "They would come in, with a hat on, of course, and they would walk into your office exactly like they were still out in the open spaces. If they didn't really know their way around, they'd stop and say, 'Is Ed in?' or 'Is John in?' or 'Is C. C. in?' Some, 'Is Charlie in?' Well, we had a standard act.

'Good morning, may I help you?'

'Yes, is Ed in?'

'Ed? Um, I don't know an Ed. Ed, did you say?'

'Merrick, Ed Merrick.'

'Oh, Mr. Merrick, you mean, Well, let me see. Have a seat out here. I'll see for you.

"So I'd walk in and I'd come back out. 'Mr. Merrick is in, but he's very busy just now and he will not be able to see you for the next thirty minutes. Shall I tell Mr. Merrick that you will wait?' Some way or other I'd have to get in three or four Mr. Merricks. Well, sometimes they would say they would come back. So, on departing, always you ended, 'Well, you say you will be back? I'll tell Mr. Merrick you'll be back.' Oh, we carried it to the nth degree, all depending on how much we knew it was deliberate. But some of the devils we knew reinforced themselves when they got downstairs on how they were going to handle it. And so when they got there, they were in their belligerent mood. Now they got 'Mr. Merrick' until they were ready to drop.

They would have loved to have done something to you. One, in particular, used to come, and he would try to figure out another way to do it. One morning, he came in, and of course it was the worst choice he ever made in his life. He walked in and he says, 'Is the preacher in?' Now don't you know we could work with that all day long! 'What preacher? Where a preacher?' We used that; we wore him out. 'Preacher? Preacher? Do you know any preacher? Preacher, no! Who's the preacher? Are you sure?' He held out as long as he could. He turned red. He sat out on the deck and wouldn't say anything. And we let him sit there. We didn't ask questions. And way late he came back to the door and stuck his head through and laughed. I guess really what he was thinking, maybe Mr. Merrick would come in, because very often they would try to stand and catch the person. If they did, they'd jump right up and walk right on with them. So finally this man had to come and ask for 'Merrick.' 'Oh? Did you mean Mr. Merrick at first?' And he didn't really return an answer, just looked. 'Well, Mr. Merrick isn't any preacher. Mr. Merrick has never been a preacher! Ha! Ha!' So we laughed the poor man right on up and down the street because Mr. Merrick wasn't there. He didn't see Mr. Merrick. And he was a long time coming back."

Once when a white woman, from a well-to-do family down on its luck, came to the Mutual on business and was required to call the secretaries by "Miss" or "Mrs.," she left in anger. She dissolved in tears in the lobby downstairs, and seeing Mr. Merrick pass by, told him she had been insulted and threatened to go and tell her uncle, a member of the Ku Klux Klan. The threat, however, provoked Mrs. Turner to nothing more than a good laugh, and it is laughter, along with her intelligence, which has carried her through difficult situations.

Her free spirit obviously brought more than a touch of grace and humor to the Mutual offices and it was rarely checked. When C. C. Spaulding was president, from 1923 until 1952, he was affectionately known as "Papa," a disciplinarian and an authoritative father figure who didn't want his Mutual girls to dance or drink or smoke and who saw they had a place at the Mutual's Clerk's Home which was properly supervised. Although he once suggested that Mrs. Turner's red dress was inappropriate for the Mutual's offices, she rarely felt disciplined (though she did not wear the red dress again).

Viola Turner is a woman of singular achievement. Pay her this compliment and she ducks her head, she winks, she claps her hands in surprise. One can see in her demeanor the lively energies of an independent woman.

Acknowledgment is made to the Southern Oral History Program of the University of North Carolina at Chapel Hill for permission to quote from an interview with Dr. Walter Weare and Mrs. Turner.

# Mademoiselle

## Ernestine Burghes Saunders

### Raleigh

*Miss Burghes felt secure walking beside her father, Reverend John R. Burghes. He was tall, he was very erect, and his strides were manly and measured like the discipline of his Germanic heritage. He acknowledged the passing of friends on the streets of Selma, Alabama, with a nod of his head, and he continued to lead her toward the jeweler's on Main Street, where she could purchase a watch. A college graduate and a new teacher, she had reason to feel confident, but still, it was reassuring to walk beside him. She was his heart, his only child, and she would never grow too old not to feel his protective authority. Once inside the store, she hesitated, a shy young black woman in the world of a white merchant and in the glitter of his gold and silver pieces locked in the cases.*

*Watches were brought out, and her father did the talking; he was known by the owner, who called him "Rev," and who now moved with a peremptory glance at the two customers. Reverend John Burghes explained that his daughter would like to buy the watch on credit and would make the payments herself. The owner fingered the watches and looked at her for several moments, as if he himself were selecting what he would have. Yes, he would sell her a watch on those terms, and as she decided on the one she wanted, he took out his book to write out the sale.*

*"Your name," he said, not looking up, his pencil waiting. "E. A. Burghes," she replied, in a low voice. "No," he said, "I have to have your name." She replied once more, a little louder, "E. A. Burghes." He put down his pencil, pushed back the book, and looked at her father. John Burghes looked directly at the white man and said nothing. The jeweler cleared his throat, leaned his arms on the counter to move closer to the young woman, and said, "Those are your initials. I want your name."*

*There was a long silence, in which the presence of the tall, dignified man and the small, shy daughter suddenly seemed as imperceptible as the ticking of the clocks. She turned to her father, and his look remained fixed on the merchant. Perhaps she was drawing strength from him, perhaps having gone through this ritual before, she knew the ending by heart. "I want to use my initials," she said, "but if you insist, my name is Ernestine Burghes." The jeweler sighed, and returned to the paper, writing out "Ernestine" in a large dark path across the page. "I gave you only my initials," she explained, "because I did not want you to call me by my first name." He looked at her, as if ready to speak, then suddenly put away his pencil and book, locked up the trays of watches, and moved quickly to the back of the store. The Reverend John Burghes put on his hat, took his daughter's arm, and the two figures moved silently toward the door. Just as they reached it, they stopped, listening, though they did not turn around. "Ernestine," the merchant laughed softly from his desk in the back. "Ernestine!"*

In Selma, Alabama, a black woman of any age was called by her first name whenever any white person wished to address her. Whites regarded the practice as a part of their southern customs, and some of them still seem surprised that the familiarity is unacceptable to black people. In Paris, France, Ernestine Burghes Saunders, born in 1903 in Selma, was addressed as "Mademoiselle," the sound ringing like a victory in her dreams.

Mrs. Saunders is a graduate of Fisk University and of Middlebury College, and she has studied at Northwestern University, the Sorbonne, Columbia University, and the University of North Carolina at Chapel Hill. For more than forty years until her

retirement in 1971 she was a teacher of
French, the last twenty-three years as Associate Professor at St. Augustine's College in
Raleigh. She speaks French and German,
and reads French, German, Portuguese,
and Spanish. Her favorite books are
Charles Dickens, from her childhood,
and Alexander Dumas, from her studies.
Former students remember her as the
first black woman they knew who spoke
French, as a learned humanist, and as a
teacher whose work was her pleasure. In
retirement, she lives near the college campus and attends Sunday services in the
small Episcopal chapel, where, unless a
faculty member knows her or a new student has heard of her reputation, she slips
quietly unnoticed from the congregation.
Her manner is shy; her mind is decisive.
The narrative of her life is told in a soft
voice, with a teacher's practice of analysis,
and with a patience which began a lifetime
ago.

"I was my father's heart. He was a Methodist minister. I know now that it was an
advantage, but when I was a child I hated
it because everybody felt that anything
done for me was done because my father
was the Reverend J. R. Burghes. He was
born in Mississippi, and his parents moved
to Selma. He mentioned the fact that his
parents lived in a German settlement, and
he spoke German as a boy. My father was a
product of one of what we call the tragic
situations in the South at that time. So
many times these children born the first
generation after slavery and during slavery
were illegitimate. So my stepmother and I
have just—he didn't tell us—but we have
come to the conclusion that his father perhaps was German. Now if you will watch
his picture, there were certain characteris-
tics that he had. I admired the fact that my
father always held his head up. I don't
know if you've come into contact with
many of these Germans. There was a walk
that they had. My father had a bearing, the
way in which he walked, the generation before Hitler. There were ever so many of
them in America in these settlements. You
had a settlement in Tennessee, and we had
very good friends, and they also came into
that group. All of them when they married
did marry black women. I like to contrast
my black grandfather and my father because each one had one common characteristic: pride. My mother's father had
eight children, three sons and five daughters. He was a slave, but at nineteen he was
freed. My grandfather was taught a trade
so that after the Civil War he went into
business for himself. He was what they
called a tinner [tinsmith]. As his children
grew up, the three sons were also taught
this trade, but they didn't stay in Selma.
They moved away. They were free. My
grandfather couldn't read. He couldn't
write. But he knew everything that was
going on because his children read the
newspaper to him every night. And when I
grew up and started taking languages, he
would have me say things to him, he had
me read to him. So one night I played a
trick on him; I didn't feel like reading so
I skipped some sentences. He said, 'Ernestine.' I said, 'Yes?' 'Go back. Re-read
what you were reading to me. Didn't sound
right.' And I didn't try to play that trick on
him anymore. He was not what you'd call
an educated man, but I never heard him
make a grammatical error. We're not sure
whether he came directly from Africa or
one of the West Indies. His speech was different from my father's, yes, but he didn't
speak with an accent like the others around
him. He spoke like the educated people in

our class. He didn't have a West Indian accent, no. Nor did he have what so many people call a southern Negro accent. But he had no white blood in him, we're sure of that because his color was black. His wife was from Talladega County. She was of mixed blood, but I imagine it was mostly Southern Cracker. She was taught to sew, and the fact that my grandmother took in sewing and was a very fine seamstress didn't quite put us in the class that we called upper class; we were definitely middle class. She was very, very strict because my aunts and my mother would frequently tell things about her to show how she reared her daughters. Now, it is said—my mother told this tale quite frequently—the day she was to be married, my grandmother came in and said, 'You promised to iron this shirt. There'll be no marriage in this house until this shirt is ironed.' So my mother had to iron the shirt.

"My mother went to the first black school that was established in Selma, Burrell Normal School. The teachers were northern whites. The [local] whites burned Burrell Normal School because it was impossible for whites to take hearing blacks called Mr. and Mrs. That would have been in the late 1890s. Mr. Sellsby, who was the principal of the school, was then transferred to Talladega College, and because of the fact that my mother was a good student, Mr. Sellsby asked my grandfather to let her go to Talladega College with him. He said he didn't have the money to do it. So he said this, 'If you will let her go, we will take her, she will help us in the house and enroll in the school.' That did take place, so she went to Talladega, but it wasn't a college then. All of these black schools when they were established were called colleges and universities because it

was the hope that they would become universities eventually. She was able to go one year. She was about eighth grade. She took the examination back in Selma and was permitted to teach, and she taught at what was called Payne University; it was a Methodist black school. She taught English until she married my father, around three years. She helped me with literature, and my father would help me with my foreign languages and with math. We read together all of the time because we subscribed to magazines. I remember *Good Housekeeping, McCall's,* and all of the stories, the old stories of Dickens, and *Delineator.* I learned to read very early, I knew how to read when I went to school, and I went to school when I was six years old. I read *Pollyanna* long before *Pollyanna* was published as a book, in one of those magazines. Pollyanna was the same age as I was, and I thought she was so silly! She did so many things, and I said, 'I wouldn't do that, and she's as old as I am!' I remember *Just David* when it came out of the serials of these magazines. And before I began each of my languages I had my first lessons with my father. In the Methodist Church you had to go through training before you were ordained as a minister, so most of his lessons were private. My father had churches in various towns in Alabama. He had a chance to pastor in Africa, and I think that was shortly after my birth, because he was to send for my mother and me, but financial affairs occurred in the Methodist Church that never gave him the type of salary that he felt he should have to take care of his family, so we never had a chance to go to Africa. But he spent two years in Monrovia, Liberia; then he returned to America and was given charge of various churches. We moved to Birmingham when I was five; then my father was sent to Florence. There were two schools. The principal of the black school was from Ohio, and she was a typical northern woman. Her husband was a physician. She stood for high scholarship. She made a magnificent salary of forty dollars a month. The superintendent asked her to resign (I overheard my mother and this principal talking together) and she said, 'They don't want a woman principal because if they have a woman principal in the school here then white women will think that they can be principals and we don't believe in women principals.' So I was a small child, that's when I began being ambitious because I said if Mrs. Suggs—she was my heroine—if she can demand what she wants, and if she will not accept less than what she wants, that's the way I'm going to be when I grow up. So she was moved from the principalship of the black school to the American Missionary Association School, and she taught there, she was the assistant principal there. The principal was Walter White's brother, George White. Now Walter White was a hero even then [White was Executive Secretary of the NAACP]. Always when my father would go to a new place, he would interview to see what school I would go to. So he had to interview with the principal of Birmingham Industrial High School, and he was told that I would have to go back to the eighth grade because every new student who came to the school even though he had passed the eighth grade had to go back. So then he went out and interviewed the president of Miles College, and he found out that the parents who wanted their children to go to college usually sent them to Miles. I went to Miles College and finished what was equivalent to junior college. One of the teachers made the statement that women couldn't learn Greek. The next day I enrolled in the Greek class. And my father, of course, gave me lessons in Greek, so I kept up with the four young men in the class. My grandfather had me reading Greek to him. He had me read Latin to him. I had six years of Latin at Miles. It was determined [after graduating from Miles] that I should go to Fisk. There were three schools to which black children went: Fisk University, Atlanta University, and Howard University. One of my aunts went to Fisk, and the younger uncle. So that was just all the thing that occurred to me to do.

"I liked Fisk, I worshipped it. People were pointed out to me. There is Yolanda Du Bois [daughter of W. E. B. Du Bois]. Another woman was Sadie Daniels, and I was told, 'She is the first woman to receive magna cum laude at Fisk.' She was one of the graduates returning, as they frequently did. The faculty was largely white because that was in 1923 and there were still not enough black people to be eligible to be members of the faculty at Fisk. One of the black teachers was Miss Lillian Cashion of Huntsville, Alabama. She influenced me so much. She had so much pride, and she taught us—well, we never had a feeling at Fisk of inferiority. We always felt that she should have been head of the English department at Fisk, but there was still this feeling that because she was a black woman that a white person should be head of the department. The faculty was largely white. The woman that was head of the English department—a Miss Dora Ann Scribner— she was New England white, and she was a rigid teacher. I remember that she would work on me. She said I never pronounced g. For example, if I said, singin', doin', willin', but the g was never sounded. So she worked on that all the time. She was simply a grammarian in the strictest sense. I don't think she had any feelings of color at all; she was just after instilling pride in everybody, black or white.

"Many of the white faculty came down with the idea of teaching pride to Negro students. Now the Fisk students resented that because so many of the Fisk students came from homes that were equal to these northern homes. And they resented the fact that these people did what they called 'looking down on us.' Now here's an illustration of that. One night we were to go to the auditorium to sing in the choir, and I wasn't particularly interested in going. So they told us, 'You should be ashamed of yourselves. As much as whites have done for you, the least you could do is to go down there.' They had to inspect us before we could go out. So I went in to the white matron who was to inspect us, and she looked at me. 'Oh, yes, Ernestine, you'll do nicely.' But that made me angry because by her saying, 'You'll do nicely,' it meant to me that I was dressed simply enough to impress the people that we needed money. Now I went to Fisk because of family tradition, but the good livers in Birmingham sent their children to Fisk, Howard, and Atlanta, and many of them sent their children to Europe if they had talent. But very few of us went to Europe then. That was one of the things which my father was very proud of, the fact that he had a chance to go to Africa and to England.

"I graduated from Fisk in '26, and I was one of the senior orators, based on grades. That was the year that the subject, 'tests and measurements,' came into being, and I was impressed by the title, so what I was to do was to compare things that made a person in life great, and I spoke to the part of tests and measurements in the life of a per-

son. My father was at my graduation. My mother didn't come. She loved me just as much, but he had a particular sort of closeness to me. When I went to Fisk, he took me there. When I went to Miles, he took me there. I was the only child, so everything I did to them was all right. Now my mother never said to me, 'Don't do this,' or 'Don't do that,' but she would say it like this: 'I wouldn't like to see a daughter of mine act like this or act like that.' And that had much more of an influence on me than telling me not to do something. It was just like the dean of women at Fisk. When we would go out, we would always have to go in a group, and she would say to this group, 'I have only one thing to say to you. No matter where you are or whatever you do, remember you are Fisk women.' We'd go out with our shoulders thrown back. We were Fisk women!"

After graduation, Miss Burghes took her first teaching job at Payne University, fulfilling a promise her father had made to the bishop. That summer she went to Northwestern University for further study, beginning a long tradition of continuing education. In 1928 she joined the faculty at Talladega College and taught French, German, and Spanish for seventeen years. During that time she enrolled at Middlebury College for summer study, receiving her master's degree in 1932. In 1933 at the age of thirty, she married Joseph W. Saunders, assistant superintendent of buildings and grounds at Talladega. Their only child, Ernestine Rebecca, was born in 1935, and after her birth Mr. Saunders encouraged his wife to fulfill her long-standing ambition to go to France, and she studied at the Sorbonne in the summer of 1937, leaving her baby at home with an elderly housekeeper and her husband. Almost a decade later, after coming to the faculty of St. Augustine's College, Mrs. Saunders enrolled in the doctoral program at Columbia University. She completed her course work at Columbia, but was discouraged from getting the degree, having been told that no black had ever earned a Ph.D. in the language department. She left Columbia and later continued her studies at the University of North Carolina at Chapel Hill when she was in her sixties. After she had completed course requirements there, she was told that she would not be a candidate for the degree because of her age. This discouragement and the illness of her husband convinced her that she must withdraw. Her disappointment in having failed to complete the degree is tempered by the pride she feels that one of her students from St. Augustine's received a doctorate from Columbia.

Mrs. Saunders concludes her story with remembrances of two experiences which stand out in her memory: studies at Middlebury College and at the Sorbonne in Paris.

"Middlebury was like Fisk, like a dream coming true. We had a couple at Talladega from Vermont, and I asked her if Middlebury accepted blacks, Negroes. (Those terms mean two completely different things. A black is a term that came into being in the sixties; before that, we were Negroes. But we resented Negroes because the average southern white can't pronounce Negro. It comes out 'Nigra.' One of the best teachers I had at the University of North Carolina—he was so nice to me—but he could not say Negro; he would say Nigra every time.) Anyway, the woman from Vermont said, 'Yes, yes, Vermont is a Christian state.' And I said, 'That's why I want to know if they accept us because you know

how Christianity is.' So I wrote to the dean, and he wrote back saying that they had had some Negro students there, but they were so fair that he wasn't sure that the student body knew that they were Negro. He said send in my credentials and then they would decide. Well, I sent in the credentials from Fisk and Miles, and I was accepted. The dean wrote back asking whether I wanted a separate room or a room with a roommate. I wrote back that I preferred a separate room because I didn't want to run the risk of coming into contact with a prejudiced roommate. So I was to leave one night, and the telegram came that day. And the telegram said, 'We have so few separate rooms, and another Negro had applied. Will you accept a room with her?' My mother said, 'You answer at once because I've been living in fear of your being in a separate room and getting sick in the night and nobody to look after you.' When I got to Middlebury, Irene Dobbs came, and she said she had received the same telegram. [Irene Dobbs Jackson is the mother of Maynard Jackson, the former mayor of Atlanta.] We were so happy to see each other. The other students were young; we were young, then. Two across from us from New York state, two down the hall, one was definitely Jewish. The other, Adeline, was one of these carefree youngsters. A Mrs. K, who lived next door to us, was from New Jersey. Everybody seemed to accept us. Mrs. K from New Jersey, we found out later, made a request; her request was that she not have to use the bathroom with the Negroes. So they divided it; they had the bathroom that the two supervisors of this house would use, that was given to us, and the other whites were to use the second bathroom. They told it to us in such a way that we weren't supposed to recognize it as segregation, but we recognized it right away. The little carefree girl, Adeline, also used our bathroom. And she was always in our room. The students as a whole—well, we were sort of a curiosity to them. They nicknamed us La Grande et La Petite. Irene was much taller than I and very well built. Everybody knew us, you see. Adeline and I met in the basement; we had our laundry to do. I said to her, 'Why is it the directress does not like your roommate?' So Adeline replied, 'Ernestine, you must remember that you and I are social outcasts.' I said, 'Adeline, are you a Jew?' She said, 'Yes.' I said, 'I would never have suspected it.' She said, 'Nobody ever knows it until I tell them. My father was an English Jew, and my mother is a German Jew, so that's why I have blonde hair and an English name.' So we got through our laundry in a little while, and we sat there and talked about one hour. Now this was in the 1930s. And she told me things I had never suspected. Everywhere I could show her where I was segregated in the South, she would say, "Well, there are certain hotels where they have signs, 'No dogs or Jews allowed.' I said, 'Well, that's what they have in Alabama, 'No dogs and niggers allowed.' I said, 'Adeline, what you're telling me is what we call 'passing' in the South, because there are some Negroes that are so fair that you'd never know it unless they announce it themselves.' She said, 'Yes, there's no need to run around with a sign on your back, I'm a Jew, or I'm a Negro.' So when we got through, I remember I ran up the stairs calling, 'Irene, Irene!' Irene had asked me before, 'Of all the students here, whom do you like the best?' I said, 'Adeline.' She said, 'Why? I like her best, too. Now do you like her because her people are rich?' I said, 'I don't

think so because I never think of money. I just think of the fact that I like her.' So that was that. So I told Irene that Adeline was Jewish. I said, 'Irene, do you know why we like Adeline so much?' She said, 'Why?' I said, 'She's a Jew.' She said, 'Well, I'm not surprised; that's why.' Then I told her about our conversation."

If Middlebury College introduced Ernestine Saunders to a broader mix of American students than she had met at Fisk, Paris and the Sorbonne introduced her to European culture and freedom for herself as an American black. She was thirty-four years old, married, and the mother of a young daughter when she sailed for France. "Arriving in France was like arriving in heaven," she remembers. "I had spent so many years dreaming of France that when I did arrive by way of the *Ile de France*, I stepped off the boat and instead of stopping with the customs officer, I wasn't even aware that I was on land. I had my small suitcase, and I was walking on air until I became conscious that three people were yelling at me. I turned around to see why, and they informed me I was passing by customs, and then I came down to earth. Everything that happened to me in France was like something happening in a dream come true.

"I stood before the grave of the writer of fables, La Fontaine, and I laughed there by his grave, as I imagined he was laughing. I met people from all over the world in a class in phonetics [at the Sorbonne]. To me, it was unreal. In a room with over a hundred people, all were understanding the French that was spoken to us in these lectures. It was wonderful, marvelous. The professors were my idea of typical Frenchmen—they carried out the theory [that] if it's not clear, it's not French. I lived at a pension for students on the Left Bank. When I first told the representative at the American Embassy I wanted help in finding a place to live, he wasn't particularly interested. I had my first experience of knowing how they regarded blacks in the same light as they regarded Josephine Baker [a black dancer from American vaudeville, she had become the toast of Paris in 1926 at the Casino de Paris and the Folies Bergere]. Josephine Baker was at the height of her popularity in France, and they had a tendency to judge all Negro women by Josephine Baker. When I told the man at the Embassy that I was a student, then he changed his attitude suddenly, and he gave me a list of places to stay, where students at the Sorbonne stayed.

"I liked the French people, but the French people are for themselves. The French criticized America because segregation was in force in America then, but they segregated us on the boat, but they didn't do it openly and we weren't supposed to recognize that they were doing it. The French people always asked this question, 'Do you want to go back to America?' But the economic situation in France as compared to the economic situation in America—I knew that I was much better off in America. I always replied, 'I'm so glad to be in France, but I shall be glad to go back to America.'

"It was the fourteenth of July. My friend and I met this French woman, and we spoke of how difficult it was to not become separated in the crowd. And she said she had become separated from the group with which she had come. I had clutched very firmly my friend with whom I had come. And the French woman seemed determined to separate us. So she did something that never had occurred to me in America, which was then called the land of prejudice. She took her fist, and she beat on my hand to make me lose the grip of my friend, but she couldn't do it because I gripped my hand so firmly on hers. My first reaction was—I didn't say it but I thought—'so this is your France, and America is the land you call the land of racial prejudice!' But I never had this to happen to me in America."

Surprised to discover what she felt to be race prejudice in a native Frenchwoman, perhaps Mrs. Saunders was better prepared to deal with the attitudes of other Americans in Paris. As she recalls it, "We were standing in line one day and a white American deliberately got in front of my friend, and she was so angered that she started to move up. She spoke in English—she saw that he spoke English—'You are ahead of me.' And he replied, 'As soon as you people get over here, you forget your place.' When she got up to the window, the Frenchman deliberately reached around the American and said, 'I'll take you next.' And when she turned she looked directly into this white American's face, and his face was red, and he was angered, and saying something under his breath."

Despite these unpleasant experiences, Ernestine Saunders still remembers her only trip to France as a dream, for she was able to study at the Sorbonne, to speak the language she loved, and to put her feet on ground where her literary giants had walked. From Selma, Alabama, to Paris, France, from Ernestine to Mademoiselle— she has achieved the fullness of an education, the extent of which even her father might never have guessed.

# ". . . For Peace and Justice, Freedom and Dignity for All People"

## Madie Hall Xuma

### Winston-Salem

Madie Hall Xuma's interest in the YWCA began in North Carolina in 1911 and has spanned the world. First introduced to the organization as a student at Shaw University in Raleigh, she later worked on the Y staff in Lynchburg, Virginia, and then returned home to lay the groundwork for a YWCA for black girls and women in Winston-Salem. Her most courageous and intense efforts were made in Johannesburg, South Africa, where, despite the opposition of the government and the white YWCA, she organized black women. Named the Zenzele YWCA, meaning "people helping themselves," the organization celebrated its fortieth anniversary in 1981. The administration building is named in Mrs. Xuma's honor. In addition to the leadership she provided for the Johannesburg YWCA, she also served eight years on the executive board of the world organization.

Today Madie Hall Xuma lives quietly in Winston-Salem, North Carolina, an ocean and a lifetime away from Johannesburg, South Africa, her home for twenty-three years. The friends she grew up with here in the South take for granted that she was a "famous" woman, married to a distinguished South African doctor, and a world leader of the YWCA. But they are more aware of her life in North Carolina and of her leadership of the local Y and of local and state garden clubs for her people. When outsiders—a reporter from New York, a university graduate student, a visiting South African—come to Winston-Salem to praise Madie Hall Xuma, her old friends are reminded of her other life, and they are pleased to recognize a prophet in their own country.

Mrs. Xuma, who continues to be known at home as Madie Hall, has been around the world and visited many of the countries which fascinated her as a child. Friends in places like Mexico, the Caribbean, England, Switzerland, Africa, and Lebanon made their countries home to Mrs. Xuma, and she still dreams of travel when she is at rest in North Carolina. But her story begins in her home state, for it was the ambition and education of her parents which provided her with the incentive to see the world.

Madie Hall was born in 1894, one of four children of Ginny Cowan Hall and H. H. Hall. Her parents met in Salisbury, North Carolina, and went to Shaw University together, where Dr. Hall graduated from Leonard Medical School. They married in 1891 and moved to Winston-Salem. Dr. Hall was the first black physician in the city, organized the black medical community, and planned for the city's first black hospital.

"At first the white doctors wouldn't help him, in no way," Mrs. Xuma explains. "But he got here at the time when they were having flu, the first flu my mother said she'd ever heard of. And they were losing so many people; they would die like flies overnight. My father didn't lose a single patient. And the help in the white homes, they would go back and tell about this black doctor; they said, 'He's treating people, and he's not losing any. All his people are getting well.' And many of the whites began to flock to him, and the white doctors wanted to know what he was using. He said, 'I learned it in school, and if you want to learn it, you'd better go back to school!' And when my younger brother, Dr. Leroy Hall, graduated from medical school, he went into practice with my father. And my father was so proud; he would stand in front of their office and read their names printed on the window. When he had an office in the home, I was just a little girl, and I was so fond of him carrying that black bag around. And when he'd come in the house, I'd go with him to see where he was going to put that black bag down. And I watched him, he let me play around in there, sometimes he had patients, sometimes he didn't. And I was watching everything he did. I wanted to be a doctor, but he kept saying, 'No, no. No girl can be a doctor.' After I finished Shaw I wrote to Howard University for admission there in the medical school and was accepted. And my brother, Leroy, had finished Livingstone College, and he applied and was accepted. So I told my father, 'I'm accepted and Leroy is accepted. Why can't I go?' He said, 'Leroy can go, but not you.' He said he had one or two women in his medical class [in 1890] and he followed them after they went out to work. And they had a hard time, going out, country practicing, winter time, and women molested. And he saw all of that if I read medicine. And he said, 'No, I'd rather you take anything else but medicine.' I gave in, and I went into teaching. He was happy with that. My mother didn't oppose him. She just wanted me to get that college education. My father's mind was always on medicine. But he was the finest and the sweetest and the kindest person I have ever known. And he was so in love with me, he just thought I was an angel from heaven. I was the first girl, and he did everything to make me happy, and offered so many suggestions and ideas, especially after my mother passed; he got closer to me. I looked after the house; my mother trained me for the business that we had, properties. My mother raised her children, and she did all the business part. She would see a house that was being sold, and she'd go

in and inquire about it. And if she could buy that house, she'd buy it. She bought a lot of property in Salisbury and built houses over there. We've got land in Asheville that she was going to build houses [on] up there. My father was sitting one night reading the paper, and he came across the section where you go and register property. And he saw this name, Ginny Hall, and he said to my mother, 'You know, I've seen this woman's name in here many times. She's got the same name you have. She sure is buying a lot of property!' And they laughed about it. My mother said, to herself, 'I think that it's time for me to tell him I'm the woman.' So she told him, she says, 'I'm that woman.' He said, 'I didn't know you were interested in real estate.' She said, 'I've always been interested in it.' So he just handed everything over to her, all the business, the rents, and the property and paying taxes. It was turned over to her, and he went on about his business of medicine. She trained me. And I think she must have known it would fall on me one day.

"My mother was born in Whiteville, North Carolina. She was three-fourths white. Her father was white, her grandfather was white, and her mother was half-white. Her mother brought her to Salisbury on the way to the mountains. My mother was about three months old. It was right after the Civil War. All of the white people were sending their servants up to the mountains with all their jewelry and their precious things because the Yankees were coming through. If you'll remember after the Civil War, there were soldiers who came down from the North, carpetbaggers, who plundered the South. So the people who lived down there [in Whiteville] thought it would be better to send their valuables with the servants up in the mountains until the Yankees had finished working that part of North Carolina. And my grandmother got very ill and couldn't continue. So they stopped off in Salisbury. The man who was driving the wagon train went out in the neighborhood to find a place to leave my grandmother and my mother, this baby, and they came across an old man who was a minister. He was a Reverend Cowan, a Baptist minister, and he had just built a two-story house, and that was something back in those days. He kindly took them in, and it was just about a month afterwards that my grandmother died and left my mother with this man and his family, and they raised her. Many years later a white lawyer from Whiteville came to Winston-Salem and saw my father, and he said, 'Do you know—' and he called her real name before she took the name of Cowan, I used to know it, but it's just gone away. And my father said, 'No, I don't know anybody by that name.' And he said, 'The reason I'm looking her up, she had a brother who was older than she was, and he used to go with a drummer who sold liquor. And after the liquor went out of the United States, they went down to Havana, Cuba, and he made a lot of money down there, as well as the white man he was working for. And he saved his money, and then when the white man died, he came back to Alabama or Georgia, one of those places. And he bought land. And the courts are going to try to dispose of this property. One afternoon Mama and Papa were sitting on the porch talking, and Papa said, 'You know there was a man in my office about two or three weeks ago, looking for a woman by the name of so-and-so. She had a brother and he had a lot of property. And nobody knew him!' And in a minute it came to her that she was the person. And

this white lawyer, when he found out that my mother was the person he was looking for, he asked her would she be willing to go to the trial about this property. She went down. And so this case came up and my mother was in the back room, and this lawyer said, 'I have a relative of this man.' They said, 'Produce her!' And he went out and got her and brought her in and when she came down the aisle, the people said, 'Ahh! She's just like him, the color and everything.' But you know, she didn't get a thing. They took everything! The whites got the property.

"My mother was active in the church and in the community, looking after people who were sick or poor or needed help. I remember my first job, when I got my first pay check. She said to me, 'Well, now you made your first pay check. What are you going to do with it?' I said, 'I don't know.' She said, 'I think you should give some of it to somebody who needs it.' And there was an old lady who lived not far from us, and my mother said, 'You can help that old lady get enough coal for the winter, so she'll have fire,' and she said, 'I'll feed her and you keep her warm.' And I took part of that check and bought coal. And the man who was looking after my father's horses and things, he'd go over there and make the fire for her every day. We had new windows put in and fixed up the house for the old lady. And that was one of the greatest things she taught me, helping people."

After Madie Hall completed two years at Shaw University (later she went to Winston-Salem Teachers College and to Columbia University for her degrees) she taught in Winston-Salem. Five years later when she became ill during a flu epidemic, her parents arranged for her to recover in

Miami, and while she was there she accepted a temporary teaching appointment at Booker T. Washington High School. During this period in Florida she met Mary McLeod Bethune, who, discovering that she was a pianist as well as a teacher, invited her to join the staff at her school in Daytona.

"Mrs. Bethune was a go-getter," Mrs. Xuma remembers. "We had vespers from five until six, and all the people from the beaches would come over to hear the black children sing the spirituals. So she was sitting there waiting for five o'clock to come. I had to take care of the little children who came there, four, five, six years old, that was my job every Sunday. So I looked at her, and she nodded her head, 'Come up here, I want to say something to you.' So I went up. She said to me, 'Don't drop dead, but on the row behind you is John D. Rockefeller. The old man himself.' She said, 'I'm going to speak today—' oh, it was so funny—'I'm going to speak today like I've never spoken before because I need some of that money he's got. This is what I want you to do: shift the children over and you sit right in front of him, so that when they pass the plate around you'll hear what he says.' She was clever like that. So that's what I did. I went back, and I sat, right in front of him. He had some woman with him; I suppose she was looking after him. She spoke that day—Oh, Lord, she got down to the dollars and the cents and the pennies! When they passed the plates around, I heard this nurse of his say, 'How much you going to put in?' He said, 'About fifty thousand dollars.' I think he said fifty; he could have said one hundred thousand. It's been so long now, but it was way up there. And she said, 'No, this is just a collection. Give her twenty dollars

and then you can give Mrs. Bethune whatever you want afterwards.' Now I heard that. Mrs. Bethune couldn't let out fast enough to hear me, what I had to say! So I told her. I told her what he said, and she said, 'I'm going to get that money,' and she devised some way to get to him, and she went over there, and when she came back, she had the check. She showed it to me. I said, 'Let me touch it. I'll never touch this much money again!' She let me look at it and turn it over in my hands; but she got the money. Now she was that kind of a person."

After finishing the year in Daytona, Madie Hall returned home, and with the death of her mother in 1930, took over the responsibilities of the house. She cared for her father until his death, and then fulfilling her parents' dream for her education, she went to New York and completed her master's degree at Columbia University in 1937; she was then forty-three years old. It was during her studies in New York that she met Dr. Alfred B. Xuma from Johannesburg, South Africa.

When Madie Hall returned to Winston-Salem, she continued to receive proposals of marriage from Dr. Xuma. "Every time he'd write me a letter, he'd ask me, and when I answered, I wouldn't mention it. So that last letter was, 'Will you marry me?' and signed his name, that's all. So I had to answer it. I was teaching first grade, and I was putting in a lot of new things that I had learned at Columbia for those children. This day that I made up my mind that I was going to write to Doctor and tell him what I was going to do. I had about two or three hours; I'd write a while, I'd get down on my knees and I'd pray a while. I said, 'Lord, tell me and show me what to do, this is a very crucial moment in my life.'

And the third time I did that, when I got up off my knees, as plain as I'm talking to you right now, I heard, 'Go, and I'll go with you.' And that was it. I put that in the letter: 'Yes, I'll marry you.' He got it, he was so happy; he sent me a cablegram and thanked me and said, 'I'll make the arrangements; don't worry about anything.'"

Madie Hall's passage to South Africa was delayed for almost a year because of the war, and in April of 1940 she finally received approval from the United States government to travel. "We went out on a Dutch ship," she remembers. "Holland and Germany were not at war when we left New York. But when we crossed the equator, that's when the Germans went into Holland and bombed Amsterdam. And the captain of this ship and all the sailors were from Holland. And I can see the captain now; he was crying like a baby; he said he didn't know what was happening to his family. And we went on to Cape Town and got there all right, but only seven of us got off at Cape Town. It was a cargo ship, and it was taking cargo out, and the German U-boats caught that ship when it got in the Indian Ocean and sank it. I read about it in the newspaper. I said, 'God was with me all the way, all the time I was there.'"

News of the sinking, the absence of her own family and friends, and a strange new country must have filled the American with great fears. But she was quickly thrust into her new life, and hours after her arrival, she was married in Cape Town. The bride played "The Wedding March" and "O Promise Me" on the church organ while the groom sang, and after the ceremony the couple left by train for Johannesburg. Mrs. Xuma met Dr. Xuma's two young children (his first wife had died several years earlier) and began family life in his eleven-room

house built in 1935 on freehold land. In 1955 the Xuma family and other residents of Sophiatown were forced by the South African government to give up their homes and be moved to Soweto, where blacks were resettled farther from the city. At the time of the government's edict, Dr. Xuma was adamant in his opposition, and his refusal to be moved was reported in the *London Daily Telegraph*, which quoted him as saying, "They will have to come and fetch me." When the government persisted in its policy of expulsion, Dr. Xuma and his family were finally forced from their home.

By this time Madie Hall Xuma had begun to win the hearts of the Africans, initially somewhat hostile to the idea of their doctor's taking an American wife. A month or two after she arrived, she invited to her home different housewives, teachers, and church workers she had met, at first calling her group The African Self-Improvement Organization. After she won their confidence and their interest, she moved to convert the organization into a YWCA. The Y concept at first had been unacceptable to the black people because of their hatred of the whites and the opposition of the white YWCA to their organization. But under Mrs. Xuma's persistent and sensitive leadership, the Zenzele group began. It continues today as one of the strongest members of the world YWCA.

In South Africa Mrs. Xuma observed apartheid restrictions more severe than the segregated customs of America, the Africans occupying the lowest place in society below the coloreds (those with mixed blood) and, at the top, the Afrikaans, or white people of Dutch descent. Government reprisals were harsh. Dr. and Mrs. Xuma were not permitted to travel together outside the country. Mrs. Xuma was jostled by white elbows on the streets of Johannesburg.

"Prejudice in South Africa is worse than in North Carolina," she observes. "I had more freedom in America. I could go many places here I couldn't go there, to theaters and picture shows. I wrote a letter in South Africa and asked to go to the theater, and I got back an insulting letter saying, 'If that's what you want, go on back to America.' But one owner of a theater, who was an Indian, went to see Doctor [her husband, Dr. Xuma] and said they'd be happy to have me, and I went and took our children. But race prejudice is more radical in South Africa, and it's out there where you can see it. We tend to slide over things [in America]. There it's the law sometimes, not on the book, but the people know it's the law. It's the worst country I have ever seen for antagonism and hate just because of the color of the skin. I was walking down Main Street to Doctor's office, and I saw some new pianos in a window, and I stopped to look at them, and then the next thing I know I was lying on the ground. Three white boys had hooked their feet in mine and pulled me down to the ground. They were just laughing. When I was studying anthropology at the university, I used to go by tram, or streetcar. They have segregated seats upstairs for the colored, and I could pass for colored. If I was the only one standing waiting at the stop, the tram would leave me there.

"We lived in Sophiatown, and the government said, 'You have to move out because we've declared this a white area.' They moved us thirteen miles further out [to Soweto]. I didn't want to go, but I had to do it, and my husband built me a beautiful ten-room, modern home. In many ways I lived better in South Africa [than in North Carolina]. In the home I didn't have much responsibility. I had four servants. I had private friends, white and black. I had more white friends there than I had had in North Carolina, and they were people at the top.

"Soon after I arrived in South Africa, my husband was elected president of the African National Congress, in December, 1940. It was more like the NAACP, trying to get the African people to work together. And the people wanted to march [to stage a protest] and Doctor said, 'We have to be careful about marching,' and he went to the government and said they wanted to march, and some thought it would stir up trouble among whites. So he said, 'To satisfy the Africans, let them march on Sunday when there are no people in the streets.' And he said to me, 'We are going to march today from the Market Place down to Gandhi Hall, and we'll have some speaking.' So we did, and I marched on the front row, but I was scared to death. That was the first and only march I heard of in South Africa. And I loved the African people, and I won over quite a number of colored people. When I went there the colored thought I would work with them, but I let them know if they worked with me they'd have to work with the African people. I came there to do a special job and to help wherever I could. But my husband didn't want me to stay [after his death] because I'd be alone, and I didn't have any help. He protected me. He said, 'You leave as quickly as you can.' I did get telephone calls after he died telling me to get out of South Africa. I was glad to get back. I felt safer in America. My home now is right here, sitting on this porch [in Winston-Salem, North Carolina]."

At home, Madie Hall Xuma often thinks

of her life in South Africa, and of her travels. Before Dr. Xuma's death, he arranged for her to have a trip around the world, and in 1966 she undertook the voyage, stopping off in Johannesburg. There she was greeted with affection by the people who had become her friends, and the newspaper celebrated "Mommy's Return," using the name No m'Bantu—Mother of the People—which was given her by an African chief when she had first arrived in Johannesburg in 1940.

The stated purpose of the YWCA—to work "for peace and justice, freedom and dignity for all people"—was her life's goal, beginning in North Carolina and continuing in South Africa. She has resigned herself to the fact that it is an ideal which has not been perfected. Despite the changes in America toward racial desegregation, Mrs. Xuma is not satisfied that here we all "live together in harmony and peace." "We have made more progress than South Africa," she concludes, "but it takes times." Madie Hall Xuma is eighty-eight years old, and now sitting on her porch she feels that her time is nearly over.

(Madie Hall Xuma died in Winston-Salem in 1982.)

# You Follow Me?

Helen Grey Edmonds

Durham

Helen Grey Edmonds is a knowledgeable, outspoken, and politically experienced woman. Her influence is broad and deep: as a historian, as a social leader of her race, as a member of leading academic and political organizations, and as a national and international speaker. For thirty-four years she was a university professor; she represented the United States Department of State on lecture tours in Europe and Africa, she served as a delegate to the United Nations, and she has been a leader in the Republican party. In 1956 she was the first black woman to give a nominating speech for a candidate for the national presidency, seconding the nomination of Dwight Eisenhower. Born in Virginia, she studied in Germany. A history teacher in a small North Carolina state university, she became widely known through her lectures and books. Forthright in expressing her conservative philosophy, particularly in economics, she has remained both solidly in the black community and detached enough to speak candidly of its shortcomings. Recognizing the legal gains from the black revolution of the sixties, she also scoffs at the "nonsense" and "hoopla" of some of its leaders. She asks for no special favors, gives none. Trained in Greek and Latin, she insists upon a disciplined and objective mind. Her interests go far beyond the American South and the race question to embrace a world view of time and history. Quick, explosive, good-humored, she listens impatiently to praise, turning aside with a laugh, "Go on! go on!" She is always teaching, whether responding to former students honoring her in a history colloquium, or speaking to newspaper reporters, or conversing with friends about contemporary events. Her speech is punctuated with frequent demands upon her listeners: "You follow me?" The slightest hesitation in their expressed understanding, and she interrupts herself to draw on lessons from history to illustrate her point. And, indeed, her listeners are well taught. Twenty-six of her former students at North Carolina Central University in Durham have earned doctorates, and more than two hundred and fifty have received the master's degree. One of her books, *The Negro and Fusion Politics in North Carolina*, is considered a standard text. She is now writing *The American Black Woman in the Political Process since 1900*, certain to be important.

The sign on the door of Dr. Edmonds' home in Durham warns, "Available after 6 P.M." Behind it she is surrounded by mounds of books and papers in every room, including the kitchen. She continues to travel all over the country—and the world—and, of course, no one believes that she is seventy-one years old.

Those visitors brave enough to press the door bell will summon her to immediate action. Laughing off the interruption, ignoring the ringing phone, urging glasses of iced tea upon her guests, she talks.

"I was born in Lawrenceville, Virginia, a little town in southside Virginia near the North Carolina line. Brunswick County had a population of about 21,000—that was back in the thirties. Of that number, two-thirds were Negroes, one-third was Caucasian. The redeeming feature for Negroes at that time was the establishment of a little college by the Episcopal Church known as St. Paul's College. That college had been established in 1888, so when I was born in 1911 it was well on the way. This institution perhaps was responsible for a certain degree of enlightenment in our county with regard to blacks. They at-

tended kindergarten, and then they had a
parochial school through the seventh grade
and then a preparatory high school. Later
on they put on a junior college and then
later a senior college. There were nine
black Episcopal colleges; we were just one.
My father's uncle, Robert Edmonds, had
come down to St. Paul's in 1888 when
Archdeacon Russell helped found the
school, to help him set up the trade part.
St. Paul's was a miniature Tuskegee-
Hampton. And my father had studied the
trade there. He was a contractor, that is,
plastering. My father made a pretty decent
wage for that time. My parents owned their
home. And my mother took care of her
church work, her house, and took care of
us. There were four children. Now I attended St. Paul's around 1918. I went there
all the way from the kindergarten through
the high school. In the high school it was
required that we live on the campus. In
high school I think I showed an aptitude
for history and the classics, Latin. In my
opinion I had the greatest high school cur-
riculum and experiences that I believe a
youngster could have. Frankly, when I left
St. Paul's after two years in the junior college, I don't think I ever had any more of
anything that was totally new.

"The mechanism for raising money
among white Episcopalians was called The
American Church Institute for Negroes,
and the head man was Dr. Robert W. Pat-
ton and his associate was Dr. James Hardy
Dillard. And both of these men were very
interested in me as a student at St. Paul's.
When I went to Morgan State University in
Baltimore, Dr. Dillard said to me, 'Now, I
hate to hurt your feelings but Latin is becoming a dying subject in the high schools.
You're planning to teach in high school.
Well, if you're going on to graduate school,

you'd better throw your concentration in
history.' This was hurting me dreadfully
because you know, I like Latin and Greek
so well. I had a major in Latin and a major
in history when I finished Morgan. I'm in-
tensely proud of that, and I regret that it's
not any more in the high schools, but times
have changed. My political science teacher
at St. Paul's was George Streeter, a writer
with the *New York Times*. He only came for
one year, but God knows, that was such a
life because I didn't even know in 1929 that
there was such an important paper as the
*New York Times*. He would bring his issues to class and would take that section
known as the Week in Review, and we'd
have to report on that entire subject. Mind-
boggling, expanding, as far as our coming
from a little town. We did a lot of public
speaking. I was on the debating team that
traveled. We had organizations and we
named ourselves after prominent literary
women. I belonged to the Sojourner Truth
[Club]. And the men in our class on the
campus belonged either to the Frederick
Douglass or the Booker Washington Club.
The whites had a high regard for St. Paul's
College. We produced more cultural activities than the white high school. We
brought celebrities there, white and black,
from everywhere, and many of the whites
in the city came to hear them. We brought
Mrs. Mary Bethune, Marian Anderson,
Langston Hughes, and of course we
brought the governor and gave many of the
common white folks the chance to shake
his hand. The audiences were not mixed.
There was a special section for them
[whites], I must tell you that. It wasn't
down front. They were not on that front
line with the blacks behind them.

"Yes, Lord, we had women faculty members, and they were good; some of them

very, very good. We had some whites, but not many though. But you need to remember these were private schools, church-related schools, which were founded immediately after the Civil War, which had some whites from the North, nobody from down South. Many of them came from their own church concerns.

"My father came from a family of seven or eight children. I know this, that one of his sisters married an Italian and moved to Flint, Michigan; another one passed for white and lived in Toledo. I looked at the whitest man in the world across the table every day! My father's grandfather was a master, I can tell you that. My father looked like Truman I used to tell him all the time. My father was—except for the right to vote which he fought very hard for in the county—apolitical, if you are talking about the national level. If you are talking about the local level, all the judges, all those who were running at the local level, they would always say, 'Uncle John, don't forget me now. don't forget to get me a few votes.' That is, when they were finally allowed in the forties. It's amusing how they called him 'Uncle John' rather than Mr. Edmonds 'cause he was as white as they were. They didn't need more than twelve or fifteen extra votes to win. They figured that my father had some kind of influence; we had property around us, people rented from us. I've often looked back, but I can't remember now what the problems were. I know we ate and slept and went to school, but I've often wondered during the Depression, how did my mother make it?

"The emphasis in our home was on individual achievement and 'do the best you can.' You were interested in the accomplishments of your people, but this thing about black is beautiful and I'm the best—

all that stuff was born in the 1960s, as I see it. I really believe it was a sense of individual achievement that stuck with us. But you know, I'm a peculiar person on race. I have never—this sounds a little vain, though, I don't know if I should say it— I have never had any problem with race. A person has been a person to me. Now where that came from I cannot say, unless it was a certain kind of security I had in myself. But I have never been out beating the racist drum.

"Now the first Grey Edmonds that we know anything about was the son of the slavemaster's daughter, and the slavemaster exiled the daughter but kept the baby. I have grave, grave caution about tracing one's roots. When you are dealing with an interracial pattern, like Johnson's book on miscegenation in Virginia and the Old South, it's difficult to really prove all of the assertions that are made and handed down. Because we are talking about people who do not bear the label of legitimacy in the sense of the marriage license, you are weaving something together. I've got a whole lot of misgivings about the line of connection from Africa on. Haley's work is a historical novel. I'm old-fashioned; I was trained in the primary school of research. The most judiciously balanced book on blacks is *From Slavery to Freedom* by John Hope Franklin. It does not satisfy the Stokely Carmichael crowd because the young militants and activists look on it as being too passive, and of course, they would have some books that they like better. 'Who gives a damn about the historical world?,' they'd say. 'They're a white man.' I don't have any objection to a white historian. You take fellows like Genovese, a little bit on the Marxist side, but he's good. I don't have any question about race in writing or race in teaching. When our students say no white person can teach me black history because they're not black, that's about the silliest answer I have ever heard in kingdom come! And I resented it when I was chairman of the department, and I resented it even as a graduate dean for seven years—for them to come to tell me that because, for instance, you mean to tell me that I'm going to say if he isn't a German he can't teach me German history? That's totally obnoxious to me. Brains are not governed by skin color or nationality.

"My sister says as a youngster I was always lecturing. She says the way I got around washing dishes at home would be immediately after dinner to grab my books and go off like I was going to study and leave the dishwashing to her. We were in our room one night and Lucy said, 'What are you thinking about now?' She had asked me some questions, and I hadn't answered. I said, 'I don't know. I've just come back from Russia and due to the fact that I've been there for two weeks I've really forgotten the English language.' And we laughed about it after that because when I finally went to Russia, it was a most interesting experience, but back then it looked like I wanted to go to faraway places and see faraway people and faraway things. I wanted to hold my own among them.

"I always liked teaching. In 1975 the Board of Governors of the University of North Carolina gave me the Oliver Max Gardner Award [for her "contribution to the welfare of the human race"]. I was the first black [to receive the award]. And just as sure as I'm sitting in this seat, I almost feel like there were some people high up in the echelon of state authority and government saying, 'This would be a good one to select.' And my entire philosophy is em-

bedded in my response. I said, 'The young must do the healing. As I view them in their search for meaning, in their search for roles and in their search for understanding, they are not, like most of us, sad. They may be disillusioned for not having created the brave new world they sought in the 1960s, but they are not sad. This generation of students will be able to master change. The youth teach me significant lessons and bring me much joy.' I am student-oriented. Make no mistake, I've had some memorable experiences. I have traveled to almost every country in Europe. I have been the guest of Mrs. Golda Meir. I have been to two White House dinners. But the memorable experiences have been my teaching at the graduate level at North Carolina Central. Nothing to me is more precious than to find a young mind that wants to be quickened and aroused.

"When I taught United States history at a sophomore level, I took the historical setting and put it in a dramatic format. We organized the Constitutional Convention, and we had the presiding officer, George Washington, and one who is Ben Franklin, who wakes up in time to pray. Then I organize the Large State Plan that's led by Governor Edmund Randolph of Virginia, then I organize the Small State Plan with Patterson of New Jersey. We had people on our campus who would always come to that, including the presidents, just to hear these kids debate the issues. We come to the Civil War, and we reproduce the activities in the Congress just prior to the Civil War. They can defend their slaves to death! They did not take a racial view on slavery. I wanted them to see slavery as an economic situation where southerners have put theirs in land earnings and human chattel while other areas of the country have put theirs in banks and shipbuilding and things of that kind. I often thought that the South was wrong in trying to justify slavery on moral grounds or Biblical grounds. I would have justified it on the economic system. Geography made it. You follow me? I wouldn't violate the rules of history because whatever we were doing the students were constructing their papers and working in the library. It was fermentation. Sometimes when I see some of my former students across the country today, I do not remember their names, but I remember the names they had in the class production of these historical events. I was teaching out in Portland, Oregon, in the summer, and there was a student there from Central in Washington, and somebody told him I was down there, and he came in and walked into my class and I couldn't think of Martin to save my life. But I said, Patterson, chairman of the Small State Plan!

"I conceived the role of a black college in 1941 when I came to North Carolina Central as being very necessary for the upward mobility of young black students. A black student finds a supportive environment on the whole on his own campus. A supportive environment for those whose gaps have not been closed. That teacher will walk a second mile. You have to take them sometimes where you find them. And you have to attempt to fill those gaps. I think there is a role for the predominantly black college and there will be until the year 2000. We have learned one factor and that factor is that many southern whites really don't care how long the black college exists. Now this is a gut reaction. There's been no attempt to do away with the black college even in North Carolina where the students stay up in arms all the time. You follow me? I haven't seen any attempt out of Raleigh

or Chapel Hill or wherever you want to say to close any of these schools, and I don't think they want them closed. They serve the purpose of closing gaps, they serve the purpose of the young present-day students who say, 'We've got to have something.' Nobody wants to fight that battle because it's a delicate battle to fight, very delicate.

"I think nothing of the separatist movement, nothing of Stokely Carmichael's movement, of Marcus Garvey's. I don't think anything of them. And, of course, you would never have heard so much about them if you had not gone through the black revolution of the sixties where the youngsters were trying to justify that black is the way, and that resurrected Garvey; and any critical historian on Garvey will tell you that Garvey was the dumbest man on economics that anybody ever heard of. And anybody who writes on Garvey and tells us about collecting tub loads of money and passing out titles—that just, to me, is nothing. I'm not interested in any separatist movement, whatsoever.

"The nature of the black revolution in the sixties was for the participation in the American dream, but particularly from a political point of view, the right to vote, to hold office, to be in decision-making positions, and the elimination of segregation in public accommodations. This was a part of the revolution which began in 1956 with Rosa Parks and the Montgomery bus situation. The black revolution didn't always stay on course as it should, because it developed some extreme radicals in the process. And in a broader context, it was not just a black revolution. Historians will place this era from about 1960 on down almost to 1980 as two decades of revolutions. Blacks were so hung up on their own that the perspective was lost by many. But you see you had Students for a Democratic Society, asking for more participatory democracy in the school system. And that SDS had a free speech movement that began in Columbia and spread across the country to Berkeley, and it worked its way back. And there were young whites, sandals and daisies in their hair, hippies, all the way through the SDS movement and then the yippies, all of this was down with middle-class values, up with our own concerns. Then you had Puerto Rican 'lords' in cities, and if you look out at the far west, you have the Mexican-Americans, and of course, the Indians. They, too, were asking. And then of course the feminist movement moved in the 1970s. I wasn't moved by the feminist movement. If they had started off with solid issues like they now have resolved, okay. But they started out just like the black revolution with a lot of hoopla. Bra burning! So, really, we have had a series of revolutions between 1960 and 1980, and the black revolution was but one part. Blacks have been so concerned about their own that they didn't fully digest all of the movements that were going on. The gains for blacks there are statutory enactments on the books that have not been taken off and the court decisions still on the law books. On the whole, I'll tell you very frankly, I enjoyed from the black revolution the very fact that I could go into any hotel in this country, and I wasn't there to socialize with the manager nor his family, but simply was utilizing the freedom, the better services, and I paid for them with good American dollars. So I was very deeply grateful to many of the students who had marched for those things because some of them would never have the money to go into a restaurant.

"Basically, at heart, I am a conservative economically. I like the idea with the Republican party. I wasn't there because Abraham Lincoln was a Republican. I became a Republican because of Dr. Shepard, president of North Carolina Central. He was an old-line Republican nationally, but he gave in to the Democrats on the state level because he knew his money had to come from the state. I was writing something about Dr. Shepard, and he sent me up to see Governor Dewey, to see his letters to Governor Dewey. That's when I met him and from that time on I said, 'Well, there's something in this party.' I like a certain class and style they had. I just couldn't stand the shouting matches in the national conventions of the Democrats! I believe that Ike was really a man for total America. I'm sure he didn't want Little Rock, but his constitutional duties required that he send the troops to Little Rock. The most challenging thing as far as I'm concerned that came from Ike was in his final address, that had nothing to do with race. Ike made a statement, 'Beware of the military-industrial complex.' Now behind that statement was a powerful indictment. I liked Nixon. I guess I had no opportunity to dislike him because of some of the greatest opportunities I received. You'll see how many committees I served on with Nixon, and I had the opportunity to serve as a delegate to the United Nations in 1970. At the United Nations I learned one thing, that there is no country in the United Nations that does not put its own vested economic interests ahead of other issues when you come down to the economics of the situation. Number two, I saw clearly in evidence the three powerful blocs: you have the Western-European and others; the Russian bloc, and the Third World. I saw in bold relief these three structures operating in the U.N. to the detriment of the United States. It was also evident that the Third World was presenting a problem which the United States could not handle, and that was the race problem. The United States never did speak forthrightly on the African race question, and the Russians used this as a whipping post for the United States because we had never cut squarely on that issue. We'd always say gradualism is the way and South Africa should look forward to the time when these people could be free. Russia was using the race question to flaunt what it considered the United States' weaknesses. And the United States needed me on the Voice of America program. We had one significant victory that I could talk about. The Russian propagandist was saying that the United States was as bad as South Africa on the race question. People asked me on their programs if when I walked in the street did white folks spit on me and that kind of thing. I never said that it was perfect over here because the black revolution hadn't come. But we had one significant event: the Supreme Court in May, 1954, had declared segregation in the public schools unconstitutional. I'm in Europe that fall, and I'm called upon to talk. I learned that I was quite a novelty to them in many of the European countries I visited. I was an asset for the government because I was visibly the color that you couldn't mistake.

"I loved Germany. I studied there. I liked the people, and if there were a European country I was going to live in, it would be Germany. When I studied in high school at St. Paul's, we studied the University of Paris in 1209, but the next university was the University of Heidelberg, and I said, 'That's where I'm going.' And I would have loved to have gone in 1929 but that was just a pipe dream! I went in '54 when we got five Ford Foundation scholarships at NCCU. I loved Heidelberg, and I loved Germany. I like the discipline and the thriftiness.

"Who are my heroes and heroines? Mrs. Mary Church Terrell, who was the first president of the Association of Colored Women's Clubs. God knows, Golda Meir was one of my heroines. I never saw such a strong woman I admired! Anna Julian, who was the wife of a famous chemist; she's black, a Ph.D. in sociology and lives in Chicago today. Rosa Parks would be one. I guess you note that some of them you thought I was going to name, I didn't name. You follow me?"

Following Helen Edmonds requires mental dexterity, and physical energy. She defies stereotypes, though she is fundamentally proud of being a black, a woman, and a southerner. If asked to choose one term to describe herself, she would likely say historian. It is a term which places her among students and teachers, and that is the place she chose for herself a long time ago.

# I Was Glad When They Said unto Me, "We Will Go into the House of the Lord."

## Viola Addington Lenoir

### Franklin

*It is a cold morning in 1907, the day before Christmas holidays begin for the school children at St. Cyprian's Episcopal Mission in Franklin, North Carolina. They have arrived in a great noise of anticipation and are taking off their coats and whispering loudly around the woodstove. Mr. Kennedy is busy at his desk but watches them from time to time. He stops what he is doing when Viola fidgets in front of him. He has watched her all week, concerned that she has seemed distracted from her work and has frequently disrupted the lesson with giggles and notes passed to her girl friends. He has waited for a chance to find out why his third-year pupil has been less than attentive to her studies.*

*"Mr. Kennedy," Viola stands at his desk. He waits a moment to let her stop shifting from one foot to the other; then he looks up and motions her with his head to speak.*

*"Mr. Kennedy, I won't be back after the holiday!" Viola begins. "I'm going to work for the Kellys!" She twists her skirt as she speaks, a tall girl for her thirteen years, already giving up her childhood.*

*"I'm sorry to hear that, Viola," Mr. Kennedy says in his quiet voice. "Is there some problem at home?"*

*"No, sir! No problem at all! My mama says it's time for me to go to work, and she's got me a job looking after the old folks at Miss Elizabeth's. I'm supposed to laugh and make them happy." And she giggles at the thought of herself entertaining two old people.*

*Mr. Kennedy does not say anything but thinks of how she has made progress in her studies and of how a third grade education will not be enough to prepare her for the kind of work he knows she would be capable of doing. Maybe she could have been a teacher, one day to take his place when he became a priest, as he already had dreams of doing. He looked*

*over her bobbing head into the small church filled with children, and did not see another child with the promise he had sensed in Viola. He stacked up his books, a signal that class would be ready to begin.*

*"Well, Viola, if that's what you and your parents think best," and he sighed, with such feeling that Viola was suddenly surprised. Had she disappointed Mr. Kennedy? Did the only teacher she'd ever had or might have in this world believe she was doing the wrong thing?*

*"It'll be just fine, Mr. Kennedy," she protested. "I'll be working at the Kellys and making money to bring home on Sunday afternoon when I visit with my own family. And I'll get to go and live in that big house!"*

*Mr. Kennedy knew the Kelly family; everyone in town did. They ran a dining room in front of their house on Main Street, and the two daughters were always busy in Franklin, Miss Lassie a clerk at the courthouse and Miss Elizabeth a well-respected teacher. She'd be in a good place. Maybe that was all he could hope for. He knew her mother had done her best for Viola and her brother, but he'd heard that her father was drinking some.*

*"Well, Viola, let's learn all we can while we can. Take your seat," Mr. Kennedy turned to the class.*

*Viola sat down, and said nothing more. Today was her last day of school, Christmas was just a few days away, after Christmas she would go to live at the Kellys'. Her teacher seemed disappointed in her. It suddenly was all too much for her to master, and she put her head on her desk and cried, quietly, so that no one noticed her at all.*

In 1980 as we visit Viola Lenoir in her home across the road from St. Cyprian's, we imagine this scene as she tells us about her childhood. Having visitors excites her and she exclaims, "I'm a big woman," laughing at her own audacity. She is friendly, loving, and full of good will. This evening we'll meet her next door neighbor, Carrie Stewart, who has recently celebrated her one hundred-and-first birthday. On Saturday we will all go to the wild game dinner the church members are preparing to serve in the town center. And on Sunday, we look forward to morning prayer at St. Cyprian's with Mrs. Lenoir and Mrs. Stewart.

Viola Lenoir was born April 1, 1894, one of two children of Callie and Ben Addington. Her mother's mother lived in their home. Her name was Caroline Obey, and Mrs. Lenoir believes that her grandmother was "almost half-Indian," perhaps of the Blackhawk tribe. Viola loved her pretty long black hair and her "keen nose." She believes that her father's mother was "a thoroughbred African; she was brought over here and sold," but she only remembers having heard this in her home and denies having any further "learning" about her ancestors. "When it comes to books," she confesses in a shy voice, "I don't know nothing about them." All she knows about Africa she says she got through reading some lessons in a Bible class she took one summer at her church school, St. Augustine's in Raleigh. When we encourage her to try to find out more information about her family, she insists, "It makes no difference." But after a pause, she looks up again and says, "But it does, and I'd like to know."

Viola's mother, like her grandmother, was a midwife and went about the community tending the sick who needed her, black and white. Mrs. Addington often took her

daughter with her, and Viola grew up playing in white homes, leading her to conclude, "I know more about your people than I do my own. I went with my mother, and I didn't see any colored people. I just don't know my own color."

Next in importance after her family was her church, St. Cyprian's.

Episcopal church work among black people in Macon County and in Franklin was begun in the 1880s by a white minister, the Reverend J. A. Deal. At that time the only place for holding church services and school for blacks was the packing house of a tannery. Mr. Deal placed an ad in a church bulletin, citing the need for a black teacher and lay reader, and Mr. James Thomas Kennedy applied and was accepted. Mr. Kennedy, born in 1865 in South Carolina to slave parents, was confirmed in the Episcopal faith when he was eighteen years old and served two years as a postulant. When he came to Franklin around 1888 he was an ordained deacon, a teacher, and a carpenter, and later carved the baptismal font still in use at St. Cyprian's. The mission was built and a school begun, emphasizing manual training for boys and cooking and sewing for girls. Basic instruction in reading, writing, and arithmetic was instituted so that around the turn of the century students like Viola Addington and Carrie McDonnell were studying in the old blue-back spellers. Mr. Kennedy later continued his studies for the ministry, and after he was ordained as a priest, he left St. Cyprian's and was given charge of a church in Asheville. St. Cyprian's, which for most of its history served a black congregation, has in recent months been enlarged by the presence of white parishioners who followed their minister from another Episcopal church in the area. Mrs. Lenoir lives for the day when St. Cyprian's will be consecrated as a parish (it has in its history been called a mission) and she can "call the bishop's hand."

The church of St. Cyprian is to Viola Lenoir "one of the most lovable churches in this county." Her affection for it began in her childhood as she came to love even the benches she swept under as one of Mr. Kennedy's pupils; it is an affection which has continued for more than eighty years, and she does not miss a Sunday of worship.

A turning point in Viola's life came in 1907, when she left school at St. Cyprian's and moved into the Kelly home to begin her chores of entertaining the older Kellys and helping prepare food for the dining room. Viola was just the girl to keep the old folks happy. "I was a trick," she laughs. "I used to cut up something awful—it tickled those old folks to death!" As she became a part of the family, the older daughter, Elizabeth, whose work teaching illiterate adults was already known in the community, took Viola under her charge and began to teach her at home, giving her what Mrs. Lenoir now regards as "a good sixth grade education." (When Jonathan Daniels wrote *A Southerner Discovers the South*, he devoted a chapter to the work of Miss Elizabeth Kelly, praising her efforts to teach mountain people who had been isolated from educational opportunities.) Although this was the first time Viola had ever lived away from home, she soon adapted to the Kellys and does not remember that she ever felt homesick. "There wasn't no time for nobody to be homesick at the time Miss T [Elizabeth] got through telling you about the different books and what was in them, telling you about the

different people. It was just like being at home." (Later, Miss Lassie opened up further opportunities for Viola Addington. when she took her to register to vote.) In addition to teaching her reading, writing and arithmetic skills, Viola feels, Miss T "taught me some good sense." Her lessons were conducted at night, after she had completed her chores in the kitchen. Mrs. Lenoir's reputation today as "the best cook in Macon County" began in the home of the Kellys, where Miss Kelly first bought her a cook book. "You know how it is," Mrs. Lenoir explains. "You read the recipes, and then you get them by heart, and you don't need the book any more."

Soon Viola was making pies and cakes for the dining room, which the family ran in front of their house. In the mountains, where people were somewhat isolated from one another, this would have been an especially popular place. One can easily imagine the scene which Viola witnessed at noon each day: local matrons in their stiff hats and manners assembling with old friends on the comfortable porch; white voile curtains tied back at the windows; light winding its way among the small tables, and chairs comfortably crowded. Peeping out from the kitchen was a tall, handsome black girl who must have had to stifle her giggles at the sight of old ladies being fussed over and eating their delicate finger sandwiches, when she knew better how good bread and syrup had tasted in her lunch pail. Looking and listening, so that after the work was over on Sunday, she could rush home to her parents full of tales of the week. "You know that had to be told," she reflects. "You'd have to tell *that* to your parents!" And while "that" would include the good and the bad, a lifetime later Mrs. Lenoir will not say to us much of what the bad parts were. The good parts were the fancy dinners and the presents she received, especially at Christmas, and having her first bath in an indoor tub.

One of the bad things which Viola learned about in the Kelly home was slavery, her first knowledge of the subject. While their daughters were away during the day, the parents passed the time with Viola, and when she wasn't making them laugh, they were making her more aware of her history, about "how bad it was. I can't tell you in words," she says, "but it wasn't pretty." Mr. and Mrs. Kelly made clear to Viola that they were not proud of slave history, but she was confused when Miss Elizabeth came home and, hearing about the conversations that had been taking place, tried to "switch around" and "smooth up" the rough parts. There must have been some confusion in the Kelly family about their obligation to interpret history to this black child, but Mrs. Lenoir's lasting impression is some notion of guilt which white people felt and her own recognition that slavery had been an injustice to her people. This recognition causes her to say today, "I wasn't no slave and I ain't gonna be one."

After ten years in the Kelly home, Viola was now a young woman of twenty-three, and she married and had a child, Caroline, named for her father's mother. She was needed at home in the evenings to care for her own family, and she began doing daywork in other white homes. In addition to helping to raise white children, from time to time she took jobs cooking in local restaurants and at the Franklin Terrace and Scott Griffith hotels. As her own daughter was growing up, she began to feel that the child knew more than the mother. "A person would have to have a little more education than I have to teach a child," she explains. "My child taught me in place of me teaching her." During Caroline's earliest years, her parents' marriage began to falter, and her mother finally decided to separate from her father. When Caroline was six years old and entering the first grade, she became conscious that other children had a father, and she came home and said, "Mama, can you buy me a daddy?" When her mother saw her child's tears because "every little girl in that school has got a daddy but me," she "got to studying" and said to herself, "Well, I guess I'll have to get out here and hunt my young'un a daddy. So I looked around here in Franklin; I couldn't see nobody I thought was fit to put over. But I decided I'd go to Waynesville where my brother lived, and ask him some questions about the men out there, you know. I was really hunting her a daddy. But I didn't want no drunkard, I didn't want no liar. I didn't want one who'd chase after women. I wanted a clean man. Well, honey, in about two years I found a winner, a grass widow just like I was. And we fell for each other. And I lived with him for thirty-two years. He was a wonderful worker in that church. And my daughter thought the world and all of him. And he did her."

Caroline graduated from high school and married and today she and her husband live in High Point. Mr. and Mrs. Lenoir went to live in Greensboro for a few years when he was sick and wanted to be close to their daughter and six grandchildren. Then, when Mr. Lenoir died in 1964, Mrs. Lenoir moved back home to Franklin.

Mrs. Lenoir is a very practical woman.

When her child wanted a daddy, she went out to find one. When her first husband mortgaged their home, Mrs. Lenoir went down to the bank and borrowed the money to buy it back. In her later years when she still lived on the mountain and had to get down to church every Sunday, she decided to build a home across the road from St. Cyprian's and secured government funding to build it. And when she saw how long her father had been dead before anyone put up a stone for him, she took matters into her own hands and went ahead and had her own stone engraved and placed in the graveyard a few feet from St. Cyprian's. She feels better, just knowing it's there.

Since she retired from her last job when she was seventy-nine years old, Mrs. Lenoir has devoted her time to participating in activities for older people in Franklin and to going to church. Sometimes she stands up at vestry meetings and does some "good preaching," reminding the members that "we are God's people and we are supposed to love each other and work together and serve God." "This is 1980," she says. "I'm cussin' 'em out from now on till I die."

Mrs. Lenoir is not one to sit back and see her hopes and dreams for St. Cyprian's go unfulfilled. She reads the Psalms every night and prays. She prays for the sick, prays for brotherhood among the people of Franklin, prays for herself. And prays that it won't rain on Sunday and keep her from going to church.

Sunday morning wakes cold and clear. Already Mrs. Lenoir has on her coat and hat and takes out the key to open up the church. Inside, it is quiet and beautiful. She takes her seat near the front and turns to her Bible. From time to time she looks over her shoulder to see how large the congregation will be today. Everyone's seated now, the prayer benches have been turned back, and the priest stands at the front. His words strike deep in the heart of Viola Lenoir.

"I was glad when they said unto me, 'We will go into the house of the Lord.'"

# When the Sun Goes Down, You're Down in a Valley like This, and You Can Look Up to the Top and See the Sunrise

## Viola King Barnett

### Mars Hill

*The bus station is filled with the noisy impatience of others waiting in line. One who has been composed for a long time stands quietly, an older woman dressed in dark Sunday clothes. In front of her, two or three passengers grumble to one another. She keeps to herself, her hands folded below her waist. She has a large pocketbook over her arm; the weight of her body is also evenly carried, in a posture of simple self-reliance. When it is her turn, she moves forward and leans toward the ticket agent, dropping her head.*

*"When does the next bus go out to Mars Hill?" she asks.*

*He does not look up from his writing. "Eight o'clock," he says in a blank voice.*

*She looks perplexed, fumbles with her ticket. Then she leans forward again, just slightly.*

*"Not till eight o'clock?" she asks.*

*The agent throws back his head and puts his hand on his hip. "You asked what time the next bus went out to Mars Hill, and I said eight o'clock!" His voice is very loud.*

*She shrinks away, her whole body seeming to diminish. "Oh, excuse me," she whispers. "I didn't mean a bit of harm."*

*No eyes in the station see her, even as she stumbles toward an empty bench.*

This is the scene we envision as Viola King Barnett remembers her conversation in the Asheville bus station and the man's response; she pauses for a long time, as if listening again to the voice of the ticket agent. As if asking the question which has troubled her for so many years: what did I do wrong?

We are strangers, and we have come asking other questions, about her life, her family, her work. Because hers is the greater question, it is all the more profound because she actually does not ask it, but looks up at us in a shy, deferential way, much as she might have looked up at the ticket agent. She has repeated the conversation with a careful regard for fact, and in her voice we hear authentically the rude voice of the man and the apologetic voice of the woman. Her story lingers at the edge of our imagination long after we have left her house on Gabriels Creek and driven down the mountain.

"I was baptized in the middle of the Swannanoa River," she says. "I think I was twelve or thirteen years old [Mrs. Barnett was born in 1891]. And I don't know just how it happened. Now at the time, old folks was queer about things because I had to go back to the mourner's bench the second time. The deacons rejected *me*! When I joined the church and told my experience, the deacons said that they didn't know whether I knew what I was talking about, that I was just too young. Here's what the preacher says, 'Deacons, now you be careful. The Bible says to suffer little children to come unto me and forbid them not, for such is the kingdom of heaven.' Next night I went back to the church, and to tell you the truth, I got down and prayed. It just seemed like, you know, when a cloud come over you and it gets dark and you can see the top of a mountain? Or another way you might say, when the sun goes down, you're down in a valley like this, and you can look up to the top and see the sunrise. I seen the light and it made me feel surer that I was right when I seen that light. So I went back the next night and joined the church again. And the older I get the more I want to be perfect. I don't want nothing to ever come before me and my Lord when I come to the end of the journey, nothing to say, 'You haven't lived as you should.' At another time, why, you sing any kind of song you want to, you say anything you want to say, and you do meanness to people if you wanted to. I never felt like going on and living as I did before. And the older I get, the closer I try to live with the Lord."

Mrs. Barnett is well known in the mountain community of Mars Hill as the woman who made it possible for black children to continue in public school after finishing the seventh grade at the two-room Long Ridge Elementary School. Yes, she remembers it very well, how she "asked around" if there was any way buses could take the children from Mars Hill and other small villages into Asheville, twenty-five miles away, where they could advance through high school. Now she turns as if to lay her hands on the letters she received from the state school superintendent; failing, she falls back upon memory to recount the story. At first, she had no encouragement from her inquiries. Then, finally, a letter came which said that buses had been secured. "You have not only made it possible for your children to attend school," the letter said, "but for all the children." She repeats the superintendent's exact words, in the same careful way that she repeated the words of the ticket agent. Suddenly, she permits herself a celebration. "Oh, I was happy!" she exclaims. "I felt like shouting!"

To appreciate what Mrs. Barnett accomplished, one would have to know how important education was among blacks, how long rural black schools had received unequal treatment, and how isolated blacks were in the North Carolina hamlets like Mars Hill. Beyond these considerations, it is important also to realize that children who could not go to school after the seventh grade had virtually no means of improving themselves—no jobs, no leadership, and no encouragement. Their horizon was no further than Bailey Mountain, as they walked the empty miles home.

Mars Hill is a small village in western North Carolina, its remoteness only partially relieved by the presence of students and faculty at Mars Hill College and by the short distance to Asheville. There have never been large numbers of black families in the Carolina mountains. Census records show that four families lived in the Mars Hill area before the Civil War; in 1870 about three hundred of the approximately eight thousand residents of Madison County were blacks. Many of them had come to the area from Tennessee, South Carolina, and eastern North Carolina to work on the railroad, clearing the land and lifting crossties for the track. Today there are only twenty-five black families living in Mars Hill. Mars Hill College is a Baptist institution, established in 1856, and given the democratic structure of the church and the vocal presence of a handful of liberal ministers in the state, the denomination has been a moderating influence for social progress. Still, the college, like so many others, did not open its doors to blacks until the sixties, when the trustees admitted the first black student. (In the late 1850s, the trustees of Mars Hill College had wanted to erect a new building on the campus. In order to secure a bank loan for this purpose, one of the trustees offered as collateral a slave named Joe, turning him over to the Asheville jail. Ironically, the first black to attend Mars Hill College was the great-great-granddaughter of Joe, the slave.)

The college did, however, provide a source of help for Viola Barnett. Some of the faculty members who employed her to do their laundry also took an interest in her and her family. When she was troubled about her children's schooling, for example, she sought advice from some of her employers. They urged her to send several of her children away to boarding schools so that they could continue past the seventh grade, and they also helped to pay the tuition. In this way she was able to send her oldest child, David, to St. Augustine's in Raleigh and several of her children to Lincoln Academy in King's Mountain. When the last of her nine children, Herbert, finished at the local Long Ridge School, she began her efforts to secure transportation to Stevens-Lee High School in Asheville, one of the best known black high schools in North Carolina. Mrs. Barnett, who had only five years of school herself, had the satisfaction of seeing her children finish high school; she is particularly proud of the fact that she has a grandson who received his doctorate from the University of Michigan and is now on the faculty of the University of North Carolina at Asheville.

White friends at the college and in the community helped Viola Barnett in another way; they helped her build what she calls "my Santy Claus house," giving her money towards the costs and asking a local contractor to help her. One winter night as she was trying to keep warm in her old house, "the paper blowing off the wall," someone knocked at the door and Mrs. Barnett welcomed a neighbor, who said, "Here's ninety-seven dollars that I've collected to help you in repairing your house."

In turn, Viola Barnett is a good neighbor. She worked until 1978 for families in Mars Hill. Despite the fact that she was already eighty-seven years old, when the wife of one of her employers died and he himself became sick, she left her home and

went to keep house for him until he recovered. One of her employers, Miss Caroline Biggers, who was dean of women, remembers with particular gratitude that when she and her sister remained at the college during the holidays, Mrs. Barnett sent her son "on the cold, snowy Christmas morning to our dormitory with a lovely fried chicken and a hot biscuit breakfast."

Viola Barnett was born August 10, 1881, on the Vanderbilt Estate in Asheville, North Carolina, where her father was the butcher for George Vanderbilt and her mother was a cook. Now a tourist attraction as the largest and most elegant mansion in the state, the Vanderbilt home still grows in Mrs. Barnett's imagination. She recalls the enormous trees lighted with candles for Christmas; she watched the stone masons carve the magnificent porch. And when her father died while she and her two sisters and brother were young, Mr. Vanderbilt asked if her mother wanted to live on the estate or complete the house her husband had begun building, and when she chose the latter, he finished her house in Brevard.

Several years later, her mother remarried. In 1907 they moved to Madison County, where her stepfather was a farmer with ninety acres and also taught school in Long Ridge, Alta Pass, and Willow Creek. Although Viola was only thirteen years old, she did not attend school again but worked on the farm. She refuses to speculate about why her stepfather did not teach her himself, replying only that he helped her "not a bit." On the farm she hoed corn and bound wheat.

"As they cut the wheat," she explains, "and lay its heads all one way, you just go on and take you up one in your arm, as much as you thought it would take to make a sheaf. And then you take a strip out of it from the top part and wrap it round there and twist it good. That's what we call binding wheat." As Mrs. Barnett describes the process, she becomes animated, snaps her fingers, and gestures with her hands and arms. All the years of using her body in hard work seem to give her a confidence of expression which she otherwise lacks in formal conversation.

She worked on the farm for about four years, and then when she was seventeen she married Oliver Barnett. They bought a small piece of land on Gabriels Creek in 1921 and raised a family of nine children, seven of whom survive. Mr. Barnett continued working somebody else's land as a sharecropper, and when he died in 1934 he was making $1.50 a day. She remembers that her husband once went to a ball game on July 4th instead of hoeing the landlord's corn, and when his absence was discovered the landlord came to Mrs. Barnett demanding to know where her husband was. When he was told, he said that Mr. Barnett could not come back to work for him but "had to find another place." "That's just life," Mrs. Barnett reflects.

Mrs. Barnett's early life was filled with new babies, caring for children, and doing laundry. Her knowledge was earned through experience. She brews a cup of queen of the meadow tea (a kind of pikewood) which is "good for kidney or bladder trouble" and penny royal tea for flu and grippe "or whatever you call it. It used to be it was grippe. Now it's called flu. And I did have flu in 1918, and I recovered just from drinking these teas and using different liniments." She has had a garden most of her life, and she plants "by the signs. When I plant my garden, I like to plant the potatoes when the nights are

dark, when the moon is old. And I like to plant my beans when the sign is in the Twins, that's in the arms. You plant your potatoes when the sign is in the feet. Plant cabbage when the sign's in the head, when it's light."

Mrs. Barnett made a profession as a laundress from knowing how to mix and how to wash, skills she learned from her mother. "Using Octagon soap and washing like I did, lots of times I made flour starch, and I would strain the starch through a flour bag. Strain the starch through that, and then I had a laundry stove that had places for your iron. We had these flat irons. I guess you know what this is now. Irons that would hang on the stove. Didn't have electricity. And I used coal in the stove and that would heat the irons. And that way, I didn't black clothes.

"I had a scrubboard, a zinc scrubboard, and the big tubs, and a big iron washpot. I set it up on rocks or else hung it up with a wire across it. And we'd bring brush and stuff from the woods, and that would heat that water. We washed first with warm water and soap, and then we'd put the clothes in and boil them with soap or powder. After we boiled them as long as we thought necessary, take them out and have three tubs of water. Take them out of the pot, in this tub to rub them. And in this tub to rinse them, the first rinse, and then the third, we'd blue the water. I used a stick of bluing most of the time. I put it in a little rag and color my water. We call that bleaching on.

"I did a lot of washing and ironing for the Mars Hill teachers and I did a lot of dresses and things for the girls. I had to go to the college and get their clothes. I'd carry them back down this road. Some folks say now they used to see me walking down this road like I have so many bundles hanging around me, they say it looked just like clothes walking by themselves. I usually go in on Monday. I didn't wash hardly of a Monday. I just go in and gather up my washing. And sometimes I'd have to make three trips up there bringing clothes and three trips up there carrying clothes [about six miles in all]. They paid me twenty-five cents a dress. I imagine that was 1918."

Now the light darkens over the mountain and ripples in the shadows off Gabriels Creek. Across the slanted fields corn shucks blow in the wind. Along the road a truck loaded with logs groans up the mountain. It's 59 degrees and a 100 percent chance of rain. The clothes are off the line. Viola Barnett draws comfort from this place.

She has been talking about race relations, how things have changed for the bet-ter. It reminds her of the ticket agent in Asheville. "Now that man is still at the bus station," she explains. "You know how he treats me now? I wasn't used to these public telephones, and I wanted to call my daughter. I put in twenty cents, put in money twice, and it didn't register. So then I just asked if he would call West Asheville. "Yes!" he says. I asked him if I could call my daughter. "Is it long distance?" I said, "No, sir." "Why sure," the ticket agent agrees.

*The woman standing at the ticket window raises her head and looks into the face of the white man. "Thank you," she says in a strong voice. "Thank you." And then she says, to no one listening, "What a change there is in people. They have seen what the Lord required."*

# The Little Country Church

## Sophia Joyce East

### Pilot Mountain

The simple cross over the door of Shady Grove Methodist Church is lighted by the sun on a November morning. The old bell sits in the grass and is silent. The cross, the bell, and the steeple identify this place as a house of worship. And there is nothing so dear to its dozen or so members as this little country church in the woods.

Inside, our eyes go up to the tapestry at the front of the room. Its bright colors are a contrast to the small white pulpit and the white cloth hanging from it, to the white walls and the white benches, about twenty in number. The tapestry depicts the Last Supper, and the table filled with the disciples is a contrast to the empty pews. It is as if, because of them, the Lord's house is filled even when it appears to be empty. Although services are held in Shady Grove on alternate Sundays, a place of worship is provided every day. It is as sacred as the great cathedrals of the world, where Evensong is often sung to but a few worshippers.

The Reverend Sophia East has just finished her earlier service down the road at Cox's Chapel, one of four churches she serves in the Asheboro area, and she comes now to greet her visitors. Early this morning she had breakfast with one of her church members who keeps the key to Shady Grove, after her two-hour drive from her home in Pilot Mountain. At first, she recalls, her congregations and other Methodists doubted that preaching was a woman's proper role. Now they listen respectfully to her sermons and call upon her when there are weddings, illnesses, and funerals. The question of the ordination of women continues among America's theologians, but here at Shady Grove it has been answered.

After she became an elder in 1964 in the United Methodist Church, following many years of service as a lay leader in her home church in Pilot Mountain and in district conferences, Sophia East moved from a temporary assignment to the four churches for which she is now pastor: Shady Grove, Cox's Chapel, McClary's Chapel, and Mitchell's Chapel. One of two black women ordained in the Western North Carolina Conference, she is to be found in the backwoods, down narrow country roads. Perhaps these roads, these fields and backwoods, are the true Bible Belt of the South.

As the morning service begins, Mrs. East has chosen I Corinthians 13 for her text:

*Though I speak with the tongues of men and of angels, and have not charity, I am become as sounding brass, or a tinkling cymbal.*

*And though I have the gift of prophecy, and understand all mysteries, and all knowledge; and though I have all faith, so that I could remove mountains, and have not charity, I am nothing.*

The service continues, and at a time the worshippers know by heart, it turns to song. Although there are no more than a dozen members present today, including a baby girl just learning to walk and to talk, the singing is strong and harmonious.

*On Christ the solid rock I stand.*
*All other ground is sinking sand.*
*All other ground is sinking sand.*
*My hope is built on nothing less*
*Than Jesus' blood and righteousness.*

There is a measured and restrained dignity in the manner of Sophia East. There is no pounding of the pulpit; no one shouts from the Amen corner. She is quiet and formal and radiates a peace at one with the autumn woods seen through the plain glass windows.

The Reverend Sophia East was born in 1906 near the place where she now has her home, a few blocks from the main street of Pilot Mountain, population not much more than one thousand. She was the middle of eleven children born to Elizabeth Kellum and James Joyce.

"My parents were married the fourth day of April in 1895," Mrs. East begins. "My daddy died in '46. He was eighty-four years old. Mama was ninety-four when she died. I think it was and is nice to live to a ripe old age. She worked until she was ninety-two in people's houses. Up until my baby sister was born (I'm ten years older than she is), Mama took in washing and ironing because she wanted to be at home with her children, and that was the only way she had of helping my daddy raise eleven children. I've known her to begin on Monday morning and wash if the weather was pretty, hang those clothes up and they'd dry, and she'd iron them at night. And she'd do that until about Friday, and she'd spend Friday afternoon patching the clothes we'd torn up or making somebody a new piece. As long as I can remember, she did that till her baby child finished high school, and that was my sister, Ruth [born in 1916]. They saw that we all got an elementary school education. I went to Salisbury and lived with my older sister and finished the tenth grade. My daddy taught school until his children came so fast he couldn't make enough money at it so he quit teaching and went to doing carpentry work. At that time they would allow a person to teach elementary school if they had finished the old blue-back speller. He just

took up carpentry. He built the first house that they owned, and I was the first child born in that house. My mother had a sister who left Pinnacle [near Pilot Mountain] with some white people she was working for, and went to Columbus, Ohio. She took a course in sewing and she worked in this home until she learned to do that, and then she got out to herself and began to sew for people, and she loaned my mama and daddy the money to buy the first lot they owned. My coming up wasn't easy for my parents. As I grew up, I wanted pretty clothes like other folks had, but I had maybe one or two nice dresses, but I didn't have them like some of the other children did in families that weren't as big as ours. That made a difference. When there's a family of eleven children and a baby coming about every two years, it makes a difference. I look back on it now and wonder how my mama and daddy did it, but they did. And we didn't suffer for the things that we needed, but there was just a lot of things that we didn't get. I loved a large family. Didn't a one of us leave home until the youngest was born. We were just a happy family; we loved each other. I followed my brothers around—I had four brothers. The older one—whatever he did, I did. If he climbed a tree, I climbed a tree. He loved me so good till he had a big old black dog, I can remember that so well. He sat down one day and made a wagon, and he hitched that dog to the wagon, and I would ride. We didn't know to ask for a whole lot. We made out with whatever we could get. We had a nice big yard to play in. The house was on an acre of ground. I can remember that we always had a cow and a nice big garden, and after my daddy taught school, it was along about the time that coal mining was becoming popular in

West Virginia, and they didn't have homes for people that wanted to go out there to work. My daddy would leave home in March and go to West Virginia and work out there building houses, helping to build houses, and he'd come home in November. And that's the way we got along.

"And I'll never forget my mother was washing this white woman's diapers. She would go and wash the family washing and then she would wash the baby diapers three times a week. And I'd go get those diapers and bring them home, she'd wash them, and when they were ready, I'd carry them back. And I'll never forget, this lady had an awful turn of diapers that time. And Mama charged her fifty cents, and she sent Mama, I think it was, thirty-five cents. And I come home and I hand Mama that thirty-five cents, and Mama said, 'You take this thirty-five cents.' And when I'd go and carry one bunch I'd bring back another—'You take this thirty-five cents back over there and these diapers and tell her there's her thirty-five cents and her baby's shit.' And I didn't have no better sense than to go over there and tell that woman that! That's a fact! I dropped them down in the back porch and told the woman what my mama said, and walked out. She didn't say nothing. Whatever she said, she said it after I left there cause she didn't say anything to me. She didn't wash for her again. That was it. No, the woman never came to our house. That was below their dignity to go to a black person's house.

"Children would fight on the street, white and black children would fight in the streets, if they met, and say ugly things to each other, but I don't know if they went back and told their parents or not. We never went back and told our parents cause we felt like if we told it we would get a spanking. The white children had this idea if you didn't do to suit them, you was called a 'nigger.' And of course black children didn't want to be called that, but we would fight back by calling them poor trash. After I got about twelve years old, I couldn't understand why—even if we had to have a one-room school—why that school building couldn't have been like the white children's building. Because my daddy paid taxes, he didn't have a lot to pay taxes on, but what he had, he paid taxes. And the school was furnished by the state, and I couldn't understand why we couldn't have the same privileges that they had when it come to schooling. We didn't have a high school in Surry County for black children till my oldest daughter finished the seventh grade, about 1938. I had four of my own children, and I raised a daughter of my sister that died and left the child, the child lacked six days of being a year old when the mother died, and I raised her along with mine. They all finished high school. And my baby daughter got a college degree from Morgan in Baltimore, my older daughter got a college degree from North Carolina A&T, and the next daughter got a college degree from Bennett.

"My mother never had time to learn to read and write. She felt all right with my children because they respected my mother. I often said, my mother was an illiterate woman, but she had good old horse sense. And she knew what was right and wrong, and she taught us that. She taught us that you don't steal and you don't lie. And why I said she did it is because she was with us more than my papa was, and she loved everyone of them. They called her Granny Lizzie, and I called her Mama. She was respected by most of the white people in this town. She never did much grumbling about what was going on. To me, Mama just wanted to be a lady. If you treated her nice, okay; if you didn't, she didn't let it stop her from trying to be a lady. And she never did much grumbling and complaining. I've seen her hurt by things people would do to us. When people snarled at us or said something maybe about . . . maybe some white person meet us and call us a little nigger or something like that. That hurt. There was this barrier [between the races] when I was growing up. But now the relationship between black and white is a whole lot better. But there was this barrier. You're a little black child, you stay in your place. And your place is to work and respect me, whether I respect you or not. [Race relations] are better in a lot of ways, and I think the integration of the schools brought it about. And of course, I think white people are beginning to realize that Negroes are human people. You know, there are just so many white people that looked on the Negroes as just a slave, and that's all. You work, and you eat what you could get, you wore what you could get. But be there to do my work, regardless of what kind of work it was. But now we grew up with this feeling of independence. We were poor, but we were taught to be independent, and not go begging. I know a white lady. I went and did some washing for her. And her tubs were in the basement, the basement was left open, the cow went in and out of the basement when she wanted to and did whatever she wanted in the basement. And when time come to eat lunch, she brought me a plate down in the basement and set it on the steps, for my lunch. I hung up the last piece and left the lunch sitting there, and

left, and she didn't know when I left, and I've never gotten paid for that washing yet!"

Like her mother, Mrs. East is a woman who does not harbor bitterness toward her adversaries, and the vocation she sought for herself in the church was one which has provided the healing power of love. From her earliest childhood, she was a faithful church-goer, for many years in Lovell's Chapel near her home, where as a young woman she helped to organize a Sunday School and where she became chairman of the Board of Trustees. From these activities in her home church, she began to take a prominent role in the broader activities of the United Methodist Church, serving in the district on the Board of Education and as an officer in the Women's Society of Church Service. In 1959 when she was fifty-three years old, she began taking courses at Bennett College in the summer, leading to her ordination as an elder.

The Reverend Sophia East has found her ministry among small groups of worshippers. She has not sought to build larger churches. What gifts have come from her members are in the form of dollar bills placed in the offering plate on Sunday morning. When a church member's employer in Asheboro gave fifteen thousand dollars toward the twenty thousand dollar cost of building a new church at Shady Grove, dedicated in 1980, Mrs. East was also pleased that her own members paid off the remaining debt within four years. She believes that "the church is becoming too much conformed with the world. We're beginning to think," she explains, "that there are things we have to put in the church in order to keep people. That's not it. Christianity should come from the heart. And I find that in reading James and Peter, they are talking to the church and reminding them of the things that the church ought to be doing and how we ought to live in order that we might bring somebody to Christ through a Christian life. Not because we put disco in the basement of the church. I don't believe in it. I don't think I ought to have to do anything toward coaxing anybody to become a Christian. You don't coax people. You live the life in their presence. You love them. And our job is serving each other."

Sophia East's daily ministry continues through the week in Pilot Mountain where she directs a meals program for senior citizens. As an older American herself (she is seventy-six), Mrs. East understands the needs of her contemporaries, and as one of God's disciples in 1982, it is fitting that her work is to meet both the physical and the spiritual needs of her people.

Sunday morning service at Shady Grove Methodist Church is almost over, and Sophia East concludes her sermon. 'There is joy and peace in knowing you have done what God wanted you to do.' Over the delicate church steeple, the sun has climbed higher in the heaven.

# The World Can't Take It Away

## Betty Hill Lyons

### Lewisville

To be very old is to remember some things like riding a steer down a country road and cooking parched corn and dancing the rang tang, and forgetting the year of your birth. Betty Hill Lyons is one hundred and four years old, an age documented by the United States Census. A census-taker going to the home of Millie and William Hill in Davie County, North Carolina, in late summer of 1880 wrote the following:

*Hill, William black male 25 factory hand cannot read cannot write*
*Hill, Millie black female 24 wife keeping house cannot read cannot write*
*Hill, Fanny black female 3 daughter*
*Hill, Betty black female 2 daughter*
*Hill, Bob black male 1 son*

A decade later the record notes the births of seven more children, but the facts of their lives are essentially unchanged.

One can imagine the scene which might have taken place as the government man came up the slanting steps of the small cabin on an August morning. Millie Hill holds her youngest child in her lap and drops her eyes. William Hill gets up from his chair and leans against the doorframe, watching. Out in the sand yard Betty and her sister look fearfully toward their mother, trapped by the distance between them and the presence of the white stranger. Does Mr. Hill hesitate in his answers? The census-taker is anxious to get on down the road. In minutes the information is completed, and as the stranger leaves the girls race to their mother's side. She holds them in her lap and rubs their heads, over and over. Mr. Hill goes inside the dark house.

Today visitors to the home of Betty Hill Lyons might go back in their imaginations to this earlier morning and compare the record. Mrs. Lyons lives in a rural North Carolina community, in Lewisville, just off the Interstate and twelve miles from a city, Winston-Salem. Her house is small and unpainted and needs repair. In front, an old bucket sits on the well. In back, a privy leans to fall down. Rutted dirt roads wind around patches of dying fields. Here is the record: Lyons, Betty Hill black female 104 widow living alone cannot read cannot write. So much time has passed. So little has changed.

Mrs. Lyons sings church hymns much of the day. Her voice is strong and insistent and heavy with memory. "Walking the light," she sings. "Beautiful light. Somewhere the dewdrops of mercy shine bright." Interrupted by the knocking, she looks up, quizzical, and rises slowly to her feet. She greets her visitors with a loud burst of shouts. Later, by the fire, she talks, and her mind goes back to Davie County, nor far from where she now lives.

"My daddy was working on somebody else's land. He didn't own nothing cause way back in them times there wasn't many colored people that owned any property at all. You just rent the land, then you had to pay. You had to give so much out of what you made, of your crop, to the man you got the land from. You got so much for your work, and he got so much for his land. My parents was hard working people. My mother loved to quilt good. That was her biggest job, quilting. There ain't none of that going on now. She cooked everything. I've been thinking about that a whole lot now, how she used to cook a batch of good stuff. Sometimes I dream about my mama. And of course my daddy was a hard worker. Cause plenty of times way back yonder he'd get up and go to the woods and cut cord wood, and some mornings after it done got cold and he done sweat, frost done got on his hair, out there in those woods. And there ain't nothing easy about farming, is it? You out there baking yourself to death in that hot sun. No, ain't nothing easy about that. You had to work from sun-up to sun-down. I worked in the fields, and I worked in the factory. We lived about a mile and a half I guess to Farmington, and I'd be down there every morning sun-up and work till sun-down and walk back home. These young folks don't know any bout walking now. You'd get out on the road that morning going to work and say, 'Ooh, Lord, I got to make all that time!' I stemmed tobacco. First picking tobacco, that's classing it out, putting the different grades separate from the other. Well, then the stemming. I was stemming, and a man standing over here made the plugs. That was a little old factory over in Davie County. And then from there back to the farm again, binding wheat and pulling fodder and shucking corn, all like that. And then from there to the kitchen, cooking, washing, and ironing, doing everything come to hand for a dollar a week. Wasn't that something! And honey, I was working, too! Dollar a week! I just thought about that the other day, all these cold days I'd have to hang them clothes out there, and they'd be stiff time I got them on the line. Till it seemed like it went against me, and I just told the people I couldn't wash no more.

"I always had the name of a good cook. Cooking turkeys, beans, rice, chicken, peas. Come off of the farm for a cook. That's how come I'm over here, come to cook for ———. They'd put on big to-dos over there at his place. Have these people come out from town. He worked a lot of

hands. Sometimes they had their school down there at they home and I'd have the teachers to cook for and beside work hands. He was a overbearing person. He liked to take advantage of people. And when I first went there, I acted like I didn't know how to make a cake. I'd have to wait on her, get all the stuff ready and hand her to get ready to bake. So after a while she turned it over to me. So Mr. ——— said I could beat her baking cakes. I made some good, nice cakes. And I made them good old pot of dumplings. Yeah, and them good turnips, cabbage, and ain't none of that good to me now! That's the truth. All my taste done left me. I'm trying to quit snuff. I just don't like it no more. So many church people think it's a sin. But it don't taste good to me since I got older. I used to take a tooth brush and rub it all in the mouth, but now I just put it in there since I ain't got no teeth. A good old tooth brush and lay it back up in your jaw and it tasted good.

"I think my mother lived to be eighty. She come to live in Winston with my brother, Henderson. I don't remember about my daddy, how old he was. He died pretty early. I reckon my mama was born in Davie County. My father was born, I think, up there bout Mt. Airy, where he come from. I know my mama was bred and born in Davie County cause her master was. See, her mama, they was slavery. My mama was, I think she said, twelve years old when they freed the colored people. Cause she said when the yankees come around to free them, she had one up in her arms. They were rough, you know, told her to put that Rebel down, she was free now. She belonged to the Bohannons of Davie County.

"I went a few days to school. I didn't

like it. They had it just in some old house, four or five miles to walk, you see. That's the reason I ain't got no learning. Too far for two young 'uns to go by theyselves through the woods, is the reason I ain't got none. Well, later on they got having it closer in an old house. There wasn't no school house for colored people at that time. I went a little bit but then because they didn't make me go, I didn't. I hated that I didn't get to go to school cause them last children that come along, they all got to go to school. When they was having school down here [adult education] I made them laugh one night. I was tired of spelling rat and cat. I wanted something else. Yes, sir! They left me a little book to study, and I got so I could print my name good fashion, but it done left me now, I wish I did know how to read and write. It'd be so much company to me if I could set down and read the Bible."

As Betty Lyons pauses in her narrative, one can almost hear the door close on a log schoolhouse in a rural county nearly one hundred years ago.

Davie County was a region of small farms in Piedmont North Carolina. In 1880, the landscape was dotted with the tin roofs of sheds and unpainted shacks, and now and then there was a manor house with chimneys at either end. Today, some of these chimneys still stand, the houses fallen into a thicket of kudzu vines and blackberry bushes. There were small villages like Pudding Ridge, Yadkinville, Smiths Grove, and Cooleemee, where the old plantation house of the Hairston family is now a show place. In 1870 Davie County had five tobacco factories, employing 105 workers; one of them, for a time, was Betty Lyons' father, William Hill.

A historian writing in 1892 described the village of Mocksville, where Mr. Hill walked to work, as slumbering away, "undisturbed by the noise, the hurry, the restlessness, and the trouble and temptation of the outside world." This reverie of the historian does not take into account the restlessness and trouble in the minds of other Davie residents like William and Millie Hill and their family of ten children. While the village fathers, unknowingly perhaps, moved in business toward the coming industrial revolution, the Hill family lived to themselves, worked a garden each season, suffered the death of a child far from the help of any doctor, and drew together in the chill of an evening as Mrs. Hill served soup bowls from the black pot hanging over the fire.

And William Hill perhaps asked no questions when his daughter Betty, herself hardly more than a child, gave birth to a son, which he and Millie would raise. Life was crowding out the needs of each one as he or she struggled for a place in the small home, and Betty was inevitably drawn down the same dirt road to the field and the factory. At the age of twenty, with the bloom of her young womanhood no more visible to the world than the tassels of corn in the field, Betty married early, and early Joe Hauser died. Now she no longer can remember the exact years of her life; with Mr. Hauser's death, she married Albert Lyons, and they worked together on a farm in the next county. All those years, eighty, ninety, one hundred, have passed like light from the morning, and today, she lives alone, a survivor.

Betty Hill Lyons understands that it makes others feel good that she has lived so long. Her own family includes the widow of her only child, six grandchildren, seventeen great-grandchildren, and three great-

great-grandchildren. The community of Lewisville in recent years has celebrated her birthdays with a program at church, and congratulatory letters are read from the President of the United States and from her United States Congressman. She has sung for programs of senior citizens, had her picture in the newspaper, and has been interviewed on a local television show. On these occasions, she dresses up in a wig, her good black dress, her fur piece, and gloves, and she has the energy to sing as loud and as long as the audience will listen. Recently, she was recognized as the oldest senior citizen at the annual Dixie Classic Fair.

But most of her days and nights are spent alone at home, where she sits and sings, and waits for a visit from a neighbor or a grandchild. She sits out on the small porch; a cat sleeps nearby in a circle of sunlight. A white man working on the road comes by to greet her, presses a $10 bill in her hand. The insurance collector comes with his book to write down another payment. By mid-morning, she walks slowly to the end of the road and to her mail box to see if the government check has come. Back home, she turns in her conversation to the past again.

Like a good story teller, she senses the conclusion to her narrative. "I sing here to myself. I tell you, if you live your life right, there's something good come on your mind all the time. Just from one good thing to another, just here by myself. The Lord has looked after me and blessed me, and I am thanking Him for it every day.

*This love I have*
*The world didn't give it to me.*
*This love I have*
*The world didn't give it to me.*
*This love I have*
*The world didn't give it*
*And the world can't take it away.*

Visitors leave, night settles, and she is again alone. Betty Hill Lyons arouses from her dreams. She leans forward and squints into the darkness. She says to herself, "I believe my fire has gone out." She rises to bend over the small stove. Removing the top, she pokes at the coals; there is renewed light and warmth. As she prepares for bed, the house is very quiet, and the fire glows.

# Ten Thousand Times Ten Thousand

Books must come to an end, but stories go on being told. The narratives and images of older black women of the South fill the landscape: "Ten thousand times ten thousand in sparkling raiment bright." The women included in *Hope and Dignity* are a representative small number of all of these. We have been able to develop fully only their stories, but we would like to pay tribute to others who have shared their homes and lives with us in many warm mornings of hospitality and conversation. Their brief biographies belong to an American epic which older black women of the South continue to write with their daily lives.

**Theresa Smith Bland**. Goldsboro, North Carolina. Mrs. Bland was born in 1907 in the small village of Genoa, North Carolina, not far from where she now lives. She was the oldest of ten children, and the responsibility for directing the lives of members of her family often fell upon her. Again and again she had the strength and discipline to take charge, even after the early deaths of two of her younger sisters. Perhaps, she speculates, it was her Indian ancestry which gave her a kind of "tribal feeling," loyally drawing the family closer together. She persuaded her father to send her to Shaw University, and when she was seventeen years old she married Charles Irwin Bland. She and Mr. Bland were students together at Shaw, and they began their marriage teaching in a country school. They continued working together (in summers in the naval shipyard in New London, Connecticut) and earned master's degrees at the University of Connecticut. At home in North Carolina they shared forty-five years teaching in the public schools. Each of their four daughters was graduated from college (one, like her father, is a school principal), two earned master's degrees, and one is working toward her doctorate. One of their granddaughters was graduated from the University of Pittsburgh Medical School. Next to education, Theresa Bland's specialty is blueberry pie.

**Katie Bunn**. Rocky Mount, North Carolina. Born in 1891 in Rocky Mount, one of ten children, Miss Bunn worked her way to attend Albion Academy, a Presbyterian school in Franklinton, North Carolina, led by Dr. J. A. Savage. She was graduated in 1913 and began teaching in a two-room school where she had one hundred children in the first grade (she taught fifty in the morning, fifty in the afternoon). While continuing to teach, she completed work for her Bachelor of Arts degree.

She did not marry but raised the daughter of her sister after her sister's death, naming her for one of her Albion teachers, a black woman who had come down from Springfield, Massachusetts, to work in the Academy. Almost twenty years after her own struggles to earn an education, she proudly sent her adopted daughter to Palmer Memorial Institute, one of the finest private institutions for black students in the South. After Miss Bunn retired from teaching, she continued to be active in her church and in the local YWCA. "One thing I'll tell you is this," Miss Bunn says. "Negroes have stuck to God, and sticking to God, they love everybody."

**Addie Bradley Byrd**. Rocky Mount, North Carolina. Mrs. Byrd was born in 1897 in Tarboro, North Carolina. Her father was a rural mail carrier and drove a horse and buggy. She was married when she was twenty-three to James Edgar Byrd, a railroad man, later a soldier in Europe during World War I. (His hero was General John Pershing, and when he came home from the battlefield, he often told his wife of General Pershing's leadership among the foot soldiers.) Mrs. Byrd was active in the Eastern Star for most of her life and became Grand District Deputy. She particularly enjoyed arranging programs which featured distinguished visitors, and she remembers the honor she felt in introducing guests from African countries and in presenting

Mary McLeod Bethune. Addie Byrd lives alone now (her husband died in 1974) in downtown Rocky Mount in a house which is more than a century old.

**Gladys Carter Campt**. Madison, North Carolina. Mrs. Campt was born in 1903 in Greensboro, North Carolina, like Mrs. Bland and Miss Bunn one of ten children. Her father was a cook on the Norfolk and Western Railroad and often prepared his specialty—Brunswick stew—at home. After her graduation from Palmer Memorial Institute, she married a Methodist minister, and they had six children. When her husband died, Mrs. Campt had four children still in elementary school. "But we worked together, and we made it," she remembers. Five of the six children graduated from college. For a number of years Mrs. Campt was a housekeeper for a wealthy woman in Madison, and although she expresses admiration and affection for her and for other wealthy families she has known, her familiarity with their lives has led her to conclude, "Rich people are the miserablest people on earth." Mrs. Campt continues to be active in church work and attends weekly lunches for senior citizens.

member of the Wilmington 10 and served a prison term, but his conviction was overturned in 1981 by a Federal Court of Appeals. "I lived," Mrs. Chavis says, "for the complete vindication of these children. God has turned our night into day." During the years of the trial and the appeals, Mrs. Chavis spent most of her energies traveling and speaking in behalf of the Wilmington 10. Now she does not awake in the night wondering whether she hears the sounds of demonstrators outside her house. She has earned her peace.

**Elisabeth Ridley Chavis**. Oxford, North Carolina. Mrs. Chavis was born in 1913 in Oxford, near the Virginia line. One of ten children, she belongs to a family whose ties in the county go back to the nineteenth century. She married Ben Chavis, the great-nephew of John Chavis, a noted Presbyterian minister and Raleigh, North Carolina, schoolmaster (1763–1838). After graduation from Fayetteville State Normal School (and later North Carolina Central University) she began a teaching career which continued for more than thirty years. Early in their married lives she and her husband worked at the Morrison Training School for Boys in the sandhills of North Carolina. There they helped to change the lives of delinquent boys, one of whom she remembers was chased to the gates of the school under a hail of bullets from law enforcement officers. (The young man grew up at Morrison and later became a successful businessman in New York City.) Mr. and Mrs. Chavis had four children of their own and took into their home three others, all of whom received advanced university degrees. One of her own children, Ben, an ordained minister, was a

**Hallie Brown Cundiff**. Boonville, North Carolina. Mrs. Cundiff was born in 1906 in Wilkesboro, North Carolina, one of six children. Hers was a home which gave shelter to a white girl without a family, and her early interracial experiences created understandings which later made possible a close friendship with Dot Snow, a white co-worker in community projects. (Mrs. Snow herself had grown up in a home which included a black girl, also in search of a family. Mrs. Cundiff and Mrs. Snow have experienced a unique and significant chapter in southern living.) After a few years of teaching and more years of cooking in a cafe, Mrs. Cundiff turned her energies to community service, beginning as a worker in Head Start in her hometown of Boonville. Through her gift of volunteer as well as paid hours, she has helped enrich the lives of poor families, black and white, and in recent years, she has worked imaginatively with the elderly. She and Dot Snow have organized clubs for senior citizens in a four-county region of the North Carolina Yadkin Valley, and now she is Site Manager for the meals program in nearby Elkin. "Older people feel that just because they're old they're out of the world," Mrs. Cundiff explains. It has been her mission to bring pleasures and comforts, as well as necessities, to them. One reason she believes that she has a special understanding of their needs is that she, too, is a senior citizen.

**Lela Bostick Goffney**. Rocky Mount, North Carolina. Mrs. Goffney was born in 1910 in Florence County, South Carolina, the third of fourteen children. As a child she worked in the field with her father and left school after the third grade. When she was fourteen she slipped off from church to be married. When her father told her not to come back, she was on her own to make a new life with her husband. The marriage failed, and she was alone to raise four of her own children and to care for two others. Each of the children was later graduated from college, receiving more than five times the formal education their mother had. To support them, she worked as a cook in a cafe and as a stemmer in a tobacco factory.

When Mrs. Goffney was twelve she heard a voice saying, "Blessed is he that dieth in the Lord for his good works will follow him." She interpreted the message to mean that she should be a minister, and when she was twenty she began preaching in the Holiness Church. Today she travels and preaches for the Tabernacle of All People. She has weathered poverty, hard work, and serious illnesses, but her philosophy continues to be "I'm not down. I'm up."

**Lucy Saunders Herring**. Asheville, North Carolina. Mrs. Herring was born in 1900 in Union, South Carolina, the ninth of twelve children. She began teaching in a Rosenwald School when she was sixteen. "As the Rosenwald schools were built throughout the South," Mrs. Herring remembers, "they were brought from the backwoods up to the main roads, and they were all painted white and were very nice buildings. Hundreds of them spotted the South about that time." In 1925 she was selected by the North Carolina Department of Public Instruction to be a Jeanes supervisor down east in Harnett County. Her first assignment was to meet with the powerful school committeemen, a group of ninety black community leaders who were used to having their way. Despite her youth, she was successful in persuading the committee of her sincere interest in bettering educational opportunities for children, and she began to work immediately, trying to secure the best teachers and retraining those she found inadequate. She walked the country roads from one school to the next and often held night meetings to keep parents informed about the progress of their children. After ten years in Harnett County she went to Asheville and became principal of the Mountain Street School (later named the Lucy S. Herring School). After fifty years in public education, she retired. She then began a collection of archival materials on "Black Highlanders" for the University of North Carolina at Asheville. For a number of years she has been writing her autobiography, *Strangers No More.*

**Mae D. Holmes**. Clinton, North Carolina. Miss Holmes was born in 1906 in Clinton. She was graduated from Shaw University and began her career in social work in New Jersey's Department of Institutions and Agencies. In 1944 she undertook the difficult task of opening the first school in North Carolina for black girls assigned by the courts. For twenty-eight years she served as Director of the Dobbs School for Girls in Kinston, transforming abandoned buildings into a gracious campus with cottages and a chapel. (The school had begun in Rocky Mount in an old facility which had housed the National Youth Administration—"a terrible site," she remembers. "We went there. We had nothing. Whatever was left over anywhere, we got. I worked like a Trojan all month, scrubbing and cleaning. And I knew it was going to be rough." But she put the buildings in order as best she could, and she set about hiring a qualified staff, a standard she insisted upon throughout her tenure.) Even after girls left the Dobbs School, Miss Holmes continued to assist them. When a call for help came, "if I didn't have any funds, I'd just pinch off a little bit of my salary and send it."

Miss Holmes often hears from alumnae of the School, and she sometimes receives photographs of their children. During her active years she worked, and served as an officer, in state and national organizations for juvenile training. Now in retirement she has returned home to Clinton and to the memories of another home and many children.

**Geneva Collins Hunt**. Greensboro, North Carolina. Mrs. Hunt was born in 1907 in Asheville, North Carolina. There she came to know a prominent white family in which there was a daughter who became a doctor. Perhaps this early example planted in her an ambition to serve others, and in 1929 she was graduated from St. Agnes Hospital Training School for Nurses in Raleigh. Later she received a Rosenwald scholarship to study hospital administration at Johns Hopkins Hospital. From 1935 to 1948 she served as Superintendent of Hospital and Nurses at the L. Richardson Memorial Hospital in Greensboro. The following year she became a First Lieutenant in the Army Nurses Corps at Walter Reed Hospital; other assignments in supervisory nursing took her to Norfolk, Philadelphia, and Welfare Island, New York.

In 1941 she married a Lutheran minister; her husband died in 1967. Mrs. Hunt has continued to make her home in Greensboro.

**Clara Beckham Lawrence**. Winston-Salem, North Carolina. Mrs. Lawrence was born in 1910 in Chester County, South Carolina, in a home without a father. This experience drew her more closely to her mother, and a bond was established which continued over a lifetime; her mother was still sharing her daughter's home in Winston-Salem when she died in her nineties. One of the attitudes instilled in Clara by her mother was that of pride: "I've always felt," she says, "that I was on equal status with anybody, regardless of color." After finishing high school, she completed nurses' training in Columbia, South Carolina, and took a course in practical nursing at Harlem Hospital in New York City. She went on to complete the B.S. degree at Johnson C. Smith University in Charlotte and the M.S.P.A. degree at North Carolina Central University in Durham. Her experiences have included serving as Supervisor of Nurses at Knoxville (Tennessee) General Hospital; public health nursing at the Charlotte Health Department and Mecklenburg County Health Department; and being Chief Nurse at the V.A. Hospital outpatient clinic in Baltimore, Maryland. For seventeen years until her retirement in 1974 she was on the nursing faculty at Winston-Salem State University.

**Mollie Huston Lee**. Durham, North Carolina. Mrs. Lee was born in 1907 in Columbus, Ohio, an only child. Her mother was from Kentucky, her father from Columbus. Her father was a businessman and a politician—as she remembered him, always campaigning for office. He was never elected to the state legislature, but he was a delegate to the Republican convention. Mrs. Lee recalled that during his campaign it was her responsibility to stand on the street corner and gather a crowd around her father so that he could speak. After being graduated from high school in 1925, she studied at Howard University and became the first black student to receive a scholarship to the School of Library Services at Columbia University. In 1935 she opened a storefront library in Raleigh, North

Carolina, providing to black patrons in the capital city their first opportunity to borrow books. Mrs. Lee's excellent training, her imagination, and her energy were directed toward increasing these library services for blacks. Today the library she began in Raleigh, named the Richard B. Harrison Library, occupies a handsome modern building and contains a significant collection of black literature that Mrs. Lee established. She also planned a public lecture series and, through her personal contacts with leading black authors, invited to Raleigh some of the most outstanding figures in American literature, among them William E. B. Du Bois, Langston Hughes, Arna Bontemps, Zora Neale Hurston, and John Hope Franklin. Her personal papers contain a valuable collection of letters from these and other writers.

Mrs. Lee also established the black library association in North Carolina and traveled throughout the state to develop other libraries. She was a member of the American Library Association Council and was recognized nationally for her work in North Carolina. In the history of public libraries in the South, her name is indelibly written. She died in Durham in 1982.

**Estelle Hoskins Liston**. Charlotte, North Carolina. Mrs. Liston has what seems to be an impeccable memory for personal history and an orderly recall of time and place. "I was born in 1892 in Camden, South Carolina," she begins.

"My father was a shoemaker who had been a slave until he was in his late teens. He served as a page to General Kennedy in the Civil War. My mother was a bit younger than my father because he was twice married and had lived with his first wife for nine years, then married my mother when she was quite young. There were seven children in the family, and I'm the youngest. We were six girls and one boy." Mrs. Liston attended school at Scotia Seminary in Concord, North Carolina, the alma mater of Mary McLeod Bethune, and at Scotia, she remembers, "There were some of the most sainted white teachers from the North who came down and taught there." After graduation, and after teaching several years, she married Hardy Liston; they had seven children. In 1943 the family moved to Charlotte, where Mr. Liston became president of Johnson C. Smith University. It was a homecoming for Mrs. Liston, who had grown up in Charlotte after her earlier years in South Carolina.

After her husband's death, Mrs. Liston continued to maintain her home near the Johnson C. Smith campus. In recent years, almost totally blind, she has spent much of the time with one of her daughters in Chicago. Now that she no longer can read, she falls back upon memory. One of her favorite passages from the literature she knows and loves is from Longfellow's *Hyperion*: "Look not mournfully into the PAST. It comes not back again. Wisely improve the PRESent. It is thine. Go forth to meet the shadowy FUTURE, without fear, and with a manly heart."

**Anna Lee McKenzie**. Southport, North Carolina. Born in 1894, Mrs. McKenzie has lived all her life on the North Carolina coast, where she became accustomed to seeing boats on the water and to addressing certain of the local men as "Captain." She does not actually like to go out on the water herself, but she likes looking at the Atlantic, and she enjoys the cool summer breezes which blow her curtains back in her house about a mile from the sea. She married William McKenzie in 1914 and worked with

him in the confectionery shop he had opened several years earlier. She supplied the shop with brown dog candy and sweet potato pies, popular with customers at "Willie's Place." Also popular were the player piano and the adjacent pool room, which her son started. When the shop closed about 1966 after Mr. McKenzie's death, local historians estimated that it was the North Carolina business longest in operation by a single owner. The shop is vacant now, but it is easy, when one sees Anna McKenzie standing in the dusty shadows, to imagine a livelier time. The old oil lamps are still in place, and the old mirror still sends back reflections.

**Margaret Ann Mills and Mary Mills**. Watha, North Carolina. Mrs. Margaret Ann Mills was born in 1890 in Pender County, where she has continued to live, close to the North Carolina coast. Her parents died during her early childhood, and an uncle "put the children out here and yonder. Sometimes we had a good home, and sometimes we didn't. I run away two or three times." She was courted by Dallas "Jack" Mills for two or three years and finally married him when she was twenty years old. They had eleven children. Mrs. Mills shares a home with her daughter, Mary, and a large number of cats.

Miss Mary Mills was born in 1914 in Pender County and started school, when she was five, in a one-teacher school house called Pineywood; she still visits her first grade teacher, Madia Murphy, who lives down the road. After finish-

ing secondary studies in nearby Burgaw, she decided to become a nurse and was trained at Lincoln Hospital in Durham. She later studied at the Medical College of Virginia and at New York University. Early in her career she was a practitioner in North Carolina; she especially remembers delivering triplets—Abraham, Isaac, and Jacob. She became a nursing administrator and in 1946 was commissioned in the Public Health Corps. Her first of many overseas assignments was in Liberia, where she assumed responsibility for two Liberian boys, whom she sent home to Watha to be raised by her mother. Wherever she went—Lebanon, Chad, Cambodia, Vietnam—she studied the language and the culture. She retired in 1976 after having achieved the highest honor in her field, the John D. Rockefeller Public Service Award. (It was her pleasure to present Mr. Rockefeller with a red rose for each of the service inductions she was invited back to attend.) When she is at home (and she continues to travel to see friends all over the world), she is active in community projects—writing the church history, raising money for the Volunteer Fire Department, and

writing articles for the local newspaper. Watha, North Carolina, is a country crossroads, but a visitor who stops at the Mills home encounters a wide world.

**Mary Lawson Newby**. Durham, North Carolina. Mrs. Newby was born in 1890 in Durham County, one of twelve children. She began teaching in a nearby one-teacher school. Her second assignment was in Morrisville, twelve miles from Durham, and she would go there on the train. "During the time I was there," Mrs. Newby remembers, "my daddy had the chance of coming to see me in the classroom. My mother and my father couldn't read. They were not educated. My daddy could figure. He knew figures, but they didn't know A from B. But they were people who believed in education." Mrs. Newby finished her teaching career in the Durham city schools. When she was thirty-one years old, she married a minister, Dangerfield Newby, Junior, who was sixty five. He was the namesake of the first black man to die at Harper's Ferry—a death which is dramatized in Stephen Vincent Benet's *John Brown's Body*. Mrs. Newby recalls her husband's having told her of his boyhood: "He was a slave boy on another farm, and his daddy was coming back to buy the freedom of his wife and two or three young ones when they killed him." The Reverend Dangerfield Newby, Jr., died in 1936. Mrs. Newby died in 1982 at the age of ninety-two.

**Theodosia Gaither Phelps**. Winston-Salem, North Carolina. Mrs. Phelps was born in 1919, the oldest of six girls. Her mother worked as a stemmer in the local tobacco factories, and the children in the family were cared for during the day by their grandmother. A bright student, she was graduated in 1934 from Atkins High School, which was the pride of the black community. When she was about sixteen, she began working as a stemmer at the R. J. Reynolds plant. She joined the local council of the CIO and worked actively for its causes; mainly her goal was to help improve the lives of black factory workers. She participated in factory work stoppages in the forties, stood up and spoke to management for workers' rights, and was singled out as a union leader. Despite the company's opposition to the union and the division it created in the community, black and white, Theodosia Phelps showed exemplary courage in continuing her efforts for workers and in helping to direct a massive voter registration drive which resulted in the election of the first black alderman in the city. After "the union went down" (it lost its charter in 1950 after union leadership was accused of being communist), she began a second career and was trained as a radiologist, taking over major responsibilities at the local black hospital. The latter half of her life has been marked by professional success in the field of radiology. As she reflects upon her earlier life, she concludes, "All the things right now that the Reynolds employees are enjoying are a result of the union."

**Duval Winston Purefoy**. Wake Forest, North Carolina. Mrs. Purefoy was born in 1903 in Youngsville, North Carolina, four miles from the town of Wake Forest, the home until 1956 of Wake Forest College. She attended the Berry O'Kelly School and Kittrell College. During her student days she acquired a reputation for girlish pranks and wit, and she has retained her delightful sense of humor. During the hours of our interview, she "saucered" her coffee in an old-fashioned way and laced her narratives with stories and jokes. "I won't going to be serious about nothing!" she explains, and she continues her stories about how she used to discipline the fraternity boys at Wake Forest College by threatening to spank them. She knew almost every student and faculty member at the College, and they knew "Duval." She has lived most of her life in Wake Forest, except for a few years in the forties when she and her husband and daughter lived in Washington, D.C., where the Purefoys had civil service jobs. Since the death of Mr. Purefoy and her daughter's move to New York City, Mrs. Purefoy has lived alone

not far from the arch which leads into the campus (now occupied by the Southeastern Baptist Theological Seminary). Her home is filled with old family furniture, handmade coverlets, and plants. On the corner of the porch are stacked a number of fishing poles. It is said in Wake Forest that Duval Purefoy would rather fish than eat. The serious side of her life includes many years in the Presbyterian Church, in which she has been an elder since she was eighteen. What Duval Purefoy has to teach us is that the road to heaven is paved with laughter.

**Lucille Zimmerman Williams**. Durham, North Carolina. Mrs. Williams was born in 1907 in Anderson, South Carolina. Her father was a Baptist minister and her mother was a "missionary worker." She attended Morrison College in Sumter, South Carolina, and Benedict College in Columbia, and was graduated from North Carolina Central University in 1958 with a B.S. in Public Health Nursing. She took her nurses' training at St. Agnes Hospital in Raleigh. In 1934 she became a field nurse with the Farm Security Administration, and she traveled from Maine to Florida providing health care for migrant workers. One of the special pleasures in her work with migrants was serving tea to West Indians on Sunday afternoon. "They wanted to be talked to," she remembers, "and they wanted to feel like they belonged." She also worked at the community hospital in Wilmington, North Carolina, and finished her career in Durham as Director of Nursing at Lincoln Hospital.

**Pauli Murray**. Durham, North Carolina. Although the Reverend Pauli Murray was born in Baltimore, where she now lives, she continues to call North Carolina home, and her legions of friends in North Carolina claim her as their own. In her autobiography, *Proud Shoes*, she tells the story of having been raised in Durham by her maternal grandparents. Following a long and successful career as a lawyer, teacher, and writer, she was ordained in 1977 in the Episcopal priesthood and serves now as an associate

*May the blessings of God's grace be upon all who have made and all who read this book. May the lives of the women whose stories are told herein, in all of their diversity and sturdiness of spirit, inspire others toward a vision of the world transformed by love and creativity to a place where each may walk in dignity and without want or fear; to the glory of God's name.* AMEN

minister at the Church of the Holy Nativity in Baltimore and as a teaching priest at the Church of the Atonement in Washington, D.C. In Durham her oldest friends still recount stories from her youth of her courageous liberalism and her free spirit: she bobbed her hair and was known to hitch-hike. She herself has described her earliest years as a "vigorous, swashbuckling activist," and says of her ministry, "My life was pointing toward this." Whether writing a textbook for civil rights or becoming one of the first women ordained in the Episcopal church, the Reverend Pauli Murray has laid down footprints, all the way from North Carolina to New York, California and Maryland.

For this book Pauli Murray has graciously provided a prayer which serves as a concluding tribute to the women we have honored and as a benediction for us all: